MISCUES
Not Mistakes

MISCUES
Not Mistakes

Reading Assessment in the Classroom

M. Ruth Davenport

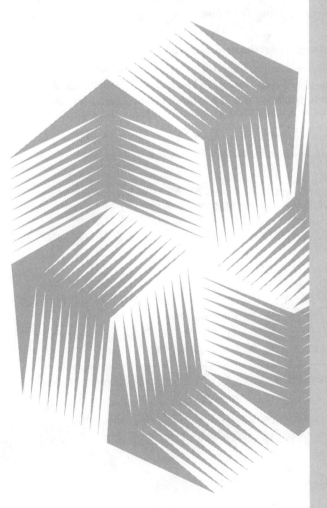

HEINEMANN
Portsmouth, NH

Heinemann
A division of Reed Elsevier Inc.
361 Hanover Street
Portsmouth, NH 03801–3912
www.heinemann.com

Offices and agents throughout the world

The author and publisher wish to thank those who have generously given permission to reprint borrowed material:

Figure 3–11 is reprinted from "Whole Language: Why Bother?" by Dorothy J. Watson in *Reading Teacher* 47 (8). Used by permission of the author.

Excerpts from *Clifford's Thanksgiving Visit* by Norman Bridwell. Copyright © 1993 by Norman Bridwell. Reprinted by permission of Scholastic Inc.

"Procedure IV Form," "Burke Reading Interview," and "Suggestions for Retelling" are reprinted from *Reading Miscue Inventory: Alternative Procedures* by Y. Goodman, D. Watson, and C. Burke. Published in 1987 by Richard C. Owen. Used by permission of Yetta Goodman.

"Holistic Evaluation of the Reader" form is adapted from "Miscue Analysis in the Classroom" by Lynn Rhodes and Nancy Shanklin in *Reading Teacher* 44 (3). Used by permission of the authors.

"The Old Man, His Son—and the Donkey" from *Country and City Book,* Bank Street College of Education, copyright © 1970 was originally published by The Macmillan Company. Reprinted by permission of The McGraw-Hill Companies.

Library of Congress Cataloging-in-Publication Data
Davenport, M. Ruth.
Miscues, not mistakes : reading assessment in the classroom / M. Ruth Davenport.
p. cm.
ISBN 0-325-00368-8 (pbk.)
1. Miscue analysis. 2. Reading (Elementary). I. Title.
LB1050.33 .D38 2002
372.48—dc21 2002005708

Editor: Lois Bridges
Production: Lynne Reed
Cover design: Jenny Jensen Greenleaf
Typesetter: Drawing Board Studios
Manufacturing: Steve Bernier

Printed in the United States of America on acid-free paper
06 05 04 EB 2 3 4 5

For Jesse and Matthew

Casey, Jesse, Cydni, Daniel, Gold, Delilah, Emily, Oliver, Lilli, Jesse, Jon, Sarah
May you always find joy in reading

Dedicated to
Shelley Harwayne
and the Children, Teachers,
Families, Staff, and Administrators
of the Schools of Manhattan
for Your Courage

Contents

Foreword

When I finished reading *Miscues, Not Mistakes,* I had the same feeling that I get when I leave classrooms where important learning and teaching are going on. Like those classrooms, this book is an exciting workout! Invitations to become involved are everywhere in those rooms, and if you don't accept a couple of them, you probably will just leave. The same is true when you dive into this book. Don't expect to sit back, thinking that the author and the readers she tells us about are going to do all the work. You will be involved, or you will close the book.

Through the holistic journey of this book, Ruth Davenport is our informed guide; she considers our needs, she challenges, she advises, and she issues invitations to dig deep. Our first such invitation is to ask ourselves an important question, "What is reading?" This isn't a question to be taken lightly; our guide shows us that our answer will be consistent with a particular model of reading, and that model will be the foundation for the reading instruction we accept and practice. Reading Instruction: Even though we've seen students who appear to learn to read despite questionable instruction, we know that reading instruction can be the "maker" or "breaker" in students becoming proficient and joyful readers. Reading Instruction: Today, a political football; and before we get our hands on that ball, we need to know what we are doing and we need a usable game plan. Ruth invites us to explore the information that supports an informed, solid, and practical plan.

Our guide asks us to respond to questions that we, in turn, will ask students: "What did you notice about your reading?" "What were you thinking as you were reading?" "Did you hesitate, repeat yourself, or say something that isn't on the page?" All this is done for the purpose of getting us to think about what we do as readers, and then to look for the thought and reading processes that parallel those of our students as they encounter difficult passages.

Ruth explains, models, and invites teachers to move comfortably into the use of a diagnostic instrument and a research paradigm that quite often changes thinking about how reading is learned and how it should be taught. In fact, through the pages of this book, teachers speak to us about their experiences with this assessment procedure.

There is no question that Ruth brings her vast experiences of listening to innumerable readers of all ages and of all reading proficiencies to this work. She also investigates her own transactions with print and she encourages readers to do the same. Also, her intimate familiarity with miscue analysis qualifies this author to suggest the most expedient ways to organize, administer, interpret, and use the results of that assessment tool.

This book is more than a how-to-do-it text. For me, the duel themes throughout, first, have to do with the importance of listening—really listening—to readers. Ruth gives teachers the means for enlightened listening, and by doing so, she addresses the second theme: The need for knowledge that leads to ownership of teaching, and curriculum. From her first invitation to the last strategy lesson, this author encourages us to listen and learn about language, about the process of reading, and, always, about students. As we use miscue analysis to do these things, she encourages us to raise questions, to interpret and reinterpret markings, to examine and reexamine coding, and to try personal adaptations—even to make changes in the forms if needed. She urges teachers to use miscue procedures in a way that meets their purposes and answers questions about their students, while remaining true to the foundational beliefs supporting those procedures.

This author is the sole of patience; she tells, offers examples, clarifies, and then offers more examples, thereby cutting through possible confusion about marking and coding. Ruth never lets the statistics of miscue analysis become more important than the readers themselves, but she does show how to *run the numbers* for those who are in situations in which a quantitative outcome is necessary.

Readers' backgrounds and language are at the heart of the miscue procedure. Ruth reminds us, for example, that LaMar comes from a ranch where his father is a farrier and so, of course, LaMar knows about horses and donkeys, which provides him the off-the-page information for the story he reads. We are reminded of the importance of praise given as truthful comments about reading successes. Building on the strengths of the reader we then turn our informed eyes and ears to the reader's needs. From the areas of concern, this teacher/researcher/author selects one strategy to present to the student. In other words, Ruth doesn't leave us with only analysis and numbers, but helps us formulate insights about the reader; those insights lead us to a reading strategy that is immediately applicable and appropriate.

After discussing the taped procedures for miscue analysis, Ruth presents a process called Over the Shoulder. An OTS isn't taped, takes less time to administer than other miscue procedures, and can be used individually with children during reading conference time. OTS is aptly named because it is relatively fast, involves a minimum of paperwork and number crunching, and it's friendly. In addition to the reading and retelling of a text, OTS also includes an important *teaching conversation*, which includes a discussion about the story, the miscues, and a selected teaching point; an OTS closes with a celebration of what the student is doing well.

Within this book there is a complete miscue assessment of a student, LaMar. This section closes the gap between theoretical assumptions about language and the reading process and the actual evaluation of a student's language and reading. The assessment closes the gap between being told how to do something and actually getting immersed in the procedure. Here the questions that users of miscue analysis frequently ask are asked and answered. Finally, keeping in mind the holistic insights gained about the reader, the author offers recommendations for instruction.

Ruth Davenport puts a great deal of store in teachers understanding their students and understanding themselves as readers. She also believes that children should understand themselves as readers. Put another way, she believes that all stakeholders in a reading community—teachers, students, and parents—should know what it is that helps readers get a handle on proficient and joyful reading. Ruth reviews procedures and offers another tool, the OTS, which will do exactly that.

With knowledge about and the ability to use Over the Shoulder and other miscue analysis procedures efficiently, you will become a stakeholder yourself; and, you will find yourself thankful that you didn't walk out of the room or close the book too soon.

Dorothy J. Watson

Acknowledgments

I'd like to offer thanks to the many individuals who shared this writing journey. Barbara Hoover, Paul Davenport, Jane Davenport, Aron Crowie, Jim Davenport, Lisa McLain, John Davenport, Holly Davenport, Helen Davenport, Ron Schossler, Cindy Schossler, Alec Ruff, Margaret Ruff, Julie Donnelly, and Sylvia Donnelly were there throughout with words of support, which means the world to me. Thanks to Matt and Jess for always checking in.

Melissa Over, April Curtis Kelly, Linda Lightburn Carter, Shelley Cimon, Christa Lazenby, and Lynne Warren are girlfriends extraordinaire who were always there with strength and wisdom. Thank you.

Thomas Fagan. Thanks.

None of this work would have taken place without the young learners with whom I have had the privilege of working. I appreciate LaMar, Josh, Claire, Ceci, and the many other readers who gave me glimpses into the fascinating process of reading.

I am grateful to the outstanding teachers who welcomed me into their worlds so that I could continue researching miscue analysis. Even during the writing, they offered me a home to continue asking questions and gathering information about using miscue analysis in the classroom setting. Enormous thanks to Mary Diener, Jacque Barthel-Hines, Debbie Mills, Heather Johnson, and Missy Rinker—master teachers all. I especially thank Julie Eckberg and Sharon Evoy for their helpful insights into Running Records. Lynne Warren and Valerie Camilli were valued editors, who I appreciate greatly.

I would also like to express my gratitude to the many undergraduate and graduate students with whom I have had the pleasure of sharing miscue analysis at Eastern Oregon University and Illinois State University. A special thank you goes out to the many teachers and school psychology students with whom I have continued to learn about miscue analysis through examining the reading process of young readers during graduate courses, summer literacy programs, conference presentations, and inservice workshops. Their insights and hard questions have helped me to continue honing my own miscue ears.

Part of this work was accomplished through the support of a Faculty Scholars research stipend from Eastern Oregon University. I appreciate the interest and support of School of Education Dean Michael Jaeger, Provost Bruce Shepard, and President Phil Creighton.

I was honored to work with Lois Bridges, editor supreme, and thank her profusely for believing this book needed to be written and for her unfailing encouragement. I am most grateful to Lynne Reed for her careful attention to the particular demands of this text. I appreciate her patience and professional rendering of the final product. It was no easy task.

To Dorothy, Ken, and Yetta, thanks for your interest and for all you've done to lead the way.

To Bill, my beloved, thanks for the laughter and love.

Introduction

It was a brisk fall evening in Central Missouri as twenty graduate students and I listened to a tape of a child reading. To our untrained ears, he sounded like a struggling reader. We shook our heads and sighed, "Too bad, he's really having a tough time."

"So, what do you think of Wayne as a reader?" Dorothy Watson's invitation got the room buzzing with speculations.

After we had heard this young boy omit the word *glasses* every time he came to it (and it was important to the story), and say *mother* every time he came to the word *mayor,* my new-to-miscue buddies and I said, "He probably didn't understand much of what he read."

"Well, let's listen to his retelling! Don't forget, miscue analysis isn't finished until we've listened to the reader retell the story!"

I will never forget the audible gasp from all of us in the room as Wayne said without hesitation a few sentences into his retelling:

> He went off and he put the signs up and he fixed them all up and then the *mayor* wanted, went back and got him and told him to fix them and then, he found the *glasses* and then he fixed them all up.

We were all astounded! "No way! How did he do that!?"

I knew this was a turning point in my understanding of reading. It was the same as remembering what you were doing when the Beatles were on the *Ed Sullivan Show* or where you were when they tore down the Berlin Wall. Flurkey (1995, 10) captures such an experience this way:

Detailed memories of the exact times and places where we experience important events have a way of staying with us; I remember what I was doing when Neil Armstrong stepped onto the moon's surface, for example. This is also true of my experiences of rethinking reading through miscue analysis.

It's a memorable moment the first time you tune in to students with a "new ear" to listen to them read, use a new language to talk about what you hear, gain a new perspective to interpret what it all means, and then change your teaching accordingly.

I had the pleasure and honor of learning miscue analysis from Dorothy Watson in 1989. She made it one of the most significant learning experiences of my life, that is, one of those milestone "Kodak moments" in my development as a teacher when I knew things had just changed dramatically for the better. I realized that I'd made a quantum leap in my understanding of reading and things would never be the same again.

Besides the fact that she kept us in stitches, the greatest part of the class was Dorothy's way of keeping us so intensely involved. I was straining to hear the miscues, I had pencil in hand practicing markings, and I was speaking a new tongue that allowed me to talk about what I heard as I took delight in and marveled at the amazingly smart things kids were doing with language. I had "miscue ears." Dorothy wrote later, "I am not sure who coined 'miscue ears' and 'miscuteers,' but I wager it was Ken [Goodman], Dave [Allen], or Dorothy Menosky" (Watson 1999, 53).

After graduate school, I returned to the classroom and shared stories about my wonderful teacher Dorothy with my young students. Late that fall we sent her some flowers and one day while the students were out to recess, I gave her a call to say hello and to see how she was doing. When the children returned, I told them, "I just got off the phone from talking with Dorothy Watson, do you remember who she is?"

Without a second thought, Danny Mac matter of factly replied, "Yeah, she's our grandteacher!"

We all agreed it was the perfect term for her! A few weeks later during silent reading time I was pouring through Ken Goodman's *Phonics Phacts* (1993) and one of my students asked me, "Who's that man in the picture on the back?" I thought for a minute and grinned. "That's *my* grandteacher!"

This book emerges from the work of my teacher and my grandteacher, as well as from the influence of other important mentors along my professional path, including: Joy Monahan, Andreé Bayliss, Genny Cramer, Carol Gilles, Carol Lauritzen, Kay Moss, Kathleen Marie Crawford, Dorothy Menosky, Carolyn Burke, and Yetta Goodman. They all have made and continue to make important contributions to my growth as a teacher, miscue researcher, and writer.

In an article by Yetta Goodman in *Primary Voices, K–6,* as is customary in the journal, she ended with her lingering questions. Among them was, "How do we help teachers and reading personnel become more familiar and comfortable with using miscue analysis?" (1995, 7). This question summarizes my motivation for writing this book.

The primary purposes of this book include:

- Making miscue analysis accessible to every classroom teacher and reading professional.
- Offering a perspective of reading as the construction of meaning through a personal transaction with text.
- Challenging the perspective of reading as something that is "right" or "wrong."
- Helping teachers change the way they listen to readers.
- Helping teachers see that readers are doing many more things to celebrate than things to be worried about.
- Offering suggestions for instruction based on evidence from miscue analysis.
- Offering an introduction to miscue analysis to parents, preservice teachers, inservice teachers, and other professionals who share the joy of reading with children.

For those of us who have come to understand unexpected responses during oral reading as miscues, not mistakes, we can answer the question, "When did you develop your miscue ears?" For those new to miscue analysis, I hope you will be able to answer that question with, "Here and now!"

Chapter 1 contains an overview of the reading process to provide a foundation for understanding the theories that support the use of miscue analysis. Chapter 2 examines the variety of miscues readers can make. To closely examine the various procedures for miscue analysis, Chapter 3 is organized around a "What, Why, How, Who, and Where" structure. Chapter 4 takes an in-depth look at all the steps in Procedure III, then Chapter 5 takes these general principles and applies them to examining a complete Procedure III with a reader named LaMar. Chapter 6 explains how to do the untaped procedures (Over the Shoulder and Procedure IV), then Chapter 7 provides examples from young readers. Chapter 8 contextualizes the use of miscue analysis in the classroom by examining one teacher's practice. It also helps move us from the evidence gathered through various procedures to instructional strategies. The chapter also considers using miscue analysis with speakers of other languages, and how to talk with parents about assessing reading through miscue analysis.

1

What Is Reading?

I feel that miscue analysis can really become a way of listening to a child read, {a way} to strengthen what they are already doing effectively and to provide strategies to support their learning.

—Karen Stack, First-Grade Teacher

This is a book about listening to readers.

How we listen, how we understand what we hear, and how we use what we observe to inform our teaching depends entirely on our answer to the question, "What is reading?" How we view the reading process influences everything we do with, for, and to students as readers. This understanding of reading determines how we interpret the changes to the text that all readers make as they read orally. When this happens, do we hear miscues or mistakes?

Miscues are unexpected responses during oral reading, such as insertions, omissions, or substitutions. We expect readers to say what is on the page, and when they alter the text in some way, they have made a miscue. Every reader, no matter how proficient, will do this when reading aloud. Two fundamental principles of miscue analysis are: all readers *make miscues* and these *changes* in the text aren't all *"bad"*! Miscues give us new understandings about the reader's dialect, background knowledge and experiences, attempts to make meaning, and active use of reading strategies. Before we examine various views of the reading process, I'd like to invite you to take a minute right now and write down your own definition. In your current understanding, What is reading?

The Language Cueing Systems

Miscues during oral reading offer us valuable insights into the reader's thinking and use of the language cueing systems. These systems help readers do the work of reading and prompt internal questions that allow the reader to monitor their process of making sense.* The following list summarizes the language cueing systems and the reader's related questions.

* The change in font indicates miscues, the voice of a reader or teacher, or lines from a text.

- *Syntax*—The structure system of language, including the rules of grammar that help us know how to string words together to make a sentence sound like English. Does this sound like language?
- *Semantics*—The meaning system of language, including what words and phrases mean and how these change over time. Does this make sense?
- *Pragmatics*—The system of social rules that lets us know what language is acceptable and expected in particular settings. What might someone say in this situation?
- *Graphophonics*—The system of relationships between the letters and their sounds, including the graphic information on the page. How do these letters and their sounds help me choose a word that makes sense here?

Total accuracy is not the goal for the reader during oral reading. In fact, it is a virtual impossibility. "Because of the differences between the language, thoughts, and meanings of the author and those of a reader, reading can never be an exact process" (Y. Goodman, Watson, and Burke 1996, 3). We want readers to focus on making sense of the text, and to do so, all the language cueing systems need to be working in harmony, each providing information to the reader in a balanced manner. To illustrate the orchestration of these information systems, consider the following sentence in a story about a student at a private boy's school and assume the blank represents a word you don't know right away.

The boy ran down the _______________.

When a reader encounters unfamiliar words, the graphophonic cueing system provides enough information from the print, so she can start making predictions; the syntactic cueing system helps the reader predict what part of speech would fit in that location in the sentence. She might think:

This word follows "the" so it could be an adjective followed by a noun, but there's only one word there, so it must be a noun.

The reader probably wouldn't consciously say, I need a noun there; she has a tacit understanding of grammar rules just by virtue of being a proficient speaker of her native language, in this case, English.

The semantic cueing system helps her select many possible choices of words that would make sense in that position in the sentence and within the overall context of the story.

Let's see . . . what could someone be running down? Could be an alley, a dune, street, sidewalk, hill, stairs, hall, path, trail . . .

The pragmatic cueing system helps her narrow the choices to those that would make sense in the context of the story, that is, within the social setting of the character.

Now what would a boy in a private school be running down? Could be a sidewalk, hill, stairs, hall . . .

Another check of the graphophonic cueing system reconfirms the initial visual information and helps the reader make the most reasonable choice among the narrowed alternatives. Using everything she knows about what has happened in the story so far, she checks the letters on the page to confirm the word is hall, checking to make sure it isn't hill.

The boy ran down the hall.

All of this decision making during reading takes place in the blink of an eye; that is: "Sampling, inferring, and predicting strategies used by readers to transact with the language cueing systems occur so rapidly as to appear simultaneous" (Y. Goodman, Watson, and Burke 1996, 6). Miscues help us take a peek inside a reader's head as all this reading work is going on and allow us to see the strategies she's using to construct meaning. These miscues are actually "part of the process of making sense of print" (K. Goodman 1996, 5).

We accept that all readers make miscues, and because we take delight in, honor, learn from, and are fascinated by the many incredibly smart ways readers construct personal meaning as they read, we refer to unexpected responses during oral reading as *miscues*, rather than using negative terms such as *mistakes* or *errors*. This is not an insignificant choice. The word we choose to label these changes in the text carries with it a great deal of meaning; that is, it reflects our philosophical and theoretical foundations and our beliefs about the reading process.

Models of the Reading Process

There are many different models of reading, or ways of viewing the reading process. These are not necessarily mutually exclusive and many of the ideas in one might resonate in another. Some situate their description of reading within the reader's head (Adams 1994), which Bloome and Dail would define as an autonomous model of reading "since it views reading as autonomous, free of the social and cultural practices that make up the particular event" (1997, 612). Other models consider both the process of reading and the context in which it takes place (K. Goodman 1996), and still others describe the cultural and social influences on reading practices and learning to read (Street 1984; Bloome 1985).

I see these definitions creating a continuum that looks something like the one shown in Figure 1–1.

The Models That Inform Miscue Analysis

We need to recognize that not only is there some overlap between the various views, but also the models listed in the figure (and the list is certainly not exhaustive!) clearly differ in whether they are describing reading as a process of saying all the words, as a process of constructing meaning, as a process of socialization and cultural transmission, or as some combination thereof. We can choose to focus our lens on the reading process from several perspectives: what happens in the head of the reader in terms of cognitive and linguistic processes, how the reading process is a transaction between the reader and the text, how the reader and the reading act are situated within a social context, and how reading is passed on as a cultural process with certain "acceptable" reading behaviors. Let's take a closer look at the views on which miscue analysis is based.

In-the-head models

↑

- Reading is a technical process—
  We read letter by letter and word by word.
- Reading is automatic information processing—
  We decode each word then comprehend each word and build an understanding of the sentence by combining all these individual meanings.
- Reading is a linguistic process—
  When we are reading, we are engaged users of language.
  Reading is an active language process.
- Reading is a transactive process—
  The reader brings meaning to the text and constructs personal meaning through a transaction with the author's text.
- Reading is a transactive sociopsycholinguistic process—
  Reading is an active search for meaning that involves the relationships between thought and language.
  Both the reader and the text are changed during reading.
- Reading is a social process—
  Reading involves social relationships between teachers and students.
- Reading is a cultural process—
  What counts as acceptable reading practice is culturally defined.
- Reading is a sociocognitive process—
  There are certain culturally acceptable ways to interpret and interact with texts.

↓

In-cultural-contexts models

FIGURE 1–1 Continuum of Models of the Reading Process

Reading Is a Linguistic Process

When Ken Goodman began to research the reading process in the early 1960s, the work done at the time was largely atheoretical reductionist research based on a view of reading as "sequential word identification" (K. Goodman 1994, 1096). What K. Goodman calls a "Copernican revolution" took place when he began looking at reading as a linguistic process. In his early research, K. Goodman (1968, 1969) asked readers to read real books, he observed their myriad miscues, and then examined what the miscues were telling him about the reading process through this new lens of linguistics. He saw that the evidence in hand (students' miscues) was contradictory to the current view of reading (saying all the words in sequence) and realized he needed to change the theory about the reading process. He came "to consider reading as an active, receptive language process and readers as users of language" (K. Goodman 1994, 1096). To describe what he saw readers doing and to compare the grammatical functions of words in the text with readers' miscues, he turned to the concepts and methods of scientific linguistics.

Reading Is a Transactive Process

Louise Rosenblatt introduced us to the notion that the reader is an active participant in the construction of meaning; that is, he plays an important role in a "transactional relationship with the text" (1978, ix). In this view of reading, the meaning is not lying on the page waiting for a reader to come pick it up, but instead, he is actively engaged in constructing personal meaning; that is, "the finding of meanings involves both the author's text and what the reader brings to it" (14).

It is important to distinguish between Rosenblatt's idea of *transaction*—a two-way exchange between the reader and the author's text—and a one-way event in which the reader picks up the author's meaning (Routman 2000; Farris 2001). "If we are to *get* meaning from a text, we must actively search for meaning, we must actually bring meaning *to* what we read. Hence reading is not a one-way process, but a two-way interaction between the mind of the reader and the language of the text" (Weaver 1980, 133, italics in original).

Rosenblatt refers to this active transaction as creating "a poem out of a text" and notes this process must be "active, self-ordering and self-corrective" (1978, 11). Her definition of *poem* is not as the literary genre, but as "an event in time. It is not an object or an ideal entity. It happens during a coming-together, a compenetration, of a reader and a text. The reader brings to the text his past experience and present personality" (Rosenblatt 1978, 12).

Rosenblatt also introduces the idea that readers take a stance during their transaction with a text. She believes that, in general, we read either to be entertained (we take an *aesthetic* stance) or to be informed (we take an *efferent* stance) (1978). *Aesthetic* reading allows us to focus on feelings and images evoked by the text. The purpose of *efferent* reading is to remember, or to take something away with us. These stances are not mutually exclusive and can occur during the same reading event.

Reading Is a Transactive Sociopsycholinguistic Process

As Ken Goodman continued to listen to readers and to investigate reading, he not only extended Rosenblatt's ideas of the reader transacting with text, he also recognized the need to go beyond linguistics to develop a more complete model of the reading process. "If reading is making sense of written language, then it is a psycholinguistic process: a theory of reading must include the relationships of thought and language" (K. Goodman 1994, 1097). As he was working with students from urban areas who spoke a variety of dialects, he also realized he had "to draw on sociolinguistics to understand the social variations in language" (1097).

Rather than see each discipline, such as psychology and linguistics, as limited to its own narrow confines, he built a theory of reading from an interdisciplinary base. He brought together the theory and research from a wide range of fields into "a unified theory of reading, writing and texts. . . . This theory comes together as a transactional sociopsycholinguistic view. If we are to understand written language we must integrate knowledge from many disciplines" (K. Goodman 1994, 1100). He drew on the best of the current thinking in the areas of human communication (sociocultural theory), language development (social–personal theory), cognition and comprehension (psycholinguistic theory), and levels of language use (linguistic theory).

In the transaction that takes place during reading, the *reader* is changed as new knowledge is assimilated, and the reader's schema is changed through comprehension. Also in the transaction that takes place between the reader and the text during reading, the *text* is changed, both in meaning intention and in oral reproduction. Because the reader brings his own schema and background to the text, his meaning will never be an exact match to the author's, plus the text will be changed through the reader's miscues.

Ken Goodman's Model of the Reading Process

Informed by his many years of research, Ken Goodman has described a model of the reading process consistent with his observations of real readers reading real books. Let's look closely at this explanation of the ways texts are organized, the cycles of the reading process, and the strategies readers use.

Text Organization

To examine how reading works, K. Goodman (1996) first considers how texts work. The language of texts is organized at three levels, at which we are provided information through different cueing systems. At the *graphophonic*, or signal level, readers get information from the print on the page; at the *lexico-grammar* level, readers assign wording to what has been written and get information about syntax, or grammatical structure of language; and at the *meaning and pragmatics* level, readers assign meaning to the text based on their experiences, their background knowledge, and their cultural and social expectations. The graphic in Figure 1–2 summarizes these different cueing systems and levels of language.

Level of Language	Cueing System	Information
Meaning and Pragmatics	Pragmatics	The social, cultural, and historical context of language in use
	Semantics	What words and phrases mean in different contexts The reader's sense of meaning • Experiential • Interpersonal • Textual
Lexico-Grammar	Syntax	Grammar • Pattern in structure • Pattern markers (word endings) • Rules Lexicon • Form • Frequency • Arrangement
Graphophonic	Orthography Written text—what we see | Phonology Oral text—what we hear Phonics The relationships between what we see and what we hear Spelling Punctuation | Sounds Intonation	Spelling Punctuation Set for ambiguity • Sound and letter • Pattern • Schwa and stress • Morphemic • Dialect and rule

FIGURE 1–2 Levels of Language, the Cueing Systems, and the Information They Provide

Graphophonics Level: Signals and Signs

Reading begins with the eye picking up an observable signal—the characters and letters on the page—and sending this input to the brain. This is the first source of information, the physical aspect of language, or the orthography, which we can directly describe. The graphophonic level of text includes the spelling system and punctuation; phonics is not included here because it is *"the set of relationships between the orthography and a specific speaker's phonology"* (K. Goodman 1996, 66, italics in original). According to Y. Goodman and Watson (1998, 120):

> Phonics is not a simplistic relationship between single letters and single sounds. Phonics is not simply a program to teach reading. Phonics is what readers learn to understand as the relationship between how they talk and how language is organized in written texts.

That is, phonics is a complex system of correspondences between the sound system and the spelling system. It is one language cueing system we use in conjunction with others to make meaning. Watson says: "Symbol–sound information should be used in concert with the other subsystems of language in order to *confirm* predictions made by the listener or reader" (1988, 7, italics in original). What we see and hear comes to our sensory systems, then these signals are interpreted as signs, or semiotics, that carry meaning.

An important aspect of K. Goodman's view of the reading process is what he calls our "set for ambiguity" (K. Goodman 1996, 66). He describes our tolerance, if you will, for information that could be interpreted in more than one way. This information could be the sounds we hear, the text we see in print, or the cues we get from the meaning system of language. Neither the sound system of language nor the written system is even close to constant—both what we hear and see in language are ambiguous. Humans have a remarkable ability to deal with this ambiguity and somehow make sense of the varied oral language we hear and written language we see.

First, K. Goodman introduces *sound* and *letter* ambiguity. As a young child learns to speak, he is surrounded by different voices with varying pitches and modulations. He must sort out "what is to be perceived as the same in all this difference" (1996, 67). For example, *car* is the same word with the same meaning, even when spoken by an older sister with a high-pitched voice, by his father who has a low voice and an East Coast accent, by his mother who has a Southern accent, and by a visitor whose first language is German. Each pronunciation of *car* will be slightly different, but the child must discern them all as the same word with the same meaning.

The written language system is also highly variable. Not only do computers offer us hundreds of different fonts, but handwriting is unique to each individual. Somehow readers are able to make sense of print when the letters aren't uniform in size, font, shape, or color. Somehow we can handle all this ambiguity when reading.

K. Goodman goes on to describe *pattern* ambiguity—that is, the fact that there is not an item-for-item match between the sound system and the graphic system. He gives a variety of examples that include homophones and homographs and, through a paragraph containing several homophones, demonstrates that we are able to use cues from the syntax and meaning of the text to understand what we are reading. When these words are in the context of connected language, we are hardly aware that there is any ambiguity. Here is K. Goodman's paragraph (1996, 69)—give it a try yourself:

The *main* feature of the *male* lion is its *red mane*. I *read* about that in a book I got in the *mail* last week. I *like* to *read* books *like* that.

Consider all the tasks with which the reader is confronted in this short passage! The reader must:

- Take words that sound the same and make them mean something different (main/mane).
- Take words that look the same and make them sound differently (read/read),
- Take words that look and sound the same, and understand that they mean something different (like/like), and
- Take words that look different and make them have the same sound but with different meanings (mail/male, red/read).

K. Goodman's point in this demonstration is that these ambiguities would have disappeared a long time ago if they made reading impossible or difficult (1996). He also points out that the so-called "silent e" at the end of words that distinguish pairs such as rat/rate or van/vane, serves as a marker to indicate the sound of the vowel—which, by the way, means that the whole pattern would need to be processed before the reader could determine which word it is and how to pronounce it. This is evidence that refutes the notion that we read letter by letter.

The other types of ambiguity K. Goodman describes are schwa and stress ambiguity, morphophonemic ambiguity, and dialect and rule ambiguity (1996). He offers an example of *schwa and stress* ambiguity using the word *man* and his own name *Goodman*. The dilemma for readers and the ambiguity they handle so readily is, when stressed, the word *man* has a short *a* sound; when combined with *Good*, it becomes unstressed and has the *schwa* sound, yet *man* is spelled the same in both contexts. Here the reader must take two words that look the same and make them have different sounds.

Morphemic ambiguity results from the decisions that have been made historically when standardized spellings were created to keep meaning relationships clear. If we consider related words, such as *confess* and *confession*, we see the spelling remains the same to keep the meaning unit, or morpheme, the same, but the pronunciation changes from *ss* to *sh*. In other words, "the morpheme is spelled more consistently than it's pronounced" (K. Goodman 1996, 72). Here the reader must take part of a word that looks the same in two different contexts, keep the same meaning in both, but change the way it is pronounced.

K. Goodman considers *dialect and rule* ambiguity to be "the most important of all aspects of signal ambiguity in English spelling" (1996, 72). Each of the regional and social dialects in our language provide another challenge for the reader. While these variations are one of the delightful aspects of language, they present another type of ambiguity, which came about when our forebears decided to standardize spelling. *There is not a universal set of phonics guidelines* because, within each dialect, there are particular relationships between the orthography (writing system) and the phonology (sound system). According to Y. Goodman, Watson, and Burke (1996, 11, italics in original):

> *Each reader must learn the set of relationships that exists between his or her oral language and its written counterparts: the phonics of language*. The relationships are not the same for all speakers because of differences in dialects, as well as idiosyncratic differences.

Regional dialects influence the way we say words that are spelled the same, such as *dog* and *fog*. For some readers, these may be pronounced differently than *smog* and *bog* based on local patterns of speech. The result is that there is no one set of phonics rules, yet prepackaged instructional materials assume there is! This is the reason we need to be aware of the dialect *of the reader* when listening to children read and when interpreting the miscues we hear. "Miscue analysis is an invaluable way of determining a reader's use of language cues and reading strategies" (Weaver 1980, 182), but when we are conducting miscue analysis and refer to *unexpected responses*, we need to keep the dialect of the reader, not the teacher, in mind. So what is *expected* are the familiar lexicon and natural syntactic patterns of the reader. We can't convey the message to students that their reading is wrong because they're using language structures, pronunciations, or words from their own dialect.

We cannot help but marvel at our capacity to deal with ambiguity in written language. Considering the different types of ambiguity in oral and written language, we have a new perspective on and appreciation of this astounding feat called reading!

Lexico-Grammar Level: Words and Syntax

This level of language, or cueing system, gives us information about words and the grammatical structure of the text (syntax). Readers use these cues to predict unfamiliar words and to assign a syntactic pattern to the text. The ways these cues are helpful become evident when readers are (shamefully) given inauthentic text that has controlled word frequency. This artificial manipulation of words results in a text that doesn't give readers the syntactic cues they need to make predictions about upcoming wording. "Authentic texts have predictable grammar and provide the reader natural grammatical cues" (K. Goodman 1996, 77).

There are three ways we get information from the grammar system of language. The first is through *patterns*. Usually these sentence patterns, or the acceptable grammatical structures, are fairly fixed so they are easy for us to predict. The second kind of information we get from the grammar, or syntactic cueing system, is *pattern markers*, which include function words, word endings, affixes, and internal changes in words. These markers provide additional information that helps us make predictions when reading, and they also give us the same clue more than once. Look at the following sentence:

The girls are riding their bicycles down the street.

Here, we see four clues that indicate plurality.—the "s" on the end of girls, the word are, the plural possessive pronoun their, and the "s" on the end of bicycles. As K. Goodman notes: "Redundancy is one way language makes up for ambiguity; it provides extra cues to the same information" (1996, 82).

The third kind of information we get from the syntactic cueing system comes from *rules*. By listening to the people in our world, we learn to speak our native language, and in doing so, we tacitly learn the grammar rules that govern that language. But the way in which we learn these rules is much more subtle than the way we learn something we can directly observe, like how to ride a bike. Language is harder to *observe* and therefore, learning to talk takes place through a series of approximations, inventions, and overgeneralizations of the *rules* we subconsciously perceive to be the guiding principles of grammar. This is why we hear young children use phrases like He goed to the store. They have begun to figure out the *rule* for past tense action in which we often use a /d/ at the end of a word, as in crawl/crawled.

Kids will use such words until, through more experience as a language user, they come to refine their understanding of the *rule* and move to more conventional usages—in this case, an irregular form (went instead of goed). When reading, sometimes the grammar rules under which a reader is currently operating may differ from the rules the author used when writing the text. Miscue analysis gives us the opportunity to observe the kinds of changes readers make in the text as a result of these wonderfully complex, yet immature understandings, of conventional grammar rules.

Meaning and Pragmatics Level: Semantics and Situation

As we continue to look at the cueing systems that make possible the process of comprehending what we read, we consider the meaning and pragmatics level of language. Watson notes: "Semantics has to do with the reader's, writer's, listener's, and speaker's sense of meaning. This subsystem emerges naturally from and along with the pragmatic system and is powerfully influenced by the culture" (1988, 6).

When examining these levels of language, or cueing systems, it is important to remember that whatever we give our readers, the *language in the text must be authentic*; that is, it must have a natural grammatical structure, use words with which readers will be familiar, and sound like the way we talk. K. Goodman refers to these qualities by saying an authentic text "has meaning potential for its intended audience, [and] it is a complete enough semiotic representation of meaning to make it possible for readers with sufficient relevant knowledge to make meaning from it" (1996, 85).

We also consider texts from the point of view of our socially agreed-on conventions of language that are needed for successful communication. We are able to make sense of texts to the extent that they follow these language characteristics. The meaning we are able to construct comes from both the writer and the reader. The writer shapes a text by communicating his intended meaning, and a reader transacts with the text by creating three types of her own meaning: experiential, interpersonal, and textual.

Experiential meaning is the most apparent type of meaning and reflects our life experiences and the ideas we've formed from previous reading and past endeavors. This kind of meaning can be made through connections between the text we're reading and ourselves, the world, or other texts (Harvey and Goudvis 2000). *Interpersonal meaning* is created when we share reactions to our experiences at the same time we are conveying our ideas. For example, when we are reading, we not only read the text itself, but may use a particular inflection that indicates to a listener that we have created interpersonal meaning; or we may miscue by using a phrase or grammatical structure that is more familiar in our pattern of speech than the one in the text. Finally, *textual meaning* is created with the help of text structure. Readers pick up cues to meaning based on how sentences are put together.

It is important to remember that all three kinds of meaning are represented by the text simultaneously in a cohesive message. According to K. Goodman "The author uses appropriate syntactic structure to represent the textual meaning, and chooses the right words and word forms to express the subtleties of interpersonal and experiential meaning" (1996, 87).

Cycles in the Reading Process

Now that we have looked at how texts are organized and the types of cues the language systems provide the reader, let's examine how we use all this information to help us make sense of what we're reading. What follows is an in-depth look at the transactive sociopsycholinguistic model of the reading process as described by K. Goodman (1996), Y. Goodman and Watson (1998), and others (e.g., Smith 1973; Weaver 1980; Y. Goodman, Watson, and Burke 1987; Wilde 2000; Routman 2000; Farris 2001).

There are some general principles about reading that frame this description of how this process works. First, as the reader is transacting with a text and interpreting what is read, he is creating a parallel text in his head. Farris states it this way (2001, 437):

> Reading is more than word recognition and the gleaning of concepts, information and ideas from text. Reading is the processing of words, concepts, information and ideas put forth by the author as they relate to the reader's previous experiences and knowledge. Only a portion of information is included by the author or a passage; it falls upon the reader to interpret the remaining information. No written text is completely self-explanatory.

While a reader is trying to understand what the author is saying, she is building her own meaning, which will always vary slightly from the author's intended meaning. This personally-constructed text governs what the reader perceives and the syntax that is assigned to what is read. As the reader is constructing both the structure and meaning of the text, sometimes the text in the reader's head must be reconstructed to maintain meaning. Multiple miscues in the same sentence (in which the later ones keep the new syntactic structure created by the earlier ones) and self-corrections give us powerful evidence of this process.

The following are some other guiding principles of the reading process from the transactive sociopsycholinguistic perspective:

- Reading is an active language process.
- Readers actively use a variety of strategies to construct meaning.
- During oral reading, everything we observe readers doing gives us evidence of their attempts to make sense of what they're reading.
- Readers use just enough of the visual information available from texts to make sense.
- Readers use both the information they *bring* to the text and information they *gain* from the text to make meaning—both are equally important to reading.
- A reader is *effective* when he makes sense of what is being read.
- A reader is *efficient* if she is able to make sense with the least amount of time and effort; that is, she does not have to recognize each individual word because she is able to make the leap toward meaning using information from her background, perceptions, and predictions.

K. Goodman (1996) describes the four cycles we go through as we move from taking in the visual input from the page to making meaning in our brains: visual, perceptual, syntactic, and semantic. Let's examine each of these cycles, remembering that they function recursively rather than in a sequential fashion.

The Visual Cycle

This cycle of the reading process is orchestrated by our eyes as they scan the print on the page from left to right. While it seems like our eyes move in a flowing motion across the page, in fact, they move along a line of print in a series of jerky movements called *saccades* (Weaver 1980). Our eyes stop at fixation points along a line of text, and during these brief pauses between saccades, they pick up the lines, curves, edges, angles, or breaks that make up words. They then transmit this light energy to the brain as a series of neural impulses. The points at which the eye fixates can be envisioned as flattened, concentric ovals, with the information at the center in sharp focus and the print toward the periphery more fuzzy.

Although, intuitively, it may seem that *what we see* is the sole source of information to help us understand what we read, in the visual cycle we recursively use what we know about text structure and meaning to make predictions about what our eyes will see. What we know about written language and fonts helps us decide what forms all the print features will take and instantaneously we are able to turn visual information into perceptual images. As needed, the brain sends the eye back to the text to scan again for more visual input, but usually these regressions come when the reader realizes a miscue has interrupted the process of constructing meaning. As Smith notes (1973, 6):

> Reading is not primarily a visual process. Two kinds of information are involved in reading, one that comes from in front of the eyeball, from the printed page, that I call *visual information*, and one that derives from behind the eyeball, from the brain, that I call *nonvisual information*. Nonvisual information is what we already know about reading, about language, and about the world in general (italics in original).

The Perceptual Cycle

It is important to remember that the process of making sense during reading is driven more by our perceptions of what we *think* we see than by actual recognition. As K. Goodman states: "What we perceive is based on what we see, but what we see is also based on what we perceive" (1996, 95). In other words, our brains make use of the images that are coming in through the eye to make predictions, and these predictions further influence the images we perceive. We select key features from this visual information and give some perceptual value to it, adjusting our expectations as we do. For example, when we see the message on a sign written in all capital letters, we continue reading expecting to see more capitals. The perceptual cycle is also recursive, and when the images we perceive don't match what we expected, we take another look, reinterpret the information, and form an alternative perception. That is, we send the eye back to the text for more visual input to allow us to make another perceptual image.

The Syntactic Cycle

The visual and perceptual cycles are closely related. Once we have processed visual information and converted it to perceptual images, we take this surface structure and make a decision about the overall sentence format. Is it a question, a command, or a statement? Surface structure is "the relationships signaled by word endings, function words, and word order" and deep structure is "the *underlying* relations among words of a sentence" (Weaver 1980, 22, italics in original). We can think of surface structure as including the vibrations in the air as someone is speaking or the marks on the page in writing. Deep structure includes the "personal interpretations one brings to a sentence, based on one's entire store of knowledge and experience" (22).

Once we are able to determine the deep structure of the sentence, we can get at the meaning of the clauses and examine layers of meaning from the interrelationships of all the clauses in the sentence. This is the *invisible* process in the reader's head. We then generate our own surface structure and wording, which may or may not match the original text. This is the *visible* product of oral reading. If we are constructing meaning, we continue through the text without regressing.

The Semantic Cycle

The goal of reading, and of all language processes, is making meaning. These cycles, as K. Goodman describes them, flow back and forth from one to the other as we process visual information, create perceptual images, assign wording and create syntactic structure, get to the deep structure, and arrive at meaning. We move seamlessly from one cycle to the other as our "brain shifts from processing language to processing meaning . . . the entire process of reading integrates around our determination to make sense of what we're reading" (1996, 105). We construct our own meaning for a text as we move from visual information to perceptions to syntactic structure and wording. If the meaning we are making is consistent with what we have understood so far in the text, and it jives with what we are expecting the text to say, we keep reading. If we can't make sense of a text or if we notice a miscue has changed the meaning-making process, we can rethink the meaning, reconsider the syntax or the wording, or back up to the point of miscue and try to fix it. We can also read ahead to look for additional cues that may make the meaning clear.

Before we look at the strategies readers use, let's recap the cycles that take place during reading, as shown in the graphic in Figure 1–3.

Psycholinguistic Strategies in the Reading Process

To be able to read, we must use both thinking processes and language processes; that is, reading is *psycholinguistic* (K. Goodman 1996). For us to make meaning during reading, we use a variety of active strategies, which are also labeled psycholinguistic because of the constant interaction between language and thought. "Reading starts with an inquiry by the reader. To help solve the major problem confronting every reader—*What does what I'm reading mean to me?*—the reader uses a number of complex plans or strategies" (Y. Goodman, Watson, and Burke 1996, 3, italics in original). In addition to *initiating* and *terminating*, the significant strategies in the reading process include *sampling*, *inferring*, *predicting*, *confirming*, *correcting,* and *integrating*.

Initiating Strategies

For us to read, we must first realize that there is something in our world to be read. For proficient readers, most often this realization is an unconscious one, but it is a necessary action. For emergent readers, the use of this strategy often begins with learning to make the distinction between print and pictures. All readers begin the reading process through this initiation, or recognition—There is something here to read—and then other strategies can be activated. We use this strategy when we begin an episode of reading; when the print changes in some way; when we differentiate between graphics, pictures, and text; or when we change our purpose as readers.

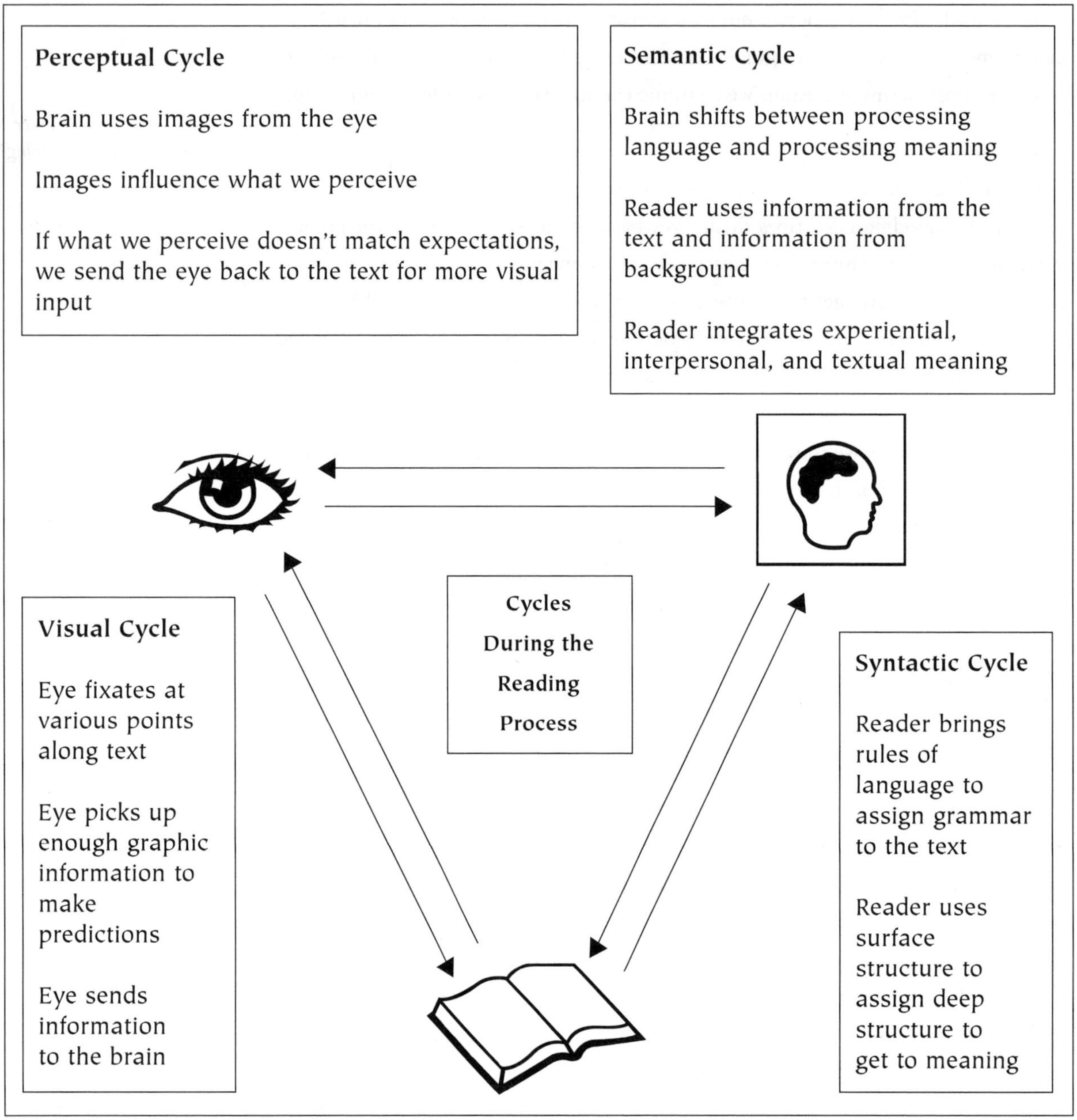
Perceptual Cycle
Brain uses images from the eye
Images influence what we perceive
If what we perceive doesn't match expectations, we send the eye back to the text for more visual input
Semantic Cycle
Brain shifts between processing language and processing meaning
Reader uses information from the text and information from background
Reader integrates experiential, interpersonal, and textual meaning
Visual Cycle
Eye fixates at various points along text
Eye picks up enough graphic information to make predictions
Eye sends information to the brain
Cycles During the Reading Process
Syntactic Cycle
Reader brings rules of language to assign grammar to the text
Reader uses surface structure to assign deep structure to get to meaning

FIGURE 1–3 Cycles During the Reading Process

Terminating Strategies

Just as we make a conscious decision to begin reading, so too do we make a deliberate choice to stop reading. Of course we stop when the text is finished, but there are many other reasons why we can choose to terminate reading. These may have to do with the physical conditions around us, like poor lighting or noisy distractions; they may have to do with our physical state, like we're too tired, bored, or hungry; they may be concerned with the text itself, for instance, it isn't as good as we thought it would be, we don't like the author's style, or we don't understand what we're reading; or the reasons we stop reading may have to do with interruptions—a knock on the front door, an appointment downtown, or our bus just arrived.

If we recognize that as adults we start and stop reading for a variety of reasons, we will honor students' reading behaviors and realize they have *rights* as readers, just as we do. For instance, it's OK for students to stop in the middle of a book that just isn't working for them. We certainly don't want students doing this with every book they read, but we also need to have realistic expectations that sometimes students make an inappropriate choice, or that there isn't a good *fit* between the content or complexity of the book and the reader.

Sampling and Selecting Strategies

When you pick up a newspaper, you don't (I would wager) read everything on the page, left to right, top to bottom. You make choices. First you scan the largest print, or headlines, to choose which article looks interesting enough to read. Within that article, you may scan until you find information you'd like to read a little more slowly, and perhaps you stop reading before the end of the article. Here we see the use of a sampling strategy (scanning), a selection strategy (choosing which article to read and which information to focus on within it), and a termination strategy (stopping before the end).

When readers just use a minimum number of graphic cues to construct meaning from a text, they are using a sampling strategy. Our common sense tells us that we need *all* the information on the page to be able to make sense of what we're reading. However, psycholinguistic research has shown that efficient readers sample the text for meaningful information and select only the *minimum* amount needed to construct meaning. "Readers sample and infer the most significant graphophonic, syntactic, semantic, and pragmatic cues, and they predict what they believe subsequent graphophonic, syntactic, and semantic structures are going to be. No reader uses all of the available cues. Reading would be too slow and inefficient if this were so" (Y. Goodman, Watson, and Burke 1996, 6). Similarly, Smith notes that (1973, 7):

> [T]he reader who concentrates on identifying every word correctly will, unless he is already very familiar with the material he is reading, be unable to read for meaning. Contrary to widespread belief, reading word perfectly is not necessary in order for comprehension to take place. Quite the reverse. A reader who concentrates on words is unlikely to be able to get any sense from the passage that he reads. It is only by reading for meaning first that there is any possibility of reading individual words correctly.

Readers use various strategies for selecting graphic information in the most efficient manner. For example, picking up beginning consonants is particularly helpful when skimming a text. Initially, they carry more information for us than do vowels. The expectations we set for the text have a great influence on what graphic cues we will actually select. As K. Goodman states: "What our brain tells the eye to look for depends on what we expect to see" (1996, 112). To make these selections from the print, we use what we know about the structure of language, the way language is written down, and what we know about the text and the meaning we have constructed up to this point. "We choose what is most useful on the basis of what we already know" (1996, 112).

Predicting and Inferencing Strategies

Because reading is a constant interaction between our thoughts and our language, we are continually making predictions and inferences. When we are actively engaged in predicting, we are anticipating what will come next in the text, using all we know about how language works and what we've read so far. We are also continually making inferences, or bringing information to the text, as we *read between the lines*. No text carries all the possible meanings or completely represents the author's meaning, so we infer as we read by filling in the gaps. These inferences might be confirmed for us later in the text, or we might discover we've made an incorrect inference.

This process is closely related to making predictions because inferences are based on what we predict will happen and predictions are based on what we have inferred so far. The background knowledge we bring to a text supports our efforts in making predictions and inferences. The more we know about a topic, the more interest we bring to the reading, which makes the text more predictable, and therefore makes it easier to understand. This cycle of actively predicting and making inferences is what led K. Goodman to refer to reading as a "psycholinguistic guessing game" (1996, 113). This term does not imply that we make wild, unreasonable guesses when we come to an unfamiliar word, but instead emphasizes the active role of inference and prediction in proficient reading.

Confirming and Disconfirming Strategies

A related part of the making predictions and inferences process is checking to see if they are supported by the text. Readers are continually taking risks as they make *psycholinguistic guesses* based on what they know so far. But along with that risk-taking comes an alertness for confirmation. This is one of the wonderful results of analyzing students' miscues: we see this very active prediction/confirmation cycle in action!

Through corrections and regressions, we are able to witness students' processes of changing their minds based on new information the text provides. If predictions are confirmed, the reader continues; if not confirmed, the reader has several choices. One course of action would be to back up, sample the text again, reread, and rethink the relevant predictions and inferences. Another alternative would be to read ahead and allow the text to teach and provide new information that might clarify the current confusion; or the reader could stop reading.

Correcting Strategies

When we hear readers correcting their miscues, we have powerful evidence of in-process understanding, or *comprehending*, rather than just observing the end product of reading—*comprehension* (Y. Goodman, Watson, and Burke 1987). As readers monitor their comprehension, they "correct when they have disconfirmed their predictions and inferences" (K. Goodman 1996, 114). These self-corrections can take place right at the point of a miscue; sometimes readers correct a miscue before they finish the word, as in the case of a corrected partial; and at other times, the reader continues reading well past the miscue. Additional information in the text may "disconfirm" for the reader an earlier prediction that resulted in the miscue. At this point, we may hear the reader pause as he reconsiders his miscue, rereads, and then corrects.

Readers do *not* have to correct all their miscues. This seems counterintuitive if your view of the reading process is one in which the reader must say all the words on the page. But, if a reader is constructing meaning, it is actually more efficient for her to continue reading than to try and fix miscues that didn't interrupt the flow of making sense of the text. We'll take a look at many examples of this type of miscue throughout this book. However, if a miscue does change the meaning or disrupts the process of making sense, then it should be corrected. As long as a reader is being effective (making meaning) and efficient (using the fewest cues to construct meaning), then we are not concerned if she leaves miscues uncorrected.

If miscues are going to be fixed, the decision needs to be made by the reader. *The teacher should not interrupt the reader at the point of miscue during oral reading.* This is disruptive to the reader's language and thought processes; that is, it "stops the reader in his linguistic tracks" (Watson 1989). Furthermore, it conveys the message that reading is saying all the words rather than constructing meaning. Interrupting also takes ownership of comprehension away from the reader—the construction of meaning and the application of correction strategies then become the teacher's, not the student's. We want readers to self-monitor for meaning, to realize when they need to self-correct, and to be able to do so independently. If the teacher is going to discuss miscues with the student, he should wait until the reader has finished the sentence or paragraph, then ask the reader to return to a miscue or difficult passage and engage in a dialogue about what was just read. As we'll see later, this is an *important* part of the teaching conversation that can take place during a reading conference.

Integrating Strategies

Y. Goodman, Watson, and Burke (1996) describe a reader's integrating strategies during which she brings prior knowledge and experience to the information she's getting from the text. Watson (2001) notes that all the reader's actions, particularly the integrating strategies, are recursive rather than linear. Integrating begins immediately as the reader starts reading. This strategy also involves bringing together all the other psycholinguistic strategies that make up the total reading process. Watson (1997) points out that it is this process of integration that makes it so critical to provide readers with authentic texts. If readers don't have supportive or "workable" texts, they don't have sufficient semantic structure to allow them to integrate what they know with the text they're reading, nor are they getting the information they need from the syntactic and pragmatic cueing systems to make reasonable predictions.

Harvey and Goudvis help us think about how actively students go about this integrating process as they try to comprehend what they are reading. They suggest that there are particular strategies we can teach students to help them become better at comprehension, including the following (2000, 6–7):

- Making connections between what they know and the new information in the text.
- Asking questions of themselves, the text, and the author.
- Drawing inferences.
- Determining which information in the text is the most important.
- Synthesizing information from within the text and across texts.
- Realizing when they are not understanding and doing something about it.

Bringing It All Together: What Is Reading?

We've seen that there are a number of different definitions of reading, and observed that they can range from *reading is saying all the words* on the page to *reading is constructing meaning* through a transaction with the text. We've seen that reading is a process of bringing together information from one's background knowledge and experience as well as using information from the language cueing systems of syntax, semantics, pragmatics, and graphophonics. The reading process is easier if we are interested, we bring background to what we are reading, and if we have a reason to read. What we personally define as reading is based on the cultural definitions of what are considered *acceptable* reading practices and social expectations about reading.

Weaver helps us understand that "reading is an active process, a deliberate search for meaning. And indeed, readers cannot get meaning from a text unless they bring meaning to it" (1980, 134). Harvey and Goudvis remind us that "reading is thinking" (2000, 5); and further, Y. Goodman, Watson, and Burke define reading this way (1987, 3):

> Reading is a problem-solving, meaning-making process. As readers, we consider the meaning the author is making while, at the same time, we are building meaning for ourselves. We use our own language, our own thoughts, and our own view of the world to understand the author's meaning. The language, thoughts, and worldviews of both the author and the reader are influenced by personal and social histories. Our interpretations are structured and directed by what we know.

Figure 1–4 summarizes the sociopsycholinguistic model of the reading process.

"OK, I think I'll read this"—*Decide to* ***ENGAGE*** *with text*
Reader *brings his own language, thought, inquiry, and culture to the reading, just as the* ***Author*** *did when she wrote the text.*

"What is there here to read?"—*Begin to* ***SAMPLE*** *text*

Eye moves across text, picking up a minimum number of graphic cues to make ***PREDICTIONS****.*
"What do I think is going to happen?"
"What is a word that would make sense here?"

"Yes, that makes sense! I understand, my predictions were right!"
Continue reading to ***CONFIRM*** *predictions*
Make ***INFERENCES*** *about meaning—****INTEGRATE*** *prior knowledge and experience.*

"Wait a minute! That doesn't make sense—That doesn't sound like language!" *Prediction is not confirmed—****REREAD, RETHINK, REPREDICT***
MONITOR UNDERSTANDING.

CONTINUE READING *when predictions are confirmed.*

FIGURE 1–4 Summary of the Reading Process

The remainder of the book, and our exploration of miscue analysis within the context of the busy classroom day, is guided by a definition of reading as "a process in which the reader and the text come together for the purpose of creating meaning" (Watson 1988, 8). Let's go on now to examine more closely the range of miscues readers can make. But as we do, let's not lose sight of the fact that the reading process is truly something of a wonder. We don't want to be like the astronomer who so carefully examines maps, charts, numbers, and diagrams that she forgets to appreciate the beauty of the stars (K. Goodman 1996).

2

What Is a Miscue?

I have taught my students to do a simple version of the miscue analysis. This helps them to become more metacognitive about their own reading, as well as understand why miscues aren't always mistakes.

—Jennifer Wilson, Seventh-Grade Language Arts

How Is a Miscue Defined?

Before we can address the "What is miscue analysis?" question, we need to find out what a miscue is so that we know what we're analyzing! A miscue is an unexpected response during oral reading. Every reader makes miscues. As we listen to readers, we often hear alterations in the text. We expect to hear readers say the words on the page and when they don't, they have made a miscue. But, as we will see, this is not always a negative thing. Others define miscue this way:

- "I found that when I asked readers . . . to read whole stories that they hadn't seen before, they made miscues—they produced unexpected responses that didn't match the text. The miscues became, for me, windows on the reading process" (K. Goodman 1994, 1096).
- "A miscue is defined as an observed response (the OR), that does not match what the person listening to the reading expects to hear (the ER). What teacher/researchers consider to be a miscue depends on their view of the reading process" (Y. Goodman, Watson, and Burke 1987, 37).
- "I'm using the term *miscue*, more comprehensive and less judgmental than the term *error*, as employed by Kenneth Goodman to refer to a reader's unexpected response to text" (Wilde 1997, 125, italics in original).

Ken Goodman began using the term *miscue* instead of *error* or *mistake* to refer to changes in the text during oral reading in order to remove the implication that the reader has done something wrong (1968). Quite often, miscues do not change the meaning of the sentence and therefore do not interrupt the reading process. If a reader is constructing meaning, a miscue may be left uncorrected. This use of the word *miscue* carries a strong message. It conveys the notion that the reader has not made a mistake, but instead has altered the text in a unique way that may or may not change the reader's understanding of the text. First-grade teacher Deborah Shadle-Talbert states: "We no longer call miscues mistakes or errors in the classroom. The children have even begun to say 'miscues'" (2000).

The word *miscue* has taken on additional meanings as we have woven it in to our professional language. Throughout this book, both in my text and in the quotations from teachers and researchers, you will see the word *miscue* used in these ways:

1. A Noun—An unexpected change from the written text during oral reading:
   The student made a *miscue* when she was reading.
2. A Verb—To make a change from the written text during oral reading:
   He will often *miscue* when reading too fast.
3. A Noun—A method of analyzing oral reading. An abbreviation of the term *miscue analysis*:
   I really enjoy teaching *miscue* to my third graders.

As we become more comfortable using the terms related to miscue analysis, we begin to share a new vocabulary and perspective on the reading process with students. First-grade teacher Sally Cummins finds her "students are also using the term 'miscue' with their reading" (2000). We can conduct a think-aloud procedure (Davey 1983) and show students what goes on in our heads as we read. To do this, we put a text on an overhead transparency, and read through a difficult passage in front of students. As we read, we stop and talk with them about the miscues we make, our questions, our confusions, our predictions, our visual images, our understanding, and our fix-up strategies when we've lost meaning.

As we continue to talk with students about their miscues, they begin to listen more carefully to their own reading, and pay closer attention to their own thinking and use of strategies during reading. Before we know it, we hear students talking about their miscues with each other off in the classroom library corner during reading workshop (see Chapter 8). In reading conferences, we notice students speculating on the reasons why they may have made a particular miscue. In the reflection circle that concludes the working time, students share their miscues and strategies for figuring out unfamiliar words.

In my class of seven-, eight-, and nine-year-old students, this talking time was full of discoveries about our reading. As students became aware of their actions and became articulate in sharing them, I put these ideas on a classroom poster titled "What do smart readers do?" The list, generated from the students' observations of their own reading process, continued to grow throughout the year, and the poster served as a resource for students when they were reading independently. These group discussions helped students to formulate hypotheses about the reasons for their miscues (I thought the word right there was going to be *through* because the word before it was *moving* but it was *though*), to become metacognitive about miscues (The word *horse* looks a lot like *house* but it doesn't make sense there), and to develop a new awareness of reading strategies (I noticed I can use a naming strategy and keep reading—I just said *Mr. Z.* and kept going). These discussions empowered each student to take ownership of his or her own reading process.

An Invitation: Take a Look at Yourself as a Reader

An important place to start in understanding students as readers is to observe ourselves during reading. I am going to present two different texts for you to read that will help you look at the things you do as a reader. When we are reading a text that is easy for us, our reading process and the strategies we use come so naturally that we may not notice them. When reading a more difficult passage, we tend to slow down the process, which allows us to bring our thought processes to a conscious level—the strategies we use, the questions we ask, and the mental convolutions that take place as we try to make sense of the text.

My purpose here is to get you to think about what you do as a reader and to compare your strategies to what students may do when they are reading a difficult text. Each time you reflect on your own reading, see if you can make a parallel to the thought processes students may go through when they are reading. OK, here's the first passage from Jung (1957, 57)—hold on to your thoughts! Please keep the following questions in mind:

- *What do you notice about your reading process?* (e.g., skipping words, rereading, reading slowly, making predictions)
- *What do you notice about your thought processes?* (e.g., asking questions, feeling confused, wondering about unfamiliar words, getting distracted)
- *What do you notice about your miscues?* (e.g., making inappropriate predictions, making corrections, making a miscue that changes the meaning, correcting miscues)

In the same way that our misconception of the solar system had to be freed from prejudice by Copernicus, the most strenuous efforts of a well-nigh revolutionary nature were needed to free psychology, first from the spell of mythological idea, and then from the prejudice that the psyche is, on the one hand, a mere epiphenomenon of a biochemical process in the brain or, on the other hand, a wholly unapproachable and recondite matter.

- *What are you thinking now?* I'm thinking that's a pretty long sentence. I had a hard time keeping track of what I'd read earlier! Did you come to any words you didn't know? Did you reread? Did you understand the overall passage?

- *What were your strategies when you came to an unfamiliar word?* Did you skip it? Did you think of what might make sense there? Did you see any chunk of the word you knew? Did you sound it out? Where did you put the accent?

Here's what went on in my head as I read this passage: I didn't know the meaning of epiphenomenon, so I continued reading to see if the rest of the text would help me. I also saw phenomenon was part of the word, and that made enough sense for me right then, so I kept going. I knew, if I needed to, I could look that one up later. I didn't know the meaning of recondite, but I looked for chunks of the word that I knew, and used the familiar to get at the unfamiliar. I saw the ite ending and figured it was an adjective (as in erudite). I also thought this because it preceded the noun matter, and because it was used in a parallel structure with unapproachable; I guessed that it means something like *out of reach.* I looked it up and found it means "hidden from sight, concealed" and "difficult or impossible for one of ordinary understanding or knowledge to comprehend" (Merriam-Webster 1990, 984). I was using context clues to create an hypothesis about the probable meaning of a word.

Similarly, Sue Peters, a school psychologist intern, noticed when reflecting on her own reading process: "I've become more aware of my own strategies and approaches, especially the use of context clues in an attempt to understand the meaning of an unfamiliar word. Rather than merely stressing the 'sound it out' strategy, I now place far more emphasis on context clues to gather meaning in a tutoring setting" (2000).

- *Did you make any miscues?* If so, did you reread and self-correct? Did your miscues make sense or change the meaning? Did you make a miscue that could have been left uncorrected?
- *Did you try to access some background knowledge to help you?* Did you think about what you knew about Copernicus to help you make sense of the passage? Did you know about Copernicus? (This example helps us think about the referents that appear in narratives that further deepen metaphorical meaning for students if they know the reference.) Were there key words that helped you access other schema (psyche, biochemical)?
- *What else did you notice about your reading?*

The previous passage served us well in getting us thinking about our own reading process, but it is from a specific disciplinary text. Let's try a paragraph from a novel to see if we use similar or different strategies as we read. Try this selection from *Cold Mountain* (Frazier 1997, 27):

She began to read, but stirring though the story's events were, she could not get food off her mind. Since the search for eggs had not gone in her favor, she had not yet eaten breakfast, though the day was coming up on midmorning. After only a few pages, she put the book into a pocket and went down to the kitchen and prowled through the pantry for something she could turn into a meal. She spent nearly two hours firing up the oven and trying to raise a loaf of wheat bread with saleratus, the only leavening she could find. When the loaf came from the oven, though, it resembled a great poorly made biscuit; its crust was of a crackerlike texture, and the remainder was sodden and tasted of uncooked flour.

Ah! Was that easier!? Consider the following as you reflect on your reading of this passage:

- *Were your strategies the same?* Were they different because you were reading a more comfortable text?
- *Were you able to visualize the woman in the kitchen?* Have you ever cooked on a wood stove? Did you think about a time you made bread and it didn't come out right?
- *Did you make any miscues?* In the first line, I read through for though and then self-corrected.
- *Would this paragraph be easier to retell because of the more familiar topic?*
- *What did you do when you came to the word* saleratus? Did you notice the author's strategy of defining the word after the comma? We find out it is a form of leavening, which helps our understanding, that is, if we know what leavening is!

Here we see a different stance as a reader (Rosenblatt 1978), in that we are reading more for an overall enjoyment of the text (aesthetic stance) rather than trying to take anything away with us (efferent stance) as we did in the psychology passage. Therefore, our anxiety level was probably lower (I know mine was!); we were able to access familiar background knowledge and common experiences. When we encountered a difficult word, we had context clues from a considerate author. We can discuss these different approaches to reading tasks with students and help them see that when our stance as a reader changes, sometimes our strategies do as well.

These are some of the purposes of this invitation:

- To help you notice your own reading process and to think about the strategies you use.
- To draw attention to your own miscues and to help you realize all readers make miscues.
- To help you think about possible reasons for miscues and how you became aware of them.

- To draw attention to your fix-up strategies.
- To help you think about how language cueing systems provide us with information as we are reading; that is, to help you see how you draw on information from what you know about the structure of language (syntax), the meanings of words (semantics), the information on the page (graphophonics), and your knowledge about how language is used in different social settings (pragmatics) to help you construct meaning.

Miscues provide important information about readers. We can listen to a reader who may appear to be struggling with a text and realize that she is either making miscues that don't change meaning or that she is correcting most of her other miscues. We develop a new perspective on what reading is and learn to value the smart things readers are doing with language rather than seeking an *accurate,* or perfect, rendition of written text during oral reading.

Through the lens of miscue analysis, we see readers who are drawing on what they know to make sense of what they are reading (Davenport 1993). Based on examining miscues of children who speak other languages, and those who speak English, we observe readers who know a great deal about how their native language works (Crowell 1995). We hear readers who make great predictions about upcoming unfamiliar words, who monitor their reading and correct their miscues, and who use their background knowledge to help them make sense of what they read (Y. Goodman, Watson, and Burke 1987). We learn to recognize when a reader is using the language cueing systems in a balanced way. For example, sometimes a reader for whom the systems are not working in harmony will overrely on print cues to the detriment of making meaning so that miscues look a lot like the text item but don't make any sense.

Now that you're getting a feel for your own reading process and miscues, let's examine the kinds of miscues readers can make.

What Are Some Different Types of Miscues?: An Introduction

There are many ways readers can change a text as they read aloud. Figure 2–1 lists some of the types of miscues that are introduced briefly here, and then examined in depth, using examples from readers, in Chapter 4.

Substitutions

- One-word substitutions: Reader substitutes one word for a word in the text.
- High-quality miscues: Do not change the meaning of the text.
- Complex miscues: Reader substitutes one phrase for a phrase in the text.
- Reversals: Reader reads the words in the text, but reverses the order of two words.

TYPES OF MISCUES

SUBSTITUTIONS

- One-word substitutions
- High-quality miscues
- Complex miscues
- Reversals
- Nonwords
- Dialect usages
- Misarticulations
- Intonation shifts
- Split syllables

OMISSIONS

- Word
- Phrase or line
- End punctuation

PARTIALS

INSERTIONS

REGRESSIONS

- Repetition
- Abandoning the correct form
- Unsuccessful attempt to correct
- Correction

PAUSES

REPEATED MISCUES

COMPLICATED MISCUES

FIGURE 2–1 Types of Miscues

- Nonwords: The miscue is a word that is not in our language.
- Dialect usages: A word commonly used by the reader in his dialect; means the same as the word in the text for which it is substituted. Certain insertions and omissions can also be dialect usages.
- Misarticulations: This is what I call *kid dialect*.
- Intonation shifts: Emphasis is put on a different syllable from where it is usually placed.
- Split syllables: Reader hesitates in the middle of a word, then finishes the word.

Omissions

- Words: Reader leaves out a word in the text.
- Phrases or lines: Reader leaves out several consecutive words or a line of text.
- End punctuation: Reader does not pause at the end of a sentence to indicate the recognition of end punctuation.

Partials

The reader begins to pronounce a word, but does not finish it and does not make another attempt to read the word.

Insertions

Reader adds one or more words to the text.

Regressions

- Repetitions: Reader reads the text correctly, then backs up and says the same word or phrase more than once.
- Abandoning the correct form: Reader says what is in the text, but then backs up and reads the same word or phrase again and makes a miscue.
- Unsuccessful attempts to correct: Reader tries more than once to correct a miscue, but continues to miscue on each attempt.
- Corrections: Reader makes a miscue, then backs up and reads the text correctly.

Pauses

Reader hesitates between words for an extended period of time then continues reading.

Repeated Miscues

Throughout the text, there is more than one occasion when the same miscue is substituted for the exact text item.

Complicated Miscues

In one sentence or phrase there are several different miscues, that is, a great deal of miscue activity.

Bringing It All Together: Listening to Our Readers

We've defined miscues, experienced making miscues ourselves, and examined why we might have made miscues. We took a brief introductory look at the types of miscues with which we will soon become very familiar.

With this new awareness of miscues, a wonderful thing begins to happen. You will never listen to students read the same way again. Even if you are not writing anything down as you listen to your readers, you will be mentally making notes about the types of miscues they are making, whether meaning was changed, and whether they are self-correcting. When this happens, you are well on your way to developing a new lens for seeing students as learners. You will have new "ears" for listening to students as readers. First-grade teacher Karen Stack observed: "I have learned much about the reading process from this class, and from the miscues that I have been doing with my students. I feel much more capable as a first-grade teacher in effectively teaching reading to my students, and I feel that I have developed miscue ears" (2000).

As we will see, students can develop miscue ears as well. Miscue analysis allows you and your students to interpret oral reading in a way that sheds new light on how wonderfully smart they are! As preschool teacher Kimberly Kay Rahn reflected: "I have discovered the valuable information that could become available for every student in your classroom through the use of miscue analysis. I no longer listen to children read as I have before" (2000).

Now that we know what miscues are, let's take a closer look at miscue analysis!

3

What Is Miscue Analysis?

Believing in children and their abilities and imparting that message creates the basis from which the seeds of success have an opportunity to develop and grow. That's what I love about miscue, it begins and ends on a positive note. It's not about pointing out mistakes. It's about creating awareness of strengths and building on those strengths. Powerful . . . truly powerful.

—Valeria Evans Pierce, Staff Developer

What

Before we examine several procedures in depth, let's look at definitions of miscue analysis and begin to explore how it helps us to better understand what reading is and what readers do. We'll also review the development of miscue analysis from the early research through the various alternative procedures.

How Is Miscue Analysis Defined?

Miscue analysis is a method of examining oral reading. It is a tool that allows us to explore why students make unexpected responses when they read. It gives us a "window on the reading process" (K. Goodman 1973, 5); that is, it provides access to a process that is usually out of our grasp and invisible. Miscue analysis gives us a way of observing readers' control of the reading process, describing their use of language, and explaining what we hear when we listen to them read. Not only can we evaluate where readers are having difficulty, but we can also appreciate their use of background knowledge and marvel at the strategies they bring to bear on their reading. We can observe how readers are using language and how they are constructing meaning.

A marvelous thing happens when teachers and researchers learn about miscue analysis. They don't hear *mistakes* any more. They come to realize that "in its interpretation of reading as a language process, miscue analysis shows that 'mistakes' aren't really mistakes; they are merely phenomena that occur in most any act of reading" (Flurkey 1995, 11). Additionally, "miscue analysis not only reveals degrees of reading proficiency; more important, it provides teacher/researchers with knowledge about the reading process itself" (Y. Goodman, Watson, and Burke 1987, 3).

As Martens reminds us, miscue analysis helps us get inside kids' heads to see how the reading process works (1995, 39):

> We no longer hear readers' stumblings, false starts, and mistakes as errors that indicate poorly learned skills or consider them to be careless lazy readers who aren't thinking or paying attention to the text. Instead, we hear sensible predictions, corrections, substitutions, and insertions evidencing readers' knowledge and control of language and the world as they transact with the text to make sense and construct meaning.

Those who understand and use miscue analysis a great deal will not only be able to analyze miscues formally, but they will also be able to use miscue analysis techniques whenever they listen to anyone read. Even if they are not writing anything down, teachers can mentally note of the types of miscues they hear. In short, miscue analysis helps us look at what *readers do* and what *reading is*.

How

Now let's take a look at the spectrum of miscue analysis procedures available, including taped and untaped methods. We'll also compare Over the Shoulder (OTS) miscue analysis (Davenport 1998) to Running Records (Clay 1993, 2000).

What Are the Different Miscue Analysis Procedures? An Overview

There are several procedures for conducting miscue analysis; some are taped, and each has a slightly different focus. We will take a brief look at all the procedures here, and later explore Procedure III, Procedure IV, and OTS in depth. Figure 3–1 contains a summary of the various miscue analysis procedures.

We are looking at Procedure III, Procedure IV, and OTS because they are the most usable for classroom teachers on a daily basis. They provide substantive information about readers, yet they are doable within the context of a busy school day in a classroom full of children (see Chapter 8).

Taped Procedures

Take more time

Procedures I and II (Y. Goodman, Watson, and Burke 1987) offer teachers the most in-depth information about a particular reader and her reading process and are the most time-consuming of the current miscue analysis procedures. These two procedures are most commonly taught in graduate courses focusing on advanced literacy assessment in general and miscue analysis in particular, and are appropriately used in most research settings (Brown, K. Goodman, and Marek 1996).

Retrospective Miscue Analysis (Y. Goodman and Marek 1996) allows readers to become involved in analyzing their own miscues. A tape recording is made as a student reads a text aloud, then she listens to her own tape while looking at the same text again. She stops the tape and talks with the teacher about her miscues

Most Complex—Taped						Least Complex—Untaped	
Original Goodman Taxonomy	Original Reading Miscue Inventory	Procedure I	Procedure II	Procedure III	Retrospective Miscue Analysis	Over the Shoulder	Procedure IV

FIGURE 3–1 Levels of Complexity of Various Miscue Analysis Procedures

when she notices that she has made changes to the text. A second tape recorder is used to record this conversation between the teacher and the student as she listens to her original reading, stops the first tape recorder, and makes comments about her miscues and strategies.

This has been shown to be a powerful method of helping readers better understand the reading process and realize it is not an error-free reproduction of what is on the page (Y. Goodman and Marek 1996). Readers also see the many things they are doing right, such as self-correcting and making miscues that don't change meaning.

Procedure III is also a taped procedure. A reader is invited to read a text aloud and retell what he remembers. Then his miscues are marked on a typescript and sentences are coded by asking the following three questions about each sentence. As the reader left the sentence, in the reader's dialect, and in the context of the passage (Y. Goodman, Watson, and Burke 1987):

- Does it sound like language?
- Does it make sense?
- Did it change the author's intended meaning?

See Appendix A for LaMar's complete Procedure III typescript.

In the original Procedure III, it is suggested that the teacher-researcher make note of the graphic similarity between the miscue and the text item by writing an *H* (for High), an *S* (for Some) or an *N* (for None) over each miscue or in the margin of the typescript beside the miscue. I found it easier to observe information about individual miscues if I made a separate tally sheet. On the sheet, each miscue is listed, and the following questions are asked (see Appendix B for LaMar's complete miscue tally form and Appendix C for a blank miscue tally form):

- Was the miscue corrected?
- Was the miscue left uncorrected?
- If left uncorrected, did the miscue change meaning?
- What is the graphic similarity between the miscue and the related text item?

Procedure III is a useful method for classroom teachers, particularly for finding out more about students for whom they have significant questions. I only conducted this more detailed procedure with a *few* students each year and used the OTS or Procedure IV daily with all my students.

Procedure III consists of the processes in the following list.

With the student:

- Talking with the student briefly about the text to be read
- Inviting the student to read, reminding her you won't be able to help her right now
- Taping a student's oral reading of a complete story; a section of a chapter book with a clear beginning, middle, and end; or a selection from a content area text that develops a clear concept
- Asking the student for a retelling of the selection (unaided retelling) and following up with the cued retelling, which is explained in Chapter 4

After the student leaves the taping session:

- Marking miscues on a typescript of the text the student read
- Tallying and examining individual miscues on the miscue tally form (or numbering each miscue and writing H, S, or N above each miscue on the typescript)
- Examining the patterns of miscues
- Coding sentences on a typescript of the text the student read
- Listening to the retelling (see Appendix D for LaMar's retelling)
- Noting the characters and events the reader remembered through the unaided and the cued retellings on the prepared retelling guide (see Appendix E)
- Transferring all information to the reader profile (see Appendix F for LaMar's reader profile and Appendix G for a blank reader profile)
- Interpreting results and determining the student's strengths and areas of concern
- Making decisions about instruction based on all the available information

Optional, but recommended, additional steps:

- Conducting a Burke Reading Interview (Y. Goodman, Watson, and Burke 1987, see Appendix H),

- Engaging the student in Retrospective Miscue Analysis (Y. Goodman and Marek, 1996). It is preferable, but not always possible, to ask the student to listen to the taped reading and discuss the miscues.

PROCEDURE III DOCUMENTS:

- Typescript: Miscues are marked and sentences are coded
- Miscue tally form: List and analysis of individual miscues (my adaptation)
- Retelling guide: List of story elements, checked according to what the student remembered in the unaided and cued retellings; comprehension score is recorded here
- Reader profile: A summary sheet that contains all the information gathered through this reading, retelling, and analysis

Untaped Procedures

Procedure IV (Y. Goodman, Watson, and Burke 1987) and the *Over the Shoulder Procedure* (Davenport 1998) are two untaped miscue analysis procedures. The reader is also referred to Rhodes and Shanklin's Classroom Reading Miscue Assessment for an alternative untaped procedure (1990). It consists of a Procedure IV and a series of follow-up questions about readers' strategies and ability to construct meaning.

The OTS procedure consists of the processes in the following list.

WITH THE STUDENT:

- Ask a student to join you in a reading conference and to bring any book he is currently reading
- Talk briefly about the text and complete the *cover page*
- Listen to the student read while looking over her shoulder at the text
- Complete the *miscue page* during the reading
- Scribe the retelling and discussion after the reading on the cover page
- Select and discuss several miscues that changed meaning
- Select a strategy to introduce or review
- Celebrate what the reader has done well

AFTER THE STUDENT HAS LEFT THE CONFERENCE:

- Complete the *insights page* and determine graphic similarity. See Appendix I for Josh's OTS Form and Appendix J for a blank form.

A Procedure IV consists of the processes in the following list.

WITH THE STUDENT:

- Ask the student to choose a book and to join you in a reading conference
- Listen as the student reads aloud while looking over his shoulder at the text
- Evaluate each sentence for semantic acceptability
- Tally the sentences as either semantically acceptable (Yes) or semantically unacceptable (No)

- Ask for a retelling of the selection—make anecdotal notes
- Discuss strategies or miscues

AFTER THE STUDENT LEAVES THE CONFERENCE:

- Calculate the comprehending score—percentage of semantically acceptable sentences (see Figure 7–2 for second-grader Claire's Procedure IV form and Appendix K for a blank form)

In Chapter 6, we will examine the "When do I use which procedure?" question. For a brief summary of this introduction to the different methods and some general guidelines and considerations to use when making the decision about which procedure to use, see Figure 3–2.

It is highly recommended that teachers learn to conduct a Procedure III before trying one of the shorter, untaped procedures (Y. Goodman, Watson, and Burke 1987). This background will provide more familiarity with types of miscues, a better understanding of readers' various uses of the language cueing systems, and a strong foundation for understanding the nature of the reading process. These areas of knowledge will help provide the "ear" for miscues that will make conducting Procedure IV and the OTS much easier! For an overview of the evidence we gain from each of these three miscue analysis procedures, see Figure 3–3.

	Procedure III	**Over the Shoulder**	**Procedure IV**
Student with whom I'm working	• Student for whom I have a lot of questions—I need more information about this student's reading process or his use of strategies	• Student for whom I have a good sense of where she is as a reader—I am collecting ongoing assessment information	• Student for whom I have no concerns as a reader—I am collecting ongoing assessment information
Time	• Half hour to conduct • 1–2 hours to analyze	• 10–15 minutes to conduct • 5 minutes to analyze	• 10–15 minutes to conduct • 5 minutes to analyze
Considerations	• More depth • Taped	• Less depth • Untaped	• Less depth • Untaped

FIGURE 3–2 Comparison of Three Miscue Analysis Procedures

Evidence Gained	Taped	Untaped	
	Procedure III	Over the Shoulder	Procedure IV
Syntactic acceptability of complete sentences	X		
Semantic acceptability of complete sentences	X		X
Semantic acceptability of individual miscues	X	X	
Retelling of passage read	X	X	X
Comprehension discussed after retelling	X	X	X
Comprehension score from retelling guide (understanding *after* the reading)	X		
Comprehending score (understanding *during* the reading)	X		X
Graphic similarity of individual miscues	X	X	
Self-corrections	X	X	
Ways reader is constructing meaning	X	X	
Ways reader is disrupting meaning	X	X	

FIGURE 3–3 Overview of Evidence Gained from Three Miscue Analysis Procedures

Please realize that I have not been out of the classroom so long that I don't remember all the demands of full-time teaching. I do. And I know that many readers will be thinking, "This is a lot to learn! When do I have time to learn it, much less have time to do this after I *do* learn it?" I understand that too. All the teachers I know who now use miscue analysis daily had a similar reaction before they began. This is one of the main purposes of this book—to help you see how you *can* use miscue analysis every day to know your readers better—especially through Procedure IV and OTS. Martens understood these apprehensions too, when she offered this invitation to teachers just beginning to learn miscue analysis (1995, 42):

> If you are hesitant to try, we want to assure you that knowledge about what miscue analysis means for instruction grows from participating in the process. Do nothing else right now than listen to your students read. Really listen. Then assume any miscue they make is for a reason. . . . It may not be easy at first but it will get easier if you continue to listen.

The more you listen, the more insights into the reading process and into your students you will have.

So the best place to start when learning miscue analysis is to tune in and listen, listen, listen, and trust that your readers are doing smart things with language and not just "making mistakes" as they read.

How Does Miscue Analysis Compare to Running Record?

Many teachers have been trained in Reading Recovery (Clay 1993, 2000; Fountas and Pinnell 1996) and use Running Records as a way of making notations about what they hear as students read aloud. Clay states that the "prime purpose of a Running Record is to understand more about how children are using what they know to get to the messages of the text, or in other words what reading processes they are using" (2000, 8). Running Records are probably the most similar to the Over the Shoulder Procedure because they have the following in common—both procedures:

- Provide ongoing reading assessment of emergent and early readers
- Offer an immediate way of writing down enough information about oral reading to be used to assess general aspects of a student's reading process
- Provide information about a reader's strengths and areas of concern
- Provide documentation about the reading process for teachers, students, and parents
- Are conducted while sitting next to the student in a one-on-one conferencing setting
- Are conducted without using a tape recorder
- Can be done with or without a prepared form

Additional purposes of OTS miscue analysis are to:

- Provide ongoing reading assessment of *all* levels of readers
- Provide a means of sharing what we know about them as readers with students
- Provide a platform for reflective talking with students about their reading
- Provide an opportunity for teaching

It is important to ask at this point, "When do I use Running Record and when do I use OTS?" A great question!

Use OTS

- When students are reading too fast to make the checks used in Running Records for each word read correctly
- When working with all students, particularly older students

Use Running Records

- When emergent readers are just getting comfortable with reading connected text
- When early readers are reading slowly
- With readers through about second grade
- When you need an *Error Ratio* or *Accuracy Rate* (These are *not* addressed by the OTS Procedure.)

Routman suggests that teachers become familiar with Running Records "and/or miscue analysis. Both are standardized procedures you will want to be familiar with for examining the strategies the reader employs in reading orally" (2000, 112). She also notes: "While running records [no capitals in original] are a great tool for developing readers, they are being increasingly misused for older, fluent readers. Such use was never intended, is unnecessary, and is not a good use of student or teacher time" (113). Although some teachers use a modified Running Record with older students, it is intended for use with students through about second grade. As Clay states (2000, 25):

> If Running Records are used with older readers there should be a special reason for taking them. They are excellent for recording the early phases of literacy acquisition but before long what the reader is doing becomes too fast and too sophisticated for teachers to observe in real time.

This is one advantage of OTS: We are able to make note of the oral reading of older students. For a comparison of OTS and Running Record, see Figure 3–4.

When teachers are trying to decide which procedure is most appropriate for assessing a student's reading, they need to consider the following:

- Which procedure will give me the type and depth of information I need?
- What are my purposes for this particular assessment? If it is a formative, ongoing assessment, I might use Running Record, Procedure IV, or OTS, depending on the age of the student. If it is a summative, formal assessment for which I need a great deal of in-depth information, I might use Procedure III.
- How well is this student reading? Is she an emergent reader? If so, Running Record might be appropriate. Is she reading so proficiently that I would not be able to keep up with her and make the checks in a Running Record for each correct word? In that case, I might use OTS. Is he a reader for whom I have no concerns and just need documentation of his reading? In that case, I might use Procedure IV.

CRITERIA OF COMPARISON	OVER THE SHOULDER PROCEDURE	RUNNING RECORD
We use this procedure when we are working with which readers?	All readers, any time	All readers at the early phase of acquiring literacy, any time
What type of text is read for the assessment session?	Any text	Any text in the classroom setting Usually a leveled book in the Reading Recovery setting
Is the session recorded?	No	No
Is there a shorthand used?	No—Write down what the reader said and what the text said when there is a miscue	Yes—Checks for each correct word, what the reader said and what the text said when there is an *error* (see Clay 2000 for scoring conventions)
What are changes in the text called?	Miscues	Errors (sometimes called miscues, see Taberski 2000)
How are unexpected responses viewed?	As valuable information about the reader's use of the language cueing systems	As valuable information about the reader's use of the language cueing systems
Is the student asked to give a retelling or discuss the reading?	Yes, after each reading	The teacher may choose to ask for a retelling
How is comprehension evaluated?	Holistically through the retelling and teaching conversation Quantitatively through an examination of corrections and miscues that did not change meaning	Teacher observes use of meaning, structure, and visual information during reading Teacher may ask for a retelling or converse with student after the reading but Clay (2000) cautions against asking "comprehension questions" because "when different teachers ask different questions, the assessment is weakened" (14); that is, it becomes difficult to compare comprehension for different students reading the same text when different questions are asked
Is there a prepared typescript?	No	No
Is there a form to be used?	Yes	Yes
Can this procedure be done without using the form?	Yes	Yes
What kinds of information are gained from this procedure?	Strategy use Use of language cueing systems Corrections	Strategy use Use of language cueing systems Self-correction Ratio

FIGURE 3–4 Comparison of OTS and Running Records

	Actions as a reader High-quality miscues Comprehension Graphic similarity between the miscue and the text item	Actions as a reader Error Ratio Accuracy Rate Comprehension
Does the teacher tell the student an unfamiliar word when she gets stuck?	Not right away —Teacher asks student what she is thinking and what word would make sense there —Teaching conversation follows and teacher may help student identify chunks of the word she knows, or he may tell her the word during the discussion and discuss its meaning if she hasn't heard it before —These miscues or any misconceptions may again be discussed after the reading and retelling —This is seen as a teaching opportunity	Not right away —When there is an "appeal" from student, teacher tells student, "You try it" —If child tries, appeals, and tries, teacher can tell her the word —This is counted as an error
Has the student read the text before?	No—Usually not —Student is invited to bring any book he is currently reading —If it is a chapter book, he continues on from where he last read	In the classroom setting, any text can be used—it can be a new book or a book that has been read before Yes—In the Reading Recovery setting, student has read the book in the previous session
What is the view of the reading process that supports the use of this procedure?	Reading is an active process of constructing meaning Readers can change the text through unexpected responses and not change the meaning the author intended	"A message-getting, problem-solving activity, which increases in power and flexibility the more it is practiced. My definition states that within the directional constraints of the printer's code, language and visual perception responses are purposefully directed by the reader in some integrated way to the problem of extracting meaning from cues in a text, in sequence, so that the reader brings a maximum of understanding to the author's message" (Clay 1991, 6).
Is special training required before a teacher uses this procedure?	It is recommended that a teacher be familiar with Procedure III and the supporting view of the reading process Also recommended are several workshops in how to conduct OTS	It is recommended that teachers attend at least three training sessions on how to conduct Running Records, working with teachers knowledgeable in this method

FIGURE 3–4 (continued)

Where

It is important to create a space and time to meet with students individually to collect the information needed to conduct miscue analysis. The setting can be a conferencing corner in your classroom. The time needed for each procedure will vary. Procedure IV and OTS can be conducted in brief conferences during the reading workshop. Procedure III requires a tape recording and can be done before or after school, or at some time when the classroom is quiet.

The Setting for Taped Procedures

If you decide you are going to conduct a Procedure III, you will need to create a comfortable, quiet setting to do so. It is difficult to get a quality recording and really be able to hear the student's voice on the tape if there is background noise, as is typical in a busy classroom. For the three or four times a year I needed to conduct a Procedure III, I got parent permission to have a student come in early or stay after school to do the taping. The sessions usually take less than an hour, especially if you are just having the student read and retell a story or content-area passage and you are not conducting any interviews at this time. Our purposes in the taped sessions are to gather assessment information and to let the student demonstrate how he independently uses problem-solving strategies when reading; therefore there is no discussion with the student during the more formal miscue analysis procedures.

The Setting for Untaped Procedures

Our purposes in the untaped sessions are to talk and teach. We discuss what we hear and observe with students, we get at their meanings, we discover their insights, and we celebrate their strengths. We suggest appropriate strategies and build new background as we see they are needed. We listen to students read, conduct an OTS or Procedure IV, and then we have lots to talk about.

Usually I see two or three students each day as I conduct my OTS conferences during our reading workshop. We'll look at this organizational structure (Hagerty 1992; Hindley 1996; Allen and Gonzalez 1998; Calkins 2001; Serafini 2001) in Chapter 8.

Why

As with everything we do as teachers, we need to examine the rationale for using miscue analysis to examine students' oral reading. Our practices, such as getting to know our students well, conducting miscue analysis, or teaching meaning-based strategy lessons, should all emerge from our belief system about learning and teaching. They should also be supported by a theoretical foundation.

Theories Guide Us

There is a strong theory base that supports the use of miscue analysis. Based on the research of Michael Halliday (1985), we understand how children come to understand language through the use of language. Similarly, children become more capable readers through reading and by having teachers bring the nature of the reading process to a conscious level for them. Based on the research of Frank Smith (1973), we understand that readers use both the print on the page (visual information) and bring to the reading their prior knowledge and background experiences (nonvisual information). Based on the work of Ken Goodman (1969), we know that all readers make changes in the text when reading orally. From his research we see that readers gain information from the language cueing systems and that reading is a language process. Louise Rosenblatt's transactional theory (1978) informs us about the changes that take place in both the text and the reader during the reading process. From David Bloome's writings (1985), we can better understand the social and cultural aspects of the reading process and the social variations in language.

The graphic in Figure 3–5 represents the dynamic relationship between our *practices*, the *theories* that support them, and the *beliefs* we hold. How does this model help us examine our rationale for using miscue analysis? Often, when we try something new as a teacher, we begin doing it because we have seen someone else do it and became intrigued with its possibilities for our students. We don't yet have the theory behind it, but we have observed another teacher being successful with this practice.

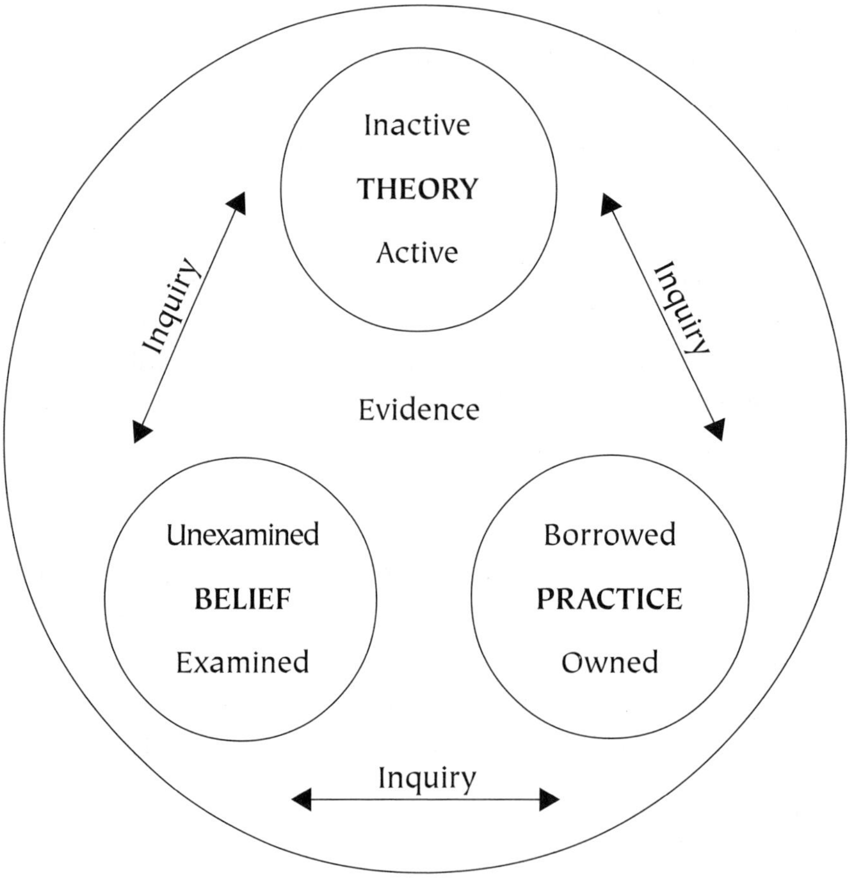

FIGURE 3–5 Belief–Theory–Practice Model (Davenport and Watson 1993; Watson 1994)

Everything we do as teachers is based on something we believe. According to Davenport and Watson (1993) there is a recursive, reciprocal relationship between the following:

- The theories to which we ascribe:
  I have heard this is a good thing to do because of what folks have found through researching this idea.
- The classroom practices:
  This is how I choose to engage my learners and assess their progress.
- The beliefs we hold:
  This is what I know to be true based on my experiences and my students' successes.

Whether or not we have taken the time to bring our beliefs about a particular practice, such as assessing readers through miscue analysis, to the conscious level and articulate them, the beliefs we hold and the theories that support them are there.

Principles of Assessment Guide Us

Rhodes and Shanklin (1993) help us think through this process of identifying what we believe about literacy assessment in general, and the assessment of reading in particular. Let's take a look at the summary in Figure 3–6 of their purposes and principles of literacy assessment and how each relates to the use of miscue analysis in the classroom.

What Do We Gain? Our Reasons for Conducting Miscue Analysis

There are many reasons for conducting miscue analysis. Most important, it informs us about an individual reader and the strategies he is using to construct meaning during reading. We see how a student deals with unfamiliar words and what he does when confronted with a variety of texts. The following list summarizes what we learn *about readers* through miscue analysis:

- They are in control of their reading process and actively construct meaning.
- They make use of the information gained from the language cueing systems to read and interpret text.
- They make use of their background knowledge and prior experience to make sense of the texts they are reading.
- They use a variety of strategies to figure out unfamiliar words.
- They are able to monitor their reading and self-correct miscues when necessary.
- They demonstrate their comprehension of what they have read through their retelling and discussion.

PURPOSES OF LITERACY ASSESSMENT	HOW THIS PURPOSE RELATES TO USING MISCUE ANALYSIS IN THE CLASSROOM
To determine what development is occurring	If we conduct miscue analysis frequently over time, we see changes in the profiles that emerge as students gain more control over their reading process.
To identify a student's strengths and weaknesses in reading and writing	Miscue analysis allows us to identify what students are doing well as readers, such as making appropriate predictions or self-corrections, and to see areas in which they need improvement—for example, in using fix-up strategies when meaning is lost.
To discover the power of your teaching	Miscue analysis helps us observe how well students are using the strategies we have shared through our focus lessons with the whole group or through our teaching during the individual reading conferences.
To learn more about the development of reading and writing	The more profiles we create of readers over time, the better sense we can gain about how reading proficiency develops.
To sharpen the quality of your observations and your confidence in them	Miscue analysis honors teachers' perceptions and observations of readers, and values the insights gained through the conversations during reading conferences.
To have information about a student as a reader and writer to share with others	The miscue analysis forms and supporting documents, like the reader profile, provide accessible evidence that can be discussed with the student and shared with parents during conferences.
To assess program strengths and weaknesses and guide staff development	Miscue analysis keeps us in tune with readers' strategies and the texts they are reading. It can also be an area in which teachers support each other in their professional growth.

FIGURE 3–6 Rhodes and Shanklin's Purposes and Principles of Literacy Assessment—how they relate to the use of miscue analysis in the classroom.

PRINCIPLES OF LITERACY ASSESSMENT	HOW THIS PRINCIPLE RELATES TO USING MISCUE ANALYSIS IN THE CLASSROOM
Assess authentic reading and writing	For miscue analysis, students read complete texts, passages of novels that stand alone, or sections of content-area texts that are of sufficient length to develop a concept.
Assess reading and writing in a variety of contexts	The contexts for miscue analysis are the books students are interested in reading, including stories or content-area texts that have relevance for them.
Assess the literacy environment, instruction, and students	Miscue analysis allows us to continue to reflect on the reading opportunities, materials, and strategies we provide our students, as well as a way of assessing students themselves.
Assess processes as well as products	The focus of all miscue analysis procedures is on the process of readers constructing meaning.
Analyze error patterns in reading and writing	Although not called *errors*, we are looking for patterns in the miscues students make during reading.
Base assessment on normal developmental patterns and behavior in reading and writing	By assessing a number of students reading a wide range of texts over an extended period of time, we gain a sense of *normal* reading developmental patterns.
Clarify and use standards in the assessment of reading and writing	Our assessment of reading through miscue analysis is guided by our theoretical stance and the standards set by professional organizations (e.g., International Reading Association and National Council of Teachers of English).
Use triangulation to corroborate data and make decisions	Miscue analysis procedures offer one view of the reader. Additional information can be gained through self-evaluation, reading inventories, and standardized tests (although these are in conflict with the theoretical stance that guides us).
Involve students, parents, and other school personnel in the assessment process	Making students and parents aware of miscue analysis and the information it provides us about young readers, then inviting student self-evaluation and parents' reflections on students' progress allows them to become invested in the assessment process as well.
Make assessment an ongoing part of everyday reading and writing opportunities and instruction	Miscue analysis is conducted daily as part of the reading workshop and is frequently modeled by the teacher through the think-aloud procedure.

FIGURE 3–6 (continued)

Miscue analysis also helps us observe the reading process of an individual student and determine how she is integrating and using the language cueing systems. These systems provide important information during reading and are the reader's tools for constructing meaning. The following list summarizes what we learn *about the reading process* through miscue analysis:

- Reading is a process of constructing meaning.
- Reading is a language process.
- Reading involves bringing meaning to the text, as well as constructing meaning through transacting with the text.
- Reading involves picking up the minimal number of graphic cues to make a prediction about the text.
- The reading process is a cycle of sampling text, reading text, making predictions about upcoming text, reading to confirm those predictions, and rereading if the prediction is not confirmed.

Finally, through miscue analysis, we gain insights into the texts we are using. If we use the same text repeatedly and several students miscue at the same point, we know the syntactic structure used by the author is one with which the students are not familiar; that is, the language style is more *book* language (Summer's here and the day is hot) than *kid* language (Boy, it's hot today!). We learn to evaluate the reading material we give students, and try to find texts written in a style that students can enter in to with ease, what Watson (1997) calls "workable" texts.

Who

We have an obligation to every student in our classroom to know him or her well as a reader. We can do so through either taped or untaped procedures of miscue analysis. By engaging students in authentic reading of complete texts and analyzing what we hear as they read orally, we consider their thought, language, and cultural background to understand them as readers.

With Whom Should We Work to Conduct Miscue Analysis? Our Students as Readers

Miscue analysis is an appropriate way to observe readers of all ages. I have taught miscue analysis to reading specialists, principals, curriculum development specialists, district language arts coordinators, school psychology interns, special education teachers, preschool teachers, adult educators, ELL teachers, and classroom teachers of every K–12 grade. All have gained a new perspective on their readers.

When conducting miscue analysis with emergent readers through adults, we gain important information about individuals' strategy use and awareness of how language works. Although miscue analysis is often used with younger readers, teachers working with middle school or high school students also see their students differently. Many times secondary teachers do not consider teaching students to be better readers as part of their responsibility, and are instead more focused on teaching their particular content area. However, middle school and secondary teachers to whom I have taught miscue analysis have come away with a remarkable new appreciation for the reading process of their older students. Kevin Nice (2000), a high school social studies teacher, sums up his experience this way:

> I have learned many things about the reading process from this class . . . I have learned that even good readers can improve upon the strategies they use. . . . I will remember that meaning is far more important than anything else in reading. I will use this information in my class a number of ways. . . . I can see myself using the Over the Shoulder form during our reading time. I want my students to gain information about History, [and] if they are not capable readers with good strategies that is one less avenue they can learn from. . . . I have a new appreciation for literature as a tool in my classroom. I can safely say that the students in my class will use better strategies and become better readers because of this [miscue analysis] class.

Who Conducts Miscue Analysis? Teachers as Learners

As teachers, it is important that we continue to be learners throughout our career. Many teachers are members of either a study group (Birchak et al. 1999) or a professional group such as TAWL (Teachers Applying Whole Language) (Davenport and Watson 1993). Many seek renewal by attending professional conferences through organizations such as the Whole Language Umbrella, National Council of Teachers of English, or the International Reading Association. Miscue analysis can be one area of professional growth that colleagues decide to pursue together.

Many literacy education researchers find miscue analysis an appropriate tool for data collection and analysis (Brown, K. Goodman, and Marek 1996). Researchers appreciate the qualitative information gained as miscues are evaluated individually based on information from the language cueing systems rather than just counting the number of *mistakes* for every 100 words, for example. The reader profile (see Appendix G) also provides quantitative information that can serve as a means of comparing a large number of students or as a way of discussing an individual student with colleagues, parents, and the student. Miscue analysis allows teachers and researchers alike (and teacher-researchers!) a way of conducting inquiry into reading and entering in to a dialogue about reading with their learners.

Getting to Know Our Readers Through Miscue Analysis

One of the results of our analysis of a student's miscues is the identification of her strengths and areas in which she could improve as a reader. The strengths may include the following:

- She is using all the language systems in harmony to help her make sense of print.
- She self-corrects miscues that change meaning.
- She leaves uncorrected miscues that don't change meaning, which demonstrates she is most likely constructing meaning.
- She uses strategies, such as rereading, when meaning is lost.
- She has a nice flow to her reading with minimal pauses or regressions, not necessarily a fast pace.
- She makes effective use of minimal cues from print.
- She activates and uses appropriate background knowledge.
- She has a familiarity with "book language" and story structure.
- She is able to understand concepts in content-area texts.
- She is able to retell a passage from a narrative or expository text in a way that demonstrates comprehension.
- She has a positive self-concept as a reader.

Any of these would be an area to call to the reader's attention and to help her apply appropriate strategies. These issues are often discussed in reading conferences as well, to help readers become metacognitive about their own reading process and use of strategies.

Getting to Know Readers Through Interviews

The foundation of a strong community of readers and learners is getting to know one another in a variety of ways (Bridges 1995). There are several interviews that have been developed that allow us insights into our students, particularly in the area of reading (Wilde 2000). For very young students, it is often difficult to access their thinking, but we need to begin discussions about their reading from the earliest encounters with print to guide the development of their metacognitive awareness of themselves as readers (Davenport 1993).

Burke Reading Interview

Formulated by Carolyn Burke (Y. Goodman, Watson, and Burke 1987), this interview is often conducted in conjunction with Procedure III (see Appendix H). Also, many teachers conduct a Burke Reading Interview with each of their students early in the school year to gain a sense of students' perceptions of the reading process, their awareness of reading strategies, and their self-concepts as readers. Some teachers have students complete the interview in writing several times a year to observe changes in these views over time (Diener 2001).

From this interview, we see a spectrum of students' understanding of the reading process ranging from "reading is making sense" to "reading is calling out all the words." We develop our understanding of students' views of reading by looking at several responses to the interview questions. For example, if they say (1) they sound out words when they come to something they don't know; (2) good readers they know sound out words when they're stuck; and (3) teachers helping readers in trouble with a word would tell them to sound it out, then we have a pretty good sense that the readers have a *word-based* view of reading. Each of these responses is focused at the word level. We would also recognize that the readers have articulated a limited awareness of possible strategies to use.

On the other hand, if we hear students say (1) when they are stuck they skip the word, go on, and think of a word that would make sense at that point in the sentence; (2) they think good readers understand what they read; or (3) their teachers would help them figure out what a word means by telling them to read more and then come back to the hard word, we can assume these readers have more of a *meaning-based* view of reading. That is, they have a sense of reading process as a process of understanding the text.

It is also interesting to observe during reading conferences whether students are using the strategies they are able to articulate in the Burke Reading Interview. Sometimes we hear readers talking about strategies, and we observe they are able to use them; sometimes we hear readers who are not able to articulate their strategies, but observe that they're using lots of appropriate ones; and sometimes we hear readers who can talk about various strategies, but don't observe them in use. The Burke Reading Interview is brief, yet very informative.

Interest Interviews

Matching students to appropriate books is always a challenge (Fountas and Pinnell 1999; Peterson 2001). Our considerations include the difficulty level and content of the material. One way to help us with the latter is to know students' interests. Early in the school year, it is helpful to conduct an interest interview with each student. Older students can interview each other and share their findings with the teacher and other students. They can also submit their answers in writing. The information gained can be used all year in helping students find texts that are enjoyable and relevant to their lives. Here are some interview questions I often use with my students:

1. What are your hobbies?
2. Are there other things you enjoy doing when you're not in school?
3. Are you involved in any sports?
4. Do you watch any sports on TV?
5. What other TV shows do you watch?
6. What are some movies you have enjoyed?
7. What would you like to share about your family?
8. Do you have responsibilities at home?
9. What kinds of reading do you do at home?
10. What are your favorite things to do at school?

11. What have you always wanted to know?
12. What have you always wanted to do?
13. Tell me about the writing you do.
14. Who is a teacher who has made a difference for you? How did he or she help you?
15. How do you choose a book?
16. Do you have a favorite book? Favorite author?
17. Anything else you'd like to tell me about yourself?
18. Anything you'd like to know about me?

That last question usually surprises students, but they often have a quick answer. I feel that I should be as forthcoming with them as I am asking them to be with me! Again, because of its length, I would not conduct this interview and tape a student's reading during the same session.

Listening to Our Readers

The best way to get to know students is to listen. Be interested, be honest, be caring, be kind. They'll notice your genuine interest and respond. We want to pay attention to their talk, not just their reading. Watch them interact with others in the classroom and on the playground. When we listen to them read, all the information we have about them as people will help us in our discussions with them as readers.

Bringing It All Together: Knowing Our Readers

The end result of all our work in miscue analysis is knowing readers well. We use the reader profile as a way of bringing together all the information we have gathered (see Appendix G). For Procedure III, the profile is quite detailed, and includes a written narrative to identify strengths and areas of concern. We also have quantitative information from our typescript and miscue tally. The reader profiles developed from the untaped procedures are less detailed and provide more qualitative information (see Figure 7–2 and Appendix K). There are notes made as the reader is giving his retelling, and comments made about the level of comprehension. A comprehension score can also be calculated from Procedure IV. Teachers also complete a Holistic Evaluation of the Reader Form (see the two-page Appendix L) for each student several times a year; this form provides information regarding the reader's ability to construct meaning and to use appropriate strategies.

From the various interviews we have available, we can get to know our students in various ways not afforded to us by the actual miscue analysis. These include knowing students' self-esteem as readers, their views of the reading process, their personal interests, and the reading they do outside of school.

Now that we have an overview of miscue analysis and different procedures, the next chapter takes an in-depth look at conducting a Procedure III.

4

How Do I Conduct Procedure III?

> *I cannot think of an aspect of miscue analysis that will not be helpful to me as a teacher. I am so excited to go back to school, have students whom I taught two years ago, and finally get to know them as readers. Though I've conducted reading inventories with students, I've never really felt like I knew what was going on in their heads as they read. Now I will be able to design lessons, either for the whole class, small groups, or even individuals, which specifically address the areas of their reading that need improvement.*
>
> —Stephanie Keolker, Fifth-Grade Teacher

In this chapter we will go through all the steps involved in conducting a Procedure III, which is an in-depth, taped miscue analysis method that serves the needs of classroom teachers in getting to know their students as readers (Y. Goodman, Watson, and Burke 1987).

Choosing the Student

Remember that we will not be conducting an in-depth Procedure III with all our students, so we need to carefully consider which students to choose. We may have observed a student who does not seem to be using proficient strategies, but it is unclear what is going on. We could benefit from more detailed information about this particular reader to better meet her needs. We're doing frequent reading conferences and listening carefully to her reading, but she's still an enigma to us.

Sometimes we have a student enter our classroom in the middle of the year. By conducting a Procedure III with this student, we quickly get up to speed in terms of the amount of information we have about him as a reader relative to all that we know about our other students.

Sometimes parents request special services for a child who is having difficulties in school. When this happens, a diagnostic team is convened to conduct a variety of assessments with this student to determine his current level of skills, which will enable them to then develop an Individual Education Plan (IEP). The team needs in-depth information about his reading strategies and abilities as a reader. If the teacher or reading specialist conducts a Procedure III, that information is readily available to all those involved in making decisions and recommendations for this learner.

Choosing a Text

When I come to a taping session for a Procedure III, I offer several texts that I think might be *just right* for this reader and let her choose which one to read. These represent my best guess at books that would be slightly challenging, so we will hear some miscues, but not so difficult that she will not be able to understand them. After she chooses a book, I have her look through it to see if she has read it before, and to see how much text there is on each page, how big the print it is, and what the pictures are. This *book walk* gives her a chance to begin making predictions and accessing appropriate schema.

I also bring a few other books to the session, some that would be easier and some that would be more difficult than the just-right books. Then, if the text she has chosen is too difficult and there is a great deal of miscue activity, I can stop her and ask her to select another book from the original offerings, or suggest another book myself. Similarly, if the book she has chosen is too easy and she is not making very many miscues, I would again stop her and we would choose another book.

Generally, we'd like to have about thirty to forty miscues to analyze; we can get a sense early on in the reading if a text and a reader are matched in an appropriate way to provide a low-stress engagement for the student and, at the same time, to result in enough miscues for our analysis. For any miscue analysis procedure, we ask the student to read a selection of text he has not read before. Depending on the age of the reader, this text is usually *at least 500* words and one of the following:

- A complete story, such as a picture book
- A passage from a chapter book that has a clear beginning, middle, and end
- A brief selection from a content-area text that develops a clear concept

As a classroom teacher, I always kept several copies of typescripts and accompanying retelling guides (see Appendices A and E) on hand. I selected texts at several levels of difficulty and prepared typescripts and retelling guides for each. When I needed to conduct an in-depth Procedure III, I could select appropriate texts for the student to read, pull the corresponding typescripts and retelling guides from my files, arrange for a time to meet with the student, set up the tape recorder, and ask the student to read for me. To continue the analysis and mark the miscues, I would use the typescript of the story the student was able to finish reading.

The following are two situations that can occur in terms of the selection we ask the student to read for a taped Procedure III:

1. The student brings any text she is currently reading, we conduct the taping session, and we borrow the book and make the typescript later. Some teachers do this by making an enlarged photocopy of the pages read and use the

copies as the typescript rather than retyping the text (Brummett and Maras 1995). The advantage here is that the student is making the choice of what to read. The disadvantage is that we do not have a prepared retelling guide to assist us in providing information during the cued retelling. I have done this many times, and I always feel the retelling may not be as good as it would have been if I had a retelling guide.

2. We have a selection of typescripts and retelling guides prepared ahead of time and we offer students copies of the books for which we have typescripts. Again, the student makes a choice about what to read, but now we have the prepared retelling guide to help us in our prompts, which leads to a better retelling.

Making the Typescript

In this section, we will take a look at how to prepare a typescript of a story a student reads. This gives us a place to write down the miscues we hear on the tape recording of the reading during a Procedure III.

A *typescript* is a copy of the text the student reads. It allows us to create a written record of the reading that we can return to repeatedly for in-depth analysis. *We make a typescript for Procedure III, but we don't for Over the Shoulder miscue analysis or Procedure IV.*

To construct a typescript, type out the complete story or passage while maintaining the same line breaks as those found in the original text. Page breaks are indicated by drawing a horizontal line at the point in the text where the break occurs. Allowing three spaces between lines leaves enough room to write down miscues above the words in the text. I have found that using a 14-point font not only makes it easier to read the typescript, but the larger-sized letters are closer to the size of normal handwriting.

We number sentences using a digit inside a circle above and slightly to the left of the first word of each sentence. We provide a short line off to the right side of the page for sentence codings. This line is opposite each sentence's end punctuation and is given the same number as the sentence. If two sentences end on the same line, their coding lines will be close together at the right margin.

For a summary of the guidelines for creating a typescript of a text, see Figure 4–1.

Making the Retelling Guide

For every typescript we prepare, we also construct a *retelling guide*. For stories, this is a list of the characters, the main events, the setting, and the main idea. For content-area passages, this is a list of the main concepts, details that develop the concept, and the main idea of the passage. We assign points to each item on the list and check off each item we hear the student mention during the retelling. Based on a total of 100 points, the total number of points we check off on the retelling guide gives us a comprehension score. Here are the steps in constructing a retelling guide for a narrative selection (a similar process would be followed for a content-area passage):

- List the main characters.
- List the setting; often a story or chapter book selection (a scene that stands alone) can have more than one setting as the scene for the action changes.
- List the main events of the story or chapter book selection, or list the main ideas for a content-area passage.
- List the overall main idea of the selection.
- Assign points to each item.

Let's say you have this configuration: 5 characters, 2 areas for the setting, 12 main events, and the main idea. You will be working with a total of 100 points, which makes calculating the percentage of comprehension easier. Add up the number of items you have (20) and divide this into 100—you will assign 5 points to each item. The numbers don't always come out neatly, but we can make adjustments as we need to; for example, add another event to the list, or use a set number of points per character and then calculate the rest of the points based on the amount remaining within our 100 points. (See Appendix E for an example of a retelling guide.)

Taping the Reading and Retelling

I've selected my student, we've arranged a time to meet where we can have a quiet setting, we've selected an appropriate text and done a book walk, I have my copy of the typescript and retelling guide, the tape recorder is set up (and has been tested), and now we're ready to begin. I like to sit next to the student rather

- Type a complete story, a complete scene from a chapter book, or a complete section from a content-area text (usually a minimum of 500 words, although some picture books may be less)
- Keep the same line breaks as in the original text
- Draw a horizontal line to indicate where page breaks occur in the original text (by hand or using the computer)
- Triple space lines
- Use a 14-point font
- Number each sentence above and to the left of the first word
- Provide a short line on the right side of the page for sentence codings opposite the end punctuation of each sentence (it is easiest to do this by hand)
- Lines can be numbered in the left margin for more detailed reference

FIGURE 4–1 Guidelines for Making a Typescript

than across the table from her because I find it helps her be more comfortable. I also have her run the tape recorder and make a recording of us talking for a minute, then we rewind the tape and listen to our voices.

This few minutes is time well spent because it desensitizes her somewhat to being taped so that she can relax a little more when reading. We always have a good laugh about how our voices sound on tape, and I usually can't resist a brief explanation as to why that is the case. She's interested to learn that the way we are used to hearing our voices is really a combination of hearing the voice from the outside air and hearing the voice through bone conduction in our heads. What we hear on the tape is only part of that—the voice from the outside air.

As taping begins, I say:

> I'd like you to read this book aloud and when you come to *something* you don't know, do whatever you would do if I wasn't here. I won't be able to help you right now.

I also let her know that I will be asking her to retell the story when she is finished. Students read differently if they know they will be asked to retell the passage (Davenport 1993). If we say something you don't know (above), instead of word you don't know, the student makes the decision regarding the linguistic level she is focusing on during the reading: either the letter, word, phrase, or sentence level (Watson 1989).

If the text is too easy and she is not making a reasonable number of miscues, I would congratulate her on her great reading strategies and ask her to read another story. Also, I do not want this to be an uncomfortable experience; if the text is clearly too difficult and there are too many miscues, I will also ask her to read another text. I try to make a smooth transition between books, say something complementary, take responsibility for choosing the wrong book, and ask her to read a different one.

If a reader skips a line or a page of text, I point this out and ask him to reread. If the reader becomes stuck and pauses for about ten to fifteen seconds, I usually ask what he is thinking, ask him to make an appropriate guess at a word that would make sense there, and suggest that he keep reading.

That's about all the talking that goes on during the taping session. We *do not tell* students words they hesitate on, even if they ask us, but encourage them to continue reading. The purpose during the taping session is to access information about strategies students are using independently; we can't do that if we suggest strategies before they start reading or if we help them along the way. All the teaching and metacognitive talking takes place in the *untaped setting,* that is, the *reading conference* (see Chapter 6).

When the student has finished reading the text, take the material, and invite her to tell you everything she can remember about the selection she read. This is the *unaided retelling*. As she is retelling, you can check off items on the retelling guide. The tape recorder is still running, so you can come back to the tape later and check off on the retelling guide any items you may miss.

After the student has stopped, ask if there is anything else she can remember. If not, you begin the *cued retelling*. Looking at items on the retelling guide that the student has not mentioned, you cue the student as to the missing details. For example, you might say, `There were three things that happened on the way home from the store. You mentioned two of them, do you remember what the last one was?` If the student mentions some event that you have not listed on your retelling guide, write it down and take it into consideration when you are calculating the comprehension score.

Follow-up questions throughout the retelling should be open-ended; here are a few examples:

- `Can you tell me more about` (character mentioned by reader)?
- `What happened after` (event mentioned by reader)?
- `Why do you think` (character mentioned by reader) `did that?`
- `Can you tell me about the story in just a few sentences` (for the main idea)?

Y. Goodman, Watson, and Burke (1987, 49) list some other suggestions for successful retellings (see Figure 4–2).

- Get to know the reader
- Become familiar with the story
- Avoid giving the reader information from the text
- Include in questions and comments only information introduced by the reader
- Don't rush yourself or the reader—think through your questions and patiently wait for the reader's reply
- Make your directions and questions very clear and avoid giving more than one question at a time
- Don't take "I don't know" for an answer—rephrase questions to get the information another way; at the same time, don't exhaust the reader with too great a focus on one topic
- Let students develop a topic and reach their own conclusions before changing the subject
- Ask open-ended questions—questions that can be answered with *yes* or *no,* or with single words, often limit the reader's presentation potential
- Retain any nonwords or name changes given by the reader

FIGURE 4-2 Suggestions for Retellings

As you are calculating the points, it is OK to give half credit for an item; for example, if a student remembers the character who teased Curtis was a boy, but he can't remember the boy's name, he gets half credit for that character. When determining the main idea of the passage, our perception of what that is might be different from what a student tells us. Write down what the student said and consider if it is reasonable to accept, or to give partial credit. The purpose of the retelling guide is to give us a sense of the student's comprehension of the text, and we need to be flexible in scoring, giving the student some benefit of the doubt when it is appropriate.

Marking the Miscues

A type of shorthand has been developed (Y. Goodman, Watson, and Burke 1987) that allows us to consistently write down, or *mark*, the miscues we hear. Listening to the tape, we mark the miscues on a typescript of the text the student read. We can return to the tape repeatedly until we are sure that the miscues are accurately represented on the typescript.

There are many different types of miscues, any of which can be self-corrected. The various miscues that were introduced in Chapter 2 (pp. 28–30) are described in depth below (after the overview summary of miscue markings), along with an explanation of how these are marked on a typescript. In each example, we examine the following four miscue features:

- What type of miscue is it?
- Was it corrected?
- If it was left uncorrected, did it significantly change the meaning of the sentence?
- What is the *graphic similarity* between the text item and the miscue?

To examine graphic similarity, we ask, How much does the miscue look like the text item? that is, How many letters are in common between the miscue and the text item? We make the determination for graphic similarity by following these guidelines:

- If we divide the miscue and the text item into roughly three parts each, and there are two of these parts in common, we say there is *High* graphic similarity—most of the letters are in common.
- If there is at least one letter in common, we say there is *Some* graphic similarity.
- If there are no letters in common, we ask, "Is there graphic similarity?"; the answer is No, there is *none.*
- We *do not ask* the question about graphic similarity for:
  –*Complex miscues:* We are not able to make a one-to-one correspondence between the several words of the miscue and the several words of the text

–*Partials:* There is not enough information

–*Insertions:* A word has been inserted so there is nothing to compare it to in the text

–*Omissions:* A word has been omitted so there is nothing to compare it to in the text

At this point, you may want to revisit the list of the types of miscues readers can make in Figure 2–1. We will examine each of these in detail, with examples from readers, in the next section. Figure 4–3 summarizes the markings we use in Procedure III.

Substitutions

Probably the most common miscue is a *substitution*, where the reader says one word for another. Sometimes several words are substituted for more than one word in the text; these complex miscues are discussed next. When marking one-word substitutions, the word is *written above* the text item. The following examples illustrate different types of substitutions.[1]

TYPE:	Substitution—One-word
CORRECTED:	No
MEANING CHANGE:	No (High-quality miscue)
GRAPHIC SIMILARITY:	High

When one word is substituted for one word, this is called a one-word substitution. Many types of miscues can be *high-quality*: that is, they *do not significantly change the meaning* of the text. In this example, one word is substituted for another, the miscue and the text item have a lot of letters in common, or High graphic similarity, and meaning is not significantly changed.

glittering
Soon, he had a room full of gleaming gold objects.

This would sound like:

Soon, he had a room full of glittering gold objects.

A common occurrence when learning to mark substitutions is a tendency to want to circle the text item, as you would if there were an omission (see "Omissions" section later in this chapter). There is an intuitive sense that because it isn't heard, it is *left out* and therefore should be marked as an omission. Resist the urge! No, we do not hear the text item, but something has been *put in* in its place. There is no need to indicate an omission. A substitution has occurred!

[1]*Note:* When discussing the miscues in the narrative, miscues and text items will appear in a different font, with a slash (/) between them, indicating the miscue first.

Type of Miscue	Example of Markings
One-word substitution	glittering Soon, he had a room full of gleaming gold objects.
Complex miscue	the woman The old man heard her words.
Reversal	"Please," said the servant at last, "or he will be gone."
Nonword	$stranded It's a seal pup I found stranded in the shallows.
Dialect usage	ⓓ done He did this experiment.
Misarticulation	additions On Monday the class met for auditions to choose who was best for each part.
Intonation shift	We want the project to succeed.
Split syllable	She set out to seek her fortune, with no companion but her trus|ty cat
Omission of word	She opened the door and turned on the porch light.
Omission of phrase or sentence	"No cheating," he yelled. He tripped over a stone. Jimmy and I stopped to tie a knot.

FIGURE 4–3 Summary of Markings for Procedure III

Type of Miscue	Example of Markings
Omission of end punctuation	"I had lemon cake for mine, and lemon makes me shiver." "I had orange soda," Rosemary said.
Partial	The sails were flapping like the wings of a wounded gull.
Insertion	I gathered my courage, Excellency, and leaped from the cliff.
Repetition	He tickled the loon who sang a tune.
Abandoning the correct form	He stops to talk to cats and dogs.
Unsuccessful attempt to correct	The Prince stopped on the slightly gummy steps.
Correction	The old man heard them laugh.
Repeated miscue	Michael showed his tambourine to a friend. (see example p. 84)
Pause	Look at that!

FIGURE 4–3 (continued)

TYPE: Substitution—One-word
CORRECTED: No
MEANING CHANGE: No (High-quality miscue)
GRAPHIC SIMILARITY: Some

High-quality miscues that have few or no letters in common can also be made, as in this example from Nicole as she substitutes a determiner for a pronoun (the/his). Because they share at least one letter in common, we say there is Some graphic similarity.

the
He loved to go into his treasure room and count his coins.

This would sound like:

He loved to go into the treasure room and count his coins.

TYPE: Substitution—One-word
CORRECTED: No
MEANING CHANGE: No (High-quality miscue)
GRAPHIC SIMILARITY: None

The following miscue was made by LaMar, a second-grader; he replaces one determiner with another (the/a), a miscue which has No graphic similarity, and is high quality.

the
They had not gone far when they saw some girls at a well.

This would sound like:

They had not gone far when they saw some girls at the well.

TYPE: Substitution—One-word
CORRECTED: No
MEANING CHANGE: Yes
GRAPHIC SIMILARITY: High

In high-quality substitutions, the reader substitutes one word for another but does not significantly change the meaning of the text. But substitutions are not always high quality; sometimes they *do change* the author's intended meaning, as in the following examples.

In the first example, fourth-grader Brooks makes substitutions that are graphically similar to the text items, but the miscues change the meaning of the sentences because they were left uncorrected. In the first sentence, she substitutes something for sometimes. At this point, we have lost the syntactic structure of the sentence. It *no longer sounds like an English sentence* because the words are strung together in the wrong order.

When examining sentences containing miscues, it is important to remember that we ask the question about syntax first (Does this sound like language?) because, if we *don't have* syntactic structure, we *can't have meaning*. We don't have the language framework to support the meaning. We will discuss these issues in depth later (see "Coding the Sentences").

Something
Sometimes I think we would both be better off if you were still a frog.

This would sound like:

Something I think we would both be better off if you were still a frog.

In the following example, the sentence appears to be an English sentence. Brooks has retained the syntactic structure by replacing an -ing form of a verb in the spot in the sentence where that is an appropriate thing to do. OK, it sounds like language. But does it *make sense* in the context of the story? *No*. Here we have lost meaning.

walking
I can't have any princes waking up Sleeping Beauty before the hundred years are up.

This would sound like:

I can't have any princes walking up Sleeping Beauty before the hundred years are up.

TYPE:	Substitution—One-word
CORRECTED:	No
MEANING CHANGE:	Yes
GRAPHIC SIMILARITY:	Some

In the following example, Nicole has made a one-word substitution that has one letter in common with the text item, therefore it has Some graphic similarity. However, this miscue changes meaning. Her phrasing indicates she also omits both commas in the sentence.

knew

No one not even Marygold was allowed into the king's treasure room.

This would sound like:

No one knew even Marygold was allowed into the king's treasure room.

Nicole lost meaning by leaving this miscue uncorrected, even though she made an appropriate prediction of a common phrase, No one knew . . .

TYPE:	Substitution—Complex miscue
CORRECTED:	No
MEANING CHANGE:	No (High-quality miscue)
GRAPHIC SIMILARITY:	Cannot determine graphic similarity

A *complex miscue* is a type of substitution in which *more than one word* replaces one or more words in the text. Although at times it seems obvious, it is impossible to determine if the reader is making word-by-word substitutions when this occurs. Therefore we *put a bracket over* the substituted word or phrase and write the complex miscue above the text. We are not able to determine graphic similarity between complex miscues and the text items because it is not clear what has been substituted for what.

Next is an example of two words substituted for two words. Meaning is not significantly lost in this high-quality complex miscue.

the woman

The old man heard her words.

This would sound like:

The old man heard the woman.

Here LaMar made a complex miscue that he left uncorrected. He appears to be focused on constructing meaning, knowing the sentence was referring to the man hearing the woman. However, some may argue that there is partial change of the author's intended meaning, which was that the woman was speaking. By saying the man heard the woman, we have lost specificity, and LaMar could be thinking the woman was shouting or singing, for example, rather than speaking.

In the next sample miscue, Stacy, an eighth grader, leaves a complex miscue uncorrected, with no change in meaning.

and touched

The Emperor reached out a thin hand to touch the pretty paper and the bird-like keel of the apparatus.

This would sound like:

> The Emperor reached out a thin hand and touched the pretty paper and the bird-like keel of the apparatus.

Sometimes readers will take two words and create a contraction, or take a contraction and split it into two words. Both instances result in complex miscues that do not change meaning. In the following two examples of high-quality miscues, the reader is perhaps predicting a structure with which he is more familiar.

> you would
> "I knew you'd say that," he said.

This would sound like:

> "I knew you would say that," he said.

Or this:

> couldn't
> She knew she could not go with them.

This would sound like:

> She knew she couldn't go with them.

Type:	Substitution—Complex miscue
Corrected:	No
Meaning Change:	Yes
Graphic Similarity:	Cannot determine graphic similarity

Sometimes complex miscues result in a *loss of meaning*, as in this example from third-grader Weston. Meaning is lost through the uncorrected nonword $shured followed by the word often (a $ is used to indicate a nonword miscue).

> And he looked to the town on the great grey cliffs
> $shured often
> that sheared off into the sea.

This would sound like:

> And he looked to the town on the great grey cliffs
> that shured often into the sea.

TYPE:	Substitution—Complex miscue
CORRECTED:	No
MEANING CHANGE:	Yes
GRAPHIC SIMILARITY:	Cannot determine graphic similarity

Complex miscues can be a substitution of *more than one word* for one word in the text, as in this miscue from second-grader Claire.

lots of
She went exploring for lost kingdoms.

This would sound like:

She went exploring for lots of kingdoms.

This is an example of a sentence that, as the reader left it, sounds like language, makes sense within the context of the story, yet results in a shift from the author's intended meaning of lost kingdoms.

TYPE:	Substitution—Reversal
CORRECTED:	No
MEANING CHANGE:	No
GRAPHIC SIMILARITY:	Cannot determine graphic similarity

One type of substitution is a *reversal*, which is *changing the order of two words next to each other in the text*. We use the *editing transposition symbol* (∽) when marking a typescript to indicate a reversal. Again, we cannot determine graphic similarity because a reversal can be seen as a type of complex miscue.

In this reversal by second-grader Shalisa, we do not see any change in meaning because both structures are commonly used and mean the same thing (asked Arthur, Arthur asked).

"Can we go to the beach tomorrow?" Arthur asked.

This would sound like:

"Can we go to the beach tomorrow?" asked Arthur.

An alternative method of marking a reversal is to use the *bracket*, as in the complex miscue marking (see preceding). Both methods of marking convey the same information.

asked Arthur
"Can we go to the beach tomorrow?" Arthur asked.

Type:	Substitution—Reversal
Corrected:	No
Meaning Change:	Yes
Graphic Similarity:	Cannot determine graphic similarity

Reversals may also result in a change of meaning, as seen in this example from LaMar.

"How can you be so mean?" asked the wife. "The two of you up there on/one poor little donkey!"

This would sound like:

"How can you be so mean?" asked the wife. "The two of you up there one on poor little donkey!"

In the following example from Stacy, the reversal results in a statement being changed to a question, which changes the meaning.

"Please," said the servant at last, "or he/will be gone?."

This would sound like:

"Please," said the servant at last, "or will he be gone?"

Type:	Substitution—Nonword
Corrected:	No
Meaning Change:	Yes
Graphic Similarity:	High

A *nonword* is a substitution with a word that is *not in the English language* (as far as you know!). It is important to remember that although a sentence with a nonword can sound like *language,* it does result in a change in meaning. A dollar sign ($) is used to designate the nonword when marking the typescript. To invent a spelling for the nonword substitution, do your best to *retain as much of the text-item spelling* as is reasonable. If there is any doubt you may not remember the pronunciation of the nonword when reading the typescript later, give yourself additional cues, such as short- or long-vowel markings or write "rhymes with . . ." in the margin.

Here is one of Weston's nonword miscues in which he changed the vowel sound of the text item, but the teacher who marked this miscue retained the same spelling as the word in the text and used the long-vowel marking.

$stränded
It's a seal pup I found stranded in the shallows.

This would sound like:

It's a seal pup I found strainded in the shallows.

In the next example, Sarah, a second grader, uses all the same letters as the text item in her miscue, but rearranges them to create this nonword.

$guardally
Ivan and Carol gradually realized that Marcella was different from all the rest of the kittens.

This would sound like:

Ivan and Carol guardally realized that Marcella was different from all the rest of the kittens.

Following is an example of a nonword substitution with Some graphic similarity from fourth-grader Brooks' typescript. To be sure she would remember how the nonword sounded, the teacher who marked this miscue gave herself a reminder in the margin.

(rhymes with "doubt her")
$router
The Prince couldn't believe his rotten luck.

This would sound like:

The Prince couldn't believe his router luck.

TYPE: Substitution—Dialect usages

Because we bring to the reading process our knowledge of the world, our culture, and our community, as well as the language we use daily in our everyday lives, we also bring our dialect usages. When the dialect of the author differs from the dialect of the reader, there may be miscues that reflect the reader's common language use. Dialect miscues are marked by writing the substitution *over the text item* and putting a *circle over the miscue* with a "d" inside.

For example, in your part of the country, what do you call a small stream of water? A creek, a crick, a branch? What do you call your mother's mother, or your father's mother?—Oma, Nana, Big Mama, Granny? How do you refer to a canned soft drink?—Soda, pop? These are considered *lexical* dialect usages, or *vocabulary variations* because the word used in one geographic area is different from the word used for the same item in a different region.

In the case of different words for grandmother, this can be a regional dialect usage, but it can also be considered a *familialect*—that is, a word specific to a particular family or clan, like Nene. Also, individuals may make up unique words that their friends and family understand, and these words become part of an *idiolect*. For example, lots of young children have a name for their special blankie, like "boonka," and my husband and I refer to a sinfully sumptuous dessert as a glup. If I were reading about desserts and said glup for pastry, this would be considered a dialect miscue because it is a word I use in my common pattern of speech and holds meaning for me. Whoever was conducting the miscue analysis might ask me about that word, or I might bring it up in my retelling, or I might have caught my miscue and self-corrected.

Sometimes a dialect usage is *phonological*, when a person is pronouncing the same word as the text item, but with a characteristic sound or *sound variation*. For example, in some regions, one might pronounce can't in a way that rhymes with paint, or store in a way that rhymes with go. My mother raises almonds in central California, and in that area, these nuts are called "amonds," pronounced with a short "a" sound and no "l" sound. If my mother read amonds for almonds, this would illustrate her dialect preference because that usage is part of her everyday speech.

Another type of dialect usage is a *syntactic* variation, in which the speaker or reader changes the structure of the sentence, such as He goed to school in place of He went to school. Another example would be: Bill be going to ride his horse for Bill was going to ride his horse. In the following case, the *n* is dropped from frozen: The lake is froze over for The lake is frozen over.

Additionally, there is a dialect usage known as the *null form,* in which the final "s" is dropped from some words, as in He lives 40 mile down the road instead of He lives 40 miles down the road. In my community in rural eastern Oregon, we buy three ton of hay for our horses instead of three tons.

Here is a sample miscue from Y. Goodman, Watson, and Burke (1987, 58) showing a dialect miscue in which one word is substituted for another.

(d)
done
He did this experiment.

This would sound like:

He done this experiment.

Type: Substitution—Misarticulation (kid dialect)

There are certain words that some readers have a hard time pronouncing even though they know what the words are and what they mean. They're just hard to say! Have you ever had a difficult time articulating words like phenomenon, statistics, or etymologist? When discussing the recent popularity of the movie *Titanic* with a friend, she repeatedly called the ship the Titantic, using a pronunciation analogous to the word gigantic. We've all heard young children use words like basketti for spaghetti. Knowing those children, we realize this is part of their regular language usage, a kind of *kid dialect* that they usually outgrow. Knowing those students and their characteristic misarticulations, we would recognize these idiosyncratic usages when listening to them read.

If readers make this type of substitution during reading, these miscues are considered *misarticulations*, or kid dialect (e.g., basketti). We *write an A* in a circle above the miscue (for articulation). By discussing the miscue after the reading and retelling, or perhaps talking about it during the retelling, we can determine if the reader knows the word and its meaning. If so, there is no loss of meaning. For example, when reading about students trying out for parts in a play, Claire read additions for auditions. When talking with her after the retelling, I asked her what you call it when you want a part in a play and go try out. She said additions. That is just her pronunciation of the word auditions (see second miscue example that follows).

Perhaps we know the reader well and recognize a misarticulation as the way the reader typically pronounces a particular word. However, if the misarticulation is not the pronunciation of a word that is part of the reader's common usage, or if through discussion the reader cannot use or define the word, we make the judgment that the reader has produced a nonword, and there is a loss of meaning.

Here are two examples of misarticulation miscues from Claire's reading. When discussing the story with her after the reading and retelling, she used the same pronunciation for these words in the conversation and was able to correctly define them. To Claire, aventure is a "real word" so I didn't mark it as a nonword.

Ⓐ
aventure
Most of all Grace loved to act out adventure stories and fairy tales.

This would sound like:

Most of all Grace loved to act out aventure stories and fairy tales.

Ⓐ
additions
On Monday the class met for auditions to choose who was best for each part.

This would sound like:

On Monday the class met for additions to choose who was best for each part.

TYPE: Substitution—Intonation shift

There are word pairs in the English language that are spelled the same, but pronounced differently, based on where the accent is placed. These are called *homographs* and include words like content, record, and project. An *intonation shift* occurs when a reader substitutes one pronunciation for another, and this type of miscue results in a change of meaning. Changing the pronunciation creates either a new word that means something different or a nonword.

An intonation shift can occur on any word. For example, if a reader said penSILL (pencíl) for pencil, this is an intonation shift that has created a nonword. When marking the typescript, we do not need to rewrite the word as a substitution. We just put an *accent mark* (´) above the accented syllable of the text item. Here is an example from Y. Goodman, Watson, and Burke (1987, 58).

We want the projéct to succeed.

This would sound like:

We want the proJECT to succeed.

TYPE: Substitution—Split syllables

Sometimes a reader will say the word in the text, but separate it into distinct sections, or *split syllables*. Perhaps this occurs because readers are looking ahead for cues to the meaning of the word, or perhaps looking back to confirm their prediction of the word, and we catch them pausing "in their linguistic tracks" (Watson 1989). This type of miscue is marked by *drawing a line* between the two syllables; generally, it does not result in a change of meaning. In the following miscue example, Claire creates a split syllable on the word trusty. This miscue did not result in a meaning change as shown by her correct use of the word in her retelling. However, the nonword miscue in the sentence does change the meaning.

$copission

She set out to seek her fortune, with no companion but her trus|ty cat—and found a city with streets paved in gold.

This would sound like:

She set out to seek her fortune, with no copission but her truss-tee cat—and found a city with streets paved in gold.

A student who habitually sounds out unfamiliar words will often make a one-syllable word into a two-syllable word, essentially creating a split syllable miscue. The following is an example from LaMar's typescript of an uncorrected substitution. However, after discussing this miscue numerous times with teachers, most of us agree that it is likely LaMar corrected this miscue in his head; it made sense to him, and he continued reading.

So he pulled l/oose and ran out into the fields.

This would sound like:

So he pulled luh-oose and ran out into the fields.

Omissions

Sometimes readers will *omit* a word, phrase, or line of text during reading. When marking the typescript, we *circle* the omitted words. In the following examples from second-grader Andrew, we see that omissions of single words *can change* meaning in some cases, and in others, meaning is not affected.

She opened the door and turned on the (porch) light.

This would sound like:

She opened the door and turned on the light.

The omission of porch only slightly changes the author's intended meaning.

safe
"You're still (alive)!" said Francine.

This would sound like:

"You're safe!" said Francine.

There are two miscues in this example. Safe is substituted for still. Alive is omitted. These miscues combine in such a way that, overall, the meaning does not significantly change. In fact, this could be marked as a complex miscue safe/still alive with a bracket over still alive. Either marking would be acceptable and would convey the same information. If a colleague reads these two ways of marking the same miscue aloud, they would both come to the ear exactly the same. Here is the alternate marking:

safe
"You're still alive!" said Francine.

This would sound like:

"You're safe!" said Francine.

In the next miscue example, Andrew has omitted the verb of the sentence, resulting in a *loss of syntax*, which *always results in a loss of meaning* because of the inappropriate language structure. However, he left it uncorrected, perhaps indicating his awareness of syntactic structure has not developed to the point that he was able to recognize this sentence did not have a verb.

Arthur (tried) not to look afraid.

This would sound like:

Arthur not to look afraid.

In the next examples, second-grader Katie leaves out a *phrase* and a *line of text*, both of which change meaning.

I went to the front (of the) room.

This would sound like:

I went to the front room.

"No cheating," he yelled.
(He tripped over a stone.)
Jimmy and I stopped to tie a knot.

This would sound like:

"No cheating," he yelled.
Jimmy and I stopped to tie a knot.

If a student inadvertently skips a line during a taped session, I usually let it go. I make an on-the-spot decision about whether to stop the student or let him continue, first waiting to see if he corrects the miscue on his own. If the omission of a line happens repeatedly and I see this is a pattern, I will stop the student (when he has finished a sentence) and ask him to go back and read the line he missed.

Omitting end punctuation can result in an intonation shift, as well as a meaning change. The end punctuation is *circled*. If other miscues occur in conjunction with the omitted or changed end punctuation, they are marked as usual. In this example, Katie omitted the period, as well as inserted and, creating a run-on sentence that slightly changes the meaning. The author intended each sentence to be said by a different character and Katie's miscues move the two lines to one speaker. Her omission of the period and insertion of and essentially eliminates the quotation mark for the second sentence.

"I had lemon cake for mine,
and lemon makes me shiver." and
"I had orange soda," Rosemary said.

This would sound like:

"I had lemon cake for mine
and lemon makes me shiver
and I had orange soda," Rosemary said.

End punctuation can be *changed*, for example from a period to a question mark. We know this by carefully listening to the reader's intonation. In the next miscue example from Stacy, she has substituted What for It, turning the sentence into a question. As a result, she raises her intonation at the end.

What
It is this man I fear. ?

This would sound like:

What is this man I fear?

End punctuation can also be *inserted* by the reader, creating a new sentence structure. In this example from LaMar, an additional substitution creates two sentences that slightly changes meaning.

well
"Look at that!" one of the men shouted. "That big boy rides while. His poor old father must walk."

This would sound like:

"Look at that!" one of the men shouted. "That big boy rides well. His poor old father must walk."

It is interesting to know that at the time of this reading, LaMar lived on a ranch with his parents and helped his father with his work as a farrier. He rode a horse every day and had surely heard someone say, That big boy rides well. In the same text, LaMar makes this miscue:

> couldn't
> "Two big people like you could carry him."

This would sound like:

> "Two big people like you couldn't carry him."

Knowing the size and weight of a donkey, LaMar knows two people couldn't pick one up. These are examples of the probable influence of a reader's background on his miscues.

Partials

Sometimes a reader will say a part of a word, resulting in a miscue called a *partial*. We usually hear a rising intonation and an abrupt ending, which lets us know what we have heard is an *attempt* at a word that was not completed. We make the distinction between partials and nonwords by carefully listening to the reader's intonation. Nonwords are considered substitutions and are usually stated with an intonation that has a ring of finality or intention: I meant to say this. Partials have a questioning tone and the articulation is usually cut off: I think it's—no, I'll just quit here in the middle of the word. Partials are marked on the typescript by *writing the first few letters* of the partial word over the text item, followed by a *dash*. If partials are left uncorrected, they have the same result as an omission and cause a change of meaning. However partials are often corrected, as in the following examples from third-grader Weston.

> Ⓒ fo-
> Their hut was covered with the finest mosses that kept them cool in the summer and warm in the winter.

This would sound like:

> Their hut was covered with the finest fo- mosses that kept them cool in the summer and warm in the winter.

> Ⓒ wi-
> The sails were flapping like the wings of a wounded gull.

This would sound like:

> The sails were flapping like the wi- wings of a wounded gull.

In the next miscue by Jenni, a second grader, an uncorrected partial has the same overall result as an omission.

re-
"I already know how to read," said D.W.

This would sound like:

"I already know how to re-," said D.W.

Insertions

Often readers will predict a phrase or common usage with which they are familiar, and if this varies slightly from the author's structure, they will *insert a word.* Insertions are *marked with a caret symbol (^),* with the inserted word written above the caret.

Here is an example from Stacy; her insertion did not change the meaning.

out
I gathered my courage, Excellency, and leaped ^ from the cliff.

This would sound like:

I gathered my courage, Excellency, and leaped out from the cliff.

However, in the same story, Stacy makes several insertions that change the syntactic structure, and therefore do result in a change of meaning. Remember, if we do not have the words strung together in the proper order to sound like the way we talk (syntactic structure), then we can't have meaning.

He does not know himself. It is only necessary that he create,

he
without knowing why he has done so, or what this thing ^ will do.

This would sound like:

He does not know himself. It is only necessary that he create,
without knowing why he has done so, or what this thing he will do.

Regressions

A *regression* occurs when a reader rereads part of the text. There are several reasons why readers back up during reading. All regressions are indicated by a line underneath the text indicating how far the reader has backed up before making another try.

TYPE: Regression—Repetition

One reason readers regress is to mark time; that is, to allow themselves an opportunity to reflect on what has been read, to look ahead and anticipate what might be coming up in the text, or to reassure themselves that what they have just said is correct. In these instances, readers simply repeat a phrase they have just read *with no miscues*, which is called a *repetition*. Repetitions are marked with a *line underneath the text* starting at the last word read, traveling left back under the text, then up in front of the first word of the repeated phrase. The line ends in a circle, with an *R* inside. There are two repetitions in the following sentence:

Ⓡ He tickled the Ⓡ loon who sang a tune.

This would sound like:

He tickled, he tickled the loon, loon who sang a tune.

In the following example from LaMar, we see an instance where a repetition is part of a previously repeated phrase. The lines under the text start immediately under the printed words, and progressively go further down on the page, indicating the chronological order of the regressions. Here LaMar repeats the phrase donkey in; next he repeats the word in; and then he continues reading.

The son got up on the Ⓡ donkey Ⓡ in back of his father.

This would sound like:

The son got up on the donkey in, donkey in, in back of his father.

TYPE: Regression—Several repetitions

Sometimes readers regress more than once. There is a line drawn under the text for each regression, which shows how far the reader read before backing up and rereading. The number of *lines under the text* is actually *one less* than the number of times we hear a phrase repeated.

The sergeant said Ⓡ bad luck always follows.

This would sound like:

The sergeant said bad luck, bad luck, bad luck always follows.

We hear bad luck three times; the first time is the reading and the next two are repetitions, so there are two lines under the text.

TYPE: Regression—Aside

When a reader makes a comment during reading that is clearly conversational, it is called an *aside*. This may often precede a regression and usually reveals the thinking behind his attempts on an unfamiliar word or difficult passage. The words the reader says are written on the typescript along with the miscues, with *quotation marks around them* to distinguish them as a spoken comment rather than text being read. In this next example, LaMar was apparently struggling with this line, predicting that it was going to read catch up with him, hence his asides as he realized the author was using a slightly different syntactic structure (catch him) than the one he was predicting (catch up with him).

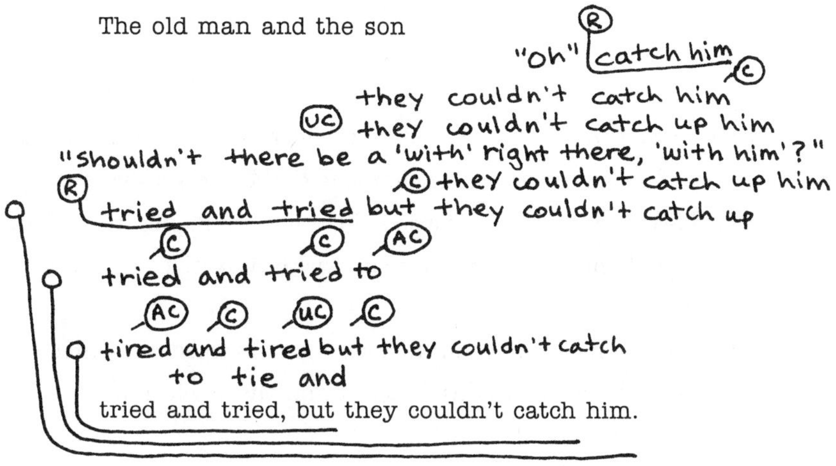

This would sound like (for clarity, new lines indicate each regression):

> The old man and the son tried to tie and,
> tired and tired but they couldn't catch
> tried and tried to
> tried and tried but they couldn't catch up
> they couldn't catch up him

"Shouldn't there be a with right there, 'with him'?"

> they couldn't catch up him
> they couldn't catch him

"Oh"

> catch him

Even with all this miscue activity, LaMar corrected all his miscues and was able to retell this part of the story! Here is a less complicated example of an aside from Claire's reading.

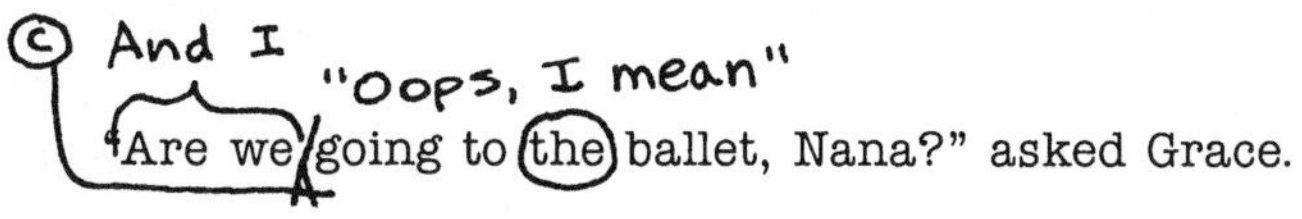

This would sound like:

"And, I, 'Oops, I mean,' Are we going to ballet, Nana?" asked Grace.

Claire's omission of the results in a slight change in meaning. When young children refer to going to ballet lessons, they often say "I'm going to ballet," and Claire may have heard one of her friends say this. The resulting meaning here is that Grace is asking her Nana if they are going to ballet lessons, not to a performance of a ballet.

TYPE: Regression—Abandoning the correct form

Abandoning the correct form occurs when the reader says what is in the text, then regresses and makes a miscue. Again, the *line under the text* shows how far the reader read before backing up. The end of the line goes up in front of the first word of the repeated phrase and ends in a circle with *AC* inside. The miscue is written over the text.

In LaMar's preceding example, his first attempt was tried to tie. He said tried correctly, then he abandons this for tired and tired, which he then corrected back to tried and tried.

Next is an example from seventh-grader Toby in which he reads the text, abandons it and miscues, then self-corrects.

(C) (AC) quite
"And you're quick and fast," Michael said.

This would sound like:

"And you're quick and fast, quite and fast, quick and fast," Michael said.

Here second-grader Linda abandons the correct response and leaves her miscue uncorrected, which results in a change of meaning. The line under the text indicates how far she went before regressing and abandoning the correct form.

(AC) take
He stops to talk to cats and dogs.

This would sound like:

He stops to talk to cats, take to cats and dogs.

Type: Regression—Unsuccessful attempt to correct

An *unsuccessful attempt to correct* occurs when the reader makes more than one attempt to correct a miscue, but never gets the text item. This type of miscue is marked with *a line under the text* showing how far the reader read before backing up and trying the text item again. There is a line in front of the first word of the repeated phrase and ends in a circle with *UC* inside.

Here are two examples from Brooks. She makes several partial attempts, and ends each unsuccessful attempt to correct with a nonword.

UC
$re-skewing
re-
res-
And I can't have any princes rescuing Snow White.

This would sound like:

And I can't have any princes res-, re-, re-skewing Snow White.

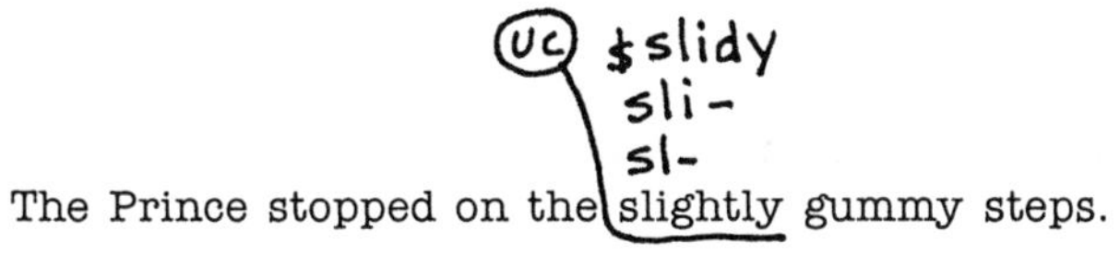

UC
$slidy
sli-
sl-
The Prince stopped on the slightly gummy steps.

This would sound like:

The Prince stopped on the sl-, sli-, slidy gummy steps.

If several unsuccessful attempts are made to correct a miscue and the reader repeats the same attempt each time, the marking is similar to multiple repetitions, with *more than one line* under the text. There is a *UC* in the circle and the repeated word is written once over the text.

This would sound like:

The clock stuck, clock stuck, clock stuck midnight.

Just as in multiple repetitions, we hear clock stuck three times, but there are only two lines under the text. The first time is the miscue and the next two times are unsuccessful attempts to correct it.

As we examine a reader's typescript or an Over the Shoulder Miscue Analysis Form (see Appendices I and J), one observation is particularly important—

the corrections the reader has made. These regressions to correct miscues that changed meaning are *critical evidence* that a reader is monitoring his reading and his comprehension. He is asking questions as he reads: Does this sound like language? and Does this make sense? If the answer is No, he does something about it. This *regulatory action* is a vital skill as a metacognitive reader (Davenport 1993).

Any of the miscues described here can be corrected. *Corrections* are marked on the typescript with a *line under the text* showing how far the reader read before regressing to correct, with the line coming in front of the first word of the repeated phrase and ending in a circle with *C* inside.

Here are several examples of corrected miscues.

TYPE: Correction—Insertion

© old
"Will you look at him!" the woman said.

This would sound like:

"Will you look at him!" the old, the woman said.

TYPE: Correction—Substitution

© the
The old man heard them laugh.

This would sound like:

The old man heard the, them laugh.

TYPE: Correction—Partial

© st-
He gets stuck.

This would sound like:

He gets st-, stuck.

TYPE: Correction—Multiple attempts

© Exca-
Ex-
Excuse me, Miss Witch.

This would sound like:

Ex-, exca-, excuse me, Miss Witch.

When a reader makes several miscues in a phrase and regresses to correct, they *may not fix* them all. When this happens, mark just the corrected miscue with its own circle with a *C* inside, and leave the circle at the beginning of the phrase open. The *open circle* indicates that more than one thing is going on in this case, and no one designation inside the circle would be appropriate for the entire phrase.

Pauses

I am cautious about letting readers pause for too long a period of time, in either a taped setting or in a conferencing setting. I try to remember that the student is probably trying to use some strategy, and I allow time for that. However, I also try to remember that beyond a certain length of time, say ten or fifteen seconds, that student has had the chance to try different strategies and still isn't getting the word. At this point, I figure they're getting pretty uncomfortable and I say, Tell me what you're thinking or Tell me what you're trying right now or What would you do if you were by yourself?

During a taping session, this is about all the talking I want to do, and I then encourage the student to try and keep reading. During a conferencing setting, this is a wonderful opportunity to find out what is in the student's head and to do some helpful talking and teaching. The student can be congratulated on using appropriate strategies, or a new strategy can be introduced, modeled, and discussed.

When readers pause during the reading for more than five seconds, a mark (∫) is used to indicate where the pause occurred. It is interesting to record the number of seconds the reader paused each time.

9 sec.
Look at ∫ that!

Repeated Miscues

Many times readers will miscue on a word and make the same miscue for the same text item repeatedly throughout the story. Rather than continuing to mark the miscue each time it occurs, you can write *RM* over the text item. If there is a one-letter difference, as in the following example, this is a new miscue and is marked as a substitution.

Mitchell
Michael showed his tambourine to a friend.

RM
Michael frowned.

Mitchell's
Michael's mother was proud.

This would sound like:

Mitchell showed his tambourine to a friend.

Mitchell frowned.

Mitchell's mother was proud.

Complicated Miscues

When miscues become complicated with various repetitions, substitutions, insertions, omissions, and so on, all on the same phrase, the easiest way to make sure you are marking the typescript correctly is to *transcribe verbatim* what the reader says. Making this transcription in the margin near the miscue is very helpful when returning to a typescript after a long period of time, or when sharing the typescript with a colleague. You may have accurately marked the many regressions, substitutions, and so on, but to look at a section of text with many markings, it begins to resemble a spiderweb. Although it may be absolutely correct, it does not tell us much at a glance. The transcription in the margin is much more informative. Here is an example from LaMar's typescript.

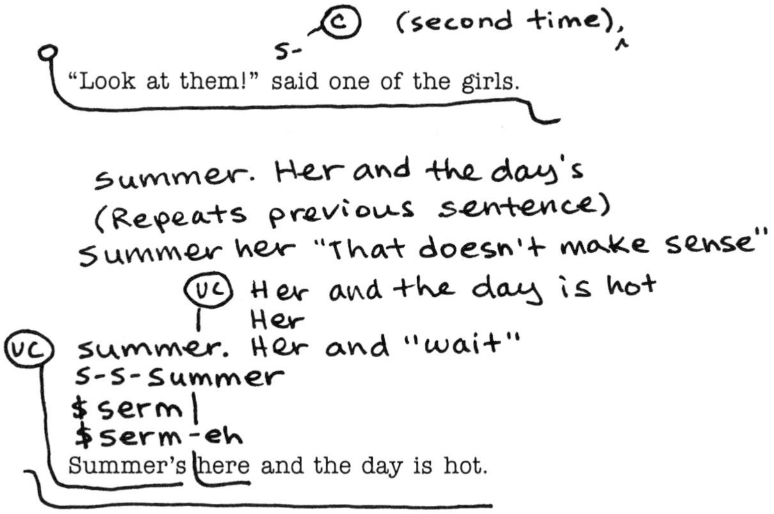

This would sound like (for clarity, a new line starts each regression):

Serm-eh
Serm
S-S-Summer
Summer
Her and "Wait"
Her
Her and the day is hot
Summer, her, "That doesn't make sense"
Look at them said one of the girls.
Summer.
Her and the day's

As we have seen, there are many types of miscues, any of which can be corrected and most of which fit under the following headings:

- Substitution
- Omission
- Partial
- Insertion
- Regression

Coding the Sentences

Your Procedure III typescript is now accurately marked, having listened to the tape as many times as you felt was needed. Now, it is time to *code* each complete sentence, regardless of whether there are miscues in the sentence.

According to Y. Goodman, Watson, and Burke (1987), there are three questions we ask about the sentence as the *reader left it*; that is, we read the sentence as it would sound *with all the miscues corrected. If miscues were left uncorrected, we read the sentence with the miscues still included.* We carefully attend to sentences in which the reader corrected some miscues but left some uncorrected and read the sentence accordingly. Then we ask these three questions about each sentence on our typescript (up to about fifty sentences):

1. In the context of the entire story, in the reader's dialect, and as the reader left it, *does it sound like language? Is it syntactically acceptable?*
   To this question we could answer: Yes/No
2. In the context of the entire story, in the reader's dialect, and as the reader left it, *does it make sense? Is it semantically acceptable?*
   To this question we could answer: Yes/No
3. In the context of the entire story, in the reader's dialect, and as the reader left it, *did it change the author's intended meaning?*
   To this question we could answer: Yes/No/Partially

For a summary of the different possible sentence codings, see Figure 4–4.

Question 1: Does it sound like language?	Question 2: Does it make sense?	Question 3: Has it changed the author's intended meaning?
Y	Y	N
Y	Y	P
Y	Y	Y
Y	N	-
N	N	-

FIGURE 4–4 Summary of Sentence Codings for Procedure III

There is a hierarchical relationship between these questions. We start with syntactic structure, because it is the framework of language that we need to support making meaning.

If we answer *Yes* to Question 1, we have sentence structure and this allows us to proceed to Question 2. If we answer *No* to Question 1, we cannot go any further. If we don't have sentence structure, we know we cannot have meaning, and we can't even ask the last question. Our coding would be NN–.

If we answer *Yes* to Question 2, we have both sentence structure (from Question 1) and meaning (from Question 2). Now we can proceed to Question 3. Our possible answers to Question 3 are:

- Y—Yes, there was a change in a major idea in the author's intended meaning.
- N—No, there was no change in the author's meaning.
- P—There was a partial change in the author's meaning. There has been some change in what the author intended, but it is not a significant change of a major idea.

Here are the possible sentence codings that would result from a *Yes* on Questions 1 and 2:

YYN YYP YYY

If we answer *No* to Question 2, it is like a red light, and we can't even ask the last question. If we don't have overall meaning (from Question 2), we can't even ask about the author's intended meaning, and our sentence coding would be YN–.

To record our sentence codings, we use the line off to the right side of the typescript. The line is written opposite the end punctuation of the sentence and has a corresponding number on it.

Let's look at some examples from readers for each of these codings.

YYN

- Yes, it sounds like language (syntactically acceptable)
- Yes, it makes sense (semantically acceptable)
- No, it didn't change the author's intended meaning

This coding is the best it can be! We want to see lots of this coding on typescripts! We know we have syntactic structure, we have meaning, and we have the author's intended meaning intact. *Every sentence is given a coding, and a sentence with no miscues in it is coded YYN.*

Here is an example from second-grader Joseph's reading:

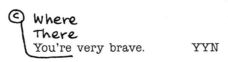

Ⓒ Where
There
You're very brave. YYN

This would sound like:

There, where, you're very brave.

To read for the sentence coding (as the reader left it):

You're very brave.

There was one miscue and it was corrected, so our coding is YYN.

A miscue can be left uncorrected and the sentence can still be coded YYN. Here is an example from second-grader Linda:

said
"OK!" says Grandpa. YYN

This would sound like (and as the reader left it):

"OK!" said Grandpa.

Although the tense has been changed from present to past, within the context of the story, this uncorrected miscue does not result in even a partial change in meaning.

YYP

- Yes, it sounds like language (syntactically acceptable)
- Yes, it makes sense (semantically acceptable)
- Partial change in the author's intended meaning

Here is an example from Joseph:

hunt
They hunted together, and they shared their food. YYP

This would sound like (and as the reader left it):

They hunt together and they shared their food.

Although this change is not significant, there is a slight change in meaning because of the mixed tenses within one sentence.

Here is another example from Linda:

six
I forgot about the sixty. YYP

This would sound like (and as the reader left it):

I forgot about the six.

The grandfather and grandson in this story are having a conversation about how old he is (sixty-nine). They are playing at a park and someone tells grandpa he's on a slide that's just for kids, to which grandpa replies, I'm only nine years old. The grandson reminds him he's sixty-nine, and he replies, I forgot about the sixty. By reading I forgot about the six, Linda has moved us to the written number of his age rather than the spoken number, resulting in a partial change in meaning.

When the reader has changed a character's name, for example from Michael to Mitchell, the first time this occurs, if there are no other miscues, I code the sentence YYP. From then on, if that same name change is the only uncorrected miscue in the sentence, I accept that the reader knows who this character is, and although she is using a different name than the one the author intended, she is constructing meaning. I code those sentences in the rest of the typescript as YYN.

If gender is changed in a title, that is a partial change in meaning, as in this example from fourth-grader Brooks:

Princess
The Prince didn't stick around to see which nasty spell the witch had in mind. YYP

This would sound like (and as the reader left it):

The Princess didn't stick around to see which nasty spell the witch had in mind.

It is always interesting to look at the sentences in the periphery to the sentence in question to try and understand what might have been going on in the reader's mind that caused her to make the miscue. In this example, the previous sentence was:

44
walking
I can't have any princes waking up Sleeping Beauty

before the hundred years are up. 44 YN-

45 Princess
The Prince didn't stick around to see which nasty

© Her
46
spell the witch had in mind. He ran deeper 45 YYP

into the forest until he came to a tiny cottage where

he saw another lady who might help him. 46 YYN

So Brooks had just said princes, which in her dialect is pronounced the same as princess—the word she used in our example. Although she maintained syntactic structure by substituting walking for waking, she left it uncorrected, which resulted in a loss of meaning (YN–). In the sentence following our example, she's probably thinking it's a princess, and she read her for he, but then she self-corrected (YYN).

YYY

- Yes, it sounds like language (syntactically acceptable)
- Yes, it makes sense (semantically acceptable)
- Yes, it changed the author's intended meaning

This is an interesting coding because it shows the reader is constructing meaning, yet has moved away from the author's meaning. Here is an example from Linda:

UC tickling
tickle-ing
tickled
tickled
tickle   said
"I think you're tricking me," she says.

This would sound like:

"I think you're tickle, tickled, tickled, tickle-ing, tickling me," she said.

To read for the sentence coding (as the reader left it):

"I think you're tickling me," she said.

YN–

- Yes, it sounds like language (syntactically acceptable)
- No, it doesn't make sense (semantically unacceptable)
- Can't ask the last question

Often when a reader leaves a nonword uncorrected in a sentence, we get this coding. Here is an example from Linda:

$ticklest
"You're the trickiest Grandpa in the world!"   YN–

This would sound like (and as the reader left it):

"You're the ticklest Grandpa in the world!"

Even though we know that ticklest is not a word, it is in the proper position in the sentence and has the appropriate structure of an adjective. It sounds as if it *could* be an adjective. So in this sense, we have sentence structure, but because it is a nonword, we have lost meaning.

Here is another example from fourth-grader Jeremy:

dark felt
That whole darn straw house fell down. YN–

This would sound like (and as the reader left it):

That whole dark straw house felt down.

All the parts of speech are in the right position in the sentence, so we have a syntactically acceptable sentence but, within the context of the story, we have lost meaning.

NN–

- No, it doesn't sound like language (syntactically unacceptable)
- No, it doesn't make sense (semantically unacceptable)
- Can't ask the last question

Sentences with this coding are the ones we hear during oral reading that don't click for us or the reader. They just don't sound like the way we talk. They have lost grammatical structure and don't make any sense. Here is an example from Joseph:

down
Let me sit by your fire and have something to eat. NN–

This would sound like (and as the reader left it):

Let me sit down your fire and have something to eat.

He lost syntactic structure when he substituted down for by. Perhaps he was predicting sit down by your fire, which would have been acceptable, but he left out the by and the sentence lost structure and meaning.

When the reader substitutes one verb for another of the same tense, for example, we usually do not lose syntactic structure and can then closely examine whether we have lost meaning. But in this next example, Joseph changes last to lets and thereby loses syntactic structure.

(C) mo- (UC) lets $laste
He wanted the food to last for a long time.

This would sound like:

He wanted mo-, the food to laste, lets for a long time.

To read for the sentence coding (as the reader left it):

He wanted the food to lets for a long time.

If the reader inserts or omits end punctuation, we still need to give a sentence coding for the *author's sentence*. An example of an inserted period is in LaMar's reading (see Appendix A, sentence 14). An example of an omitted period comes from Weston's reading:

The Fisherman's wife hurried down to the sand. And behind her followed the people of the town.

He omitted the period and read this as:

The Fisherman's wife hurried down to the sand and behind her followed the people of the town.

Each of these sentences in the typescript would be coded YYN even though they were combined into one sentence by the reader.

Determining sentence codings, like everything else associated with miscue analysis, gets easier with practice. In my university courses, I always have students work in pairs when working through all the steps in Procedure III so that they can have another set of "miscue ears" and "analysis eyes" to help make decisions about the miscue (replay and replay that tape!), how to mark it, what the appropriate sentence coding is, and what the graphic similarity is between the miscue and the text item.

Tallying the Miscues

Once the typescript has been marked and the sentences have been coded, we are ready to tally individual miscues. I use the miscue tally form (see Appendix C), which is my addition to the original Procedure III. Often, we do not start tallying miscues or coding sentences right from the beginning of the reading. Sometimes it takes readers a paragraph or two to get into the author's style and language structure or the setting of the story, or to access background for a concept being discussed in a content-area selection (Menosky 1971). Therefore, we generally see a lot of miscue activity at the beginning of passages (see LaMar's typescript in Chapter 5).

So we can choose to begin the sentence coding and miscue tally a little way into the text, but once we begin, we *work with all consecutive sentences* and miscues from that point on. We usually examine about fifty sentences and about *thirty to forty* miscues. If we do more, that's fine, we just have more information to consider.

Whether we are listening informally to readers in a conferencing setting or analyzing miscues in a more systematic way through the taped procedure described here, we make the determination as to whether the miscue was acceptable; that is, we ask the question, **Did the miscue change the meaning of the text?** An important point to remember is that miscues are judged as acceptable or not acceptable in view of the *everyday language* of the reader. As Y. Goodman, Watson, and Burke (1987, 66–67, italics in original) note:

> Acceptability of miscues is determined by what is acceptable within the dialect of the reader, not what is the norm within the culture and language of the teacher. All readers react to the acceptability of language according to their own expectations. Language is judged by what *sounds right* to the language user. When the language a reader or speaker hears *sounds right*, it usually falls within the range of the individual speaker's language use and the use of language that is part of the community. . . . In other words, the acceptability questions are answered in terms of whether the miscue would be syntactically or semantically acceptable *within the reader's dialect*—not the dialect approved by the school, teacher, or text. The issue, as it relates to reading, is the gaining of information and meaning—not the use of an approved dialect.

Here are some guidelines for completing the miscue tally form (see Appendix C):

- Select the point from which you will tally individual miscues; usually, this is from the beginning of the text, but sometimes we start a few paragraphs into the reading
- From that point on, tally the following miscues (and the sentence number in which the miscue occurs):
  - Substitutions (one-word, complex miscues, reversals, nonwords, dialect usages, misarticulations)
  - Omissions (word)—in the *Reader Said* column, put a dash (–), and in the *Text Said* column, write the word or phrase that was left out
  - Partials
  - Insertions—in the *Reader Said* column, write in the word the reader inserted, and in the *Text Said* column, put a dash
  - Repeated miscues—write down the miscue the first time (for example, name changes), then don't tally the remaining occurrences of this exact miscue

    - If there are several attempts at a word, write down the first attempt
    - Do not tally end punctuation miscues, pauses, or split syllables
- Check the column that is appropriate for that individual miscue in terms of whether it was corrected, and if not, whether the miscue resulted in a meaning change or a partial meaning change
- Check the column that is appropriate for that individual miscue in terms of the graphic similarity between the miscue and the text item
- Some miscues we cannot code for graphic similarity on the tally sheet—either there is too much going on (complex miscues), so we cannot assume a one-to-one correspondence between the miscue and the text item; or there is not enough linguistic information to make this determination (omissions, insertions, or partials). *Do not code* complex miscues, omissions, insertions, and partials for graphic similarity.

After all the miscues (up to about forty) have been tallied, bring the totals for each column down to the bottom of the page. If you are using more than one miscue tally form, combine page totals for a grand total for each column. This is the information to transfer to the reader profile form (see Appendix G).

Running the Numbers and Completing the Reader Profile

The purpose of the reader profile is to pull together all the information we have about the reader through our use of Procedure III, including data from these documents:

- The typescript (sentence codings)
- The miscue tally form (column totals)
- The retelling guide (comprehension score) (see Chapter 5)

The next sections contain directions for completing each part of the reader profile form.

Number of Sentences Coded

I usually consider about fifty sentences to be sufficient to get the information I'm seeking through a Procedure III. Record the number of sentences you coded. If your student read 120 sentences and you coded all of them, that's great—you'll have that much more information about your reader.

Comprehending in Process

In miscue analysis we are interested in what the student is understanding *during* the reading. We refer to this as *comprehending* and contrast that with what the student understood after the reading (see Comprehension later in these directions) (Y. Goodman, Watson, and Burke 1987).

To calculate the numbers for the Comprehending section, we return to our sentence codings. This time, we consider each coding as a whole. Count up the number of times a sentence had the *complete* coding YYN, YYY, and so on. Follow the same procedures as before to calculate the percentages for each type of coding. The first line is for the raw number of times that coding appeared within our 110 coded sentences. The second line is for the percentage of that particular coding within the total number of coded sentences.

Comprehending in Process (Sentence Codings)

81	74%	YYN
8	7%	YYP
1	1%	YYY
12	11%	YN–
8	7%	NN–

DO ✓

Syntactic Acceptability

Look at your sentence codings (YYN, YN–), then the first letter in each coding. These letters tell you about the syntactic acceptability of that sentence. Count up the number of *Y*s and the number of *N*s in that first position. We'll use Brooks' reader profile numbers for our examples. Her typescript had 110 sentences, with 102 *Y*s and 8 *N*s in the first position. The first column on the reader profile is for the *raw* number and the second column is for *the percentage* number.

The Syntactic Acceptability section would look like this:

Syntactic Acceptability

102	93%	Acceptable
8	7%	Unacceptable

To calculate the percentages:

$$\frac{\text{Number of syntactically acceptable sentences}}{\text{Number of sentences coded}} \times 100$$

For the acceptable sentences *(Ys),* we have 102 divided by 110, which comes out to 0.927; we multiply this by 100 and get 92.7, then round up to 93. For the unacceptable sentences (*N*s), we have 8 divided by 110, which is 0.07, we multiply by 100 to get 7. We double-check to make sure that these two percentages add up to 100, which they do (93 + 7).

DO ✓

Semantic Acceptability

We conduct the same procedure to get percentages for the Semantic Acceptability section and the Meaning Change section. To make our calculations for this section, we look at sentence codings and count up all the *Ys* and *N*s in the second position (YYN, Y*N*–, YYP, N*N*–).

Semantic Acceptability

103	94%	Acceptable
7	6%	Unacceptable

Meaning Change

To calculate the numbers for this section, we now look to the last letter (or the dash) in our sentence codings (YY*N*, YN–, YY*P*, NN–). We run the numbers the same way as before to find the percentages. For the *No Meaning Change* number, we add up all the *N*s. For the *Partial Meaning Change* number, we add up all the *P*s. For the *With Meaning Change* section, we *add all the Ys and all the dashes together*.

Meaning Change

81	74%	No Meaning Change
8	6%	Partial Meaning Change
21	20%	With Meaning Change

Comprehension

Up to this point in completing the reader profile, all our information has come from the sentence codings on the typescript. For the comprehension score, we look to the retelling guide and bring over the student's percentage of comprehension. This represents what the student understood *after* the reading, as told through the unaided and cued retellings.

Comprehension 70%

Corrections

This important information about the reader comes from the miscue tally form. As a reminder, we again write down the number of miscues tallied. Then we calculate our percentages from the raw numbers for:

- The number of miscues corrected
- The number of miscues uncorrected, with no meaning change
- The number of miscues uncorrected, with a meaning change
- The number of miscues uncorrected, with a partial meaning change

Corrections—number of miscues tallied: *72*

48	67%	Corrected
8	11%	Uncorrected—No Meaning Change
4	5%	Uncorrected—Partial Meaning Change
12	17%	Uncorrected—Meaning Change

Graphic Similarity

Now we are ready to bring information from the miscue tally form to the reader profile. We first record the number of miscues tallied and the number of miscues coded for graphic similarity. Remember, these numbers will be different because of the four kinds of miscues we cannot code for graphic similarity: complex miscues, omissions, insertions, and partials. Now we record the raw numbers of each kind of graphic similarity coding: High, Some, and None. We calculate the percentages in the same manner as before. For example, to calculate the percentage of miscues corrected, divide the number of miscues corrected by the total number of miscues coded for graphic similarity, then multiply by 100.

GRAPHIC SIMILARITY

Number of miscues tallied: *72*

Number of miscues coded for graphic similarity: *57*

41	72%	High
9	16%	Some
7	12%	None

Comments

The last section of the reader profile is an open-ended invitation for the teacher to record any relevant observations, such as:

- There were a high number of self-corrected omissions.
- There were many times the reader paused for more than ten seconds.
- The reader did not make a significant number of miscues that changed meaning, but there were many repetitions of text read correctly.

Identifying Strengths and Areas of Concern

Now the most important work begins. After completing all the steps in Procedure III, we are ready to step back from all this and say, What does it all mean? What does all this tell me about my reader? Then, on to another important question, What strategies are most appropriate for this reader right now to address the areas of concern?

We undertake the task of answering these questions in Chapter 8, where we look at evidence from each of the three procedures we're learning to see how that data can lead us to conclusions about readers and which instructional strategies will meet their needs.

Bringing It All Together: The Reader Profile

Our summary document from Procedure III, the reader profile, becomes a powerful tool for sharing what we know about students with readers, parents, colleagues, and/or IEP teams. At a glance, we can see all we know from conducting the analysis of readers' miscues. We can also look across several readers' profiles and compare patterns that emerge, which informs our instruction and helps us form temporary groups for Guided Reading lessons.

Now that we know how to conduct all the Procedure III steps, let's look at LaMar's reading through our new "eyes."

5

Procedure III with LaMar

I have learned a lot about readers that I didn't know before. My ears are now tuned to miscues not as mistakes but as information about what a reader is doing as they read. I hope to share this information with my colleagues to change their views of readers and with students to change their view of themselves as readers.

—Stephanie Hamilton, Title I Reading Teacher

Following the framework introduced in Chapter 4, let's go through a Procedure III (Y. Goodman, Watson, and Burke 1987) I conducted with an eight-year-old student named LaMar. In this chapter we will:

- Address how I decided to conduct this in-depth procedure with him.
- Examine the setting for the reading and the choice of text he read.
- "Listen" to his reading through a verbatim transcription.
- Mark his miscues on a typescript (I already had this text made up as a typescript).
- Analyze the miscues.
- Code the sentences.
- Examine the self-corrections and uncorrected miscues.
- Determine the graphic similarity of one-word substitution miscues.
- Complete the retelling guide as we "listen" to his retelling through a verbatim transcription.
- Run the numbers and complete the reader profile form.
- Determine LaMar's strengths and areas of concern as a reader.

Choosing the Student

In October 1994, LaMar joined my multiage classroom of twenty-four students (ages seven, eight, and nine). He had been home-schooled by his parents, and they decided to have him now attend a public school. After a few weeks, they were interested in knowing how he was doing, and I decided to use a Procedure III to be able to give them a clear picture of LaMar as a reader.

I had LaMar stay after school one afternoon, and we chatted about how things were going for him. He said he was starting to make some friends and he thought things were "going fine." I let him know what we were going to be doing together: I was going to ask him to read a little bit for me, and then we would talk about what he read.

Choosing a Text

I chose "The Old Man, His Son, and the Donkey" (Macmillan Company 1970; see Appendix M) as the text for LaMar to read. I predicted the story would be slightly challenging, so I would hear some miscues, but not so difficult that he would not be able to comprehend it. I knew he had some experience with donkeys and horses because of his upbringing in a ranching community. His mother said she read to him often, so I speculated he would have some background listening to this type of tale and would therefore be somewhat comfortable with the *storybook language.* I asked LaMar to flip through the typescript to see if he had read the story before and to see how many pages there were to read, and then he was ready to begin.

I had made multiple copies of typescripts and retelling guides for a variety of stories and whenever I needed to conduct a Procedure III, it was a simple task to just pull a copy from the file. So, in this instance, LaMar was actually reading from a typescript of the story rather than a book. This is why, on the tape, we hear him start off with `Name, Date, whatever.` He's reading off the top of the typescript!

Generally, we have students read from the book if it is available, because we gain additional information about them as readers when we see how they handle a book or use picture cues. The task of developing your selection of typescripts will be an ongoing process, one I encourage you to share with colleagues.

Making the Typescript

I brought three stories with me to the tape-recording session—one that was my best guess of a text that was probably just right for LaMar, one that might be a little more challenging, and one that would be a little easier. Then, I asked him to read the *just right* story. If he had started reading and made an inordinate number of meaning-change miscues, I would have asked him to read the easier one; or if he had not made very many miscues, I would have asked him to read the harder one. However, I let him get into the story a little bit before I made that call, because the beginning of a text often has more miscue activity while a reader is figuring out the author's style of language (Menosky 1971). Past sentence seven, he became more comfortable with the language of the folk tale.

If you don't already have a typescript for the book the student reads, you can make one after the reading by making a photocopy (Brummett and Maras 1995). However, this doesn't always give us the space between lines or the wider margins needed to mark miscues and make notes and transcriptions. I have found it is easiest to number the sentences, mark the miscues, and code the sentences if I type up a copy of the story, using a larger font and triple spacing. While this takes a little time initially, once you have made the typescript and the accompanying retelling guide, they are available to use repeatedly. For complete directions on constructing a typescript, see Chapter 4.

Making the Retelling Guide

Because the story I had LaMar read was one I use frequently, I already had a retelling guide. The purposes of the retelling guide are to estimate a comprehension score and to help us cue the student to discuss other details in the story that they haven't yet mentioned in our conversation. Chapter 4 provides instructions on how to make a retelling guide.

Taping the Reading and Retelling

After LaMar and I talked a minute, we were ready to begin. One advantage to having him stay after school was that it was quiet, so there wasn't a lot of background noise on the tape (except for a few train whistles!). I let LaMar test the tape recorder and listen to his voice. Then, as I asked him to read, I reminded him I would be talking with him about the story when he was finished. This is the usual invitation I use:

> I'd like you to read this aloud and when you come to something you don't know, do whatever you would do if I wasn't here. I won't be able to help you right now. When you're finished reading, I'll ask you what you remember from the story, and we can talk about it.

If I say something you don't know rather than a word you don't know, students decide which linguistic unit they're going to focus on when they're reading. When LaMar finished reading the story, I asked him to tell me everything he could remember, and as he started in, he had to make sure he didn't have to say every word! I assured him he didn't; he just had to talk about the main events and who was in the story. In one long stream of talk, he included a great deal of important information in the correct sequence. He told me so much, I didn't ask anything else, except if there was a moral to the story. He wasn't sure what *moral* meant, so I told him it was the last thing the father was talking about, sort of the lesson we learn from this story, and he was able to tell me.

I've used this reading many times in my miscue analysis classes and every time I do, I realize I could have done a better job on the retelling. I could have followed up with cues to the details he had left out, although there weren't many! Invariably, my students say the same thing when reflecting on their experiences learning Procedure III: "I could have done better on the retelling!" They often have difficulty "getting the retelling right" and find it the hardest part of learning how to do miscue analysis. One reason I keep using LaMar's reading as a teaching example is that we learn so much from him about how proficient reading works, even when on the surface, it may appear he is having difficulty. I also think it provides us clear exemplars of just about every type of miscue.

Marking the Miscues

After LaMar finished reading and retelling the story, his parents came to pick him up, then I listened to the tape and marked the miscues on the typescript. There were several places in his reading where I had to listen to a sentence many times to be sure I had marked all the miscues correctly. I'll walk you through his reading now, as we examine the miscue markings.

Let's take a look at LaMar's completed typescript first, just to get the big picture (see Appendix A). From the examples in Chapter 4, you probably recognize certain markings, such as the one we use for a regression. We draw a line under the text as far as the reader went, then bring it to the point in the text to which the reader returned. The letter inside the circle at the end of that line tells us what is going on in the regression, such as *C* for Correction or *R* for Repetition; miscue markings are shown in Figure 4–3. Soon this shorthand becomes very familiar.

Now that you have the overview of LaMar's typescript, I'd like to invite you to listen to LaMar at this URL: <http://www.heinemann.com/miscues> and to try the markings yourself either using the blank typescript (Appendix A) or the following chart (see Figure 5–1). Let's go through LaMar's reading line by line and I'll discuss what's going on. In the left column I've written what we actually hear him say as he's reading. The line from the typescript where you can practice the miscue markings is in the second column, and the same line with my markings is in the third column.

FIGURE 5–1 Procedure III with LaMar

Now I invite you to take a look at the list of miscue markings again if needed (see Figure 4–3); cover up the right column on the following chart and try your hand at marking LaMar's miscues. Listen to LaMar's reading online URL: <http://www.heinemann.com/miscues>. If it isn't available, it would help to read the first column aloud to get a better sense of what I heard LaMar say as he was reading. Following each sentence is a discussion of the miscues, a speculation on why he may have made them, and a description of the markings. Because of space constraints on this chart, I've not been able to use the same line breaks as those that appear on the complete typescript. My focus here is on the markings.

WHAT WE HEAR LAMAR SAY	TYPESCRIPT—HAVE A GO AT MARKING!	MY TYPESCRIPT MARKINGS
1. An old farmer and his son were taking their donkey to town to sell, "That doesn't make sense" —to sell —(I adjust his microphone—he says "I know")—donkey to, "Oh yeah"	An old farmer and his son were taking their donkey to town to sell.	An old farmer and his son were (AC) donkey to taking their donkey to town (R) to sell. "That doesn't make sense" "I Know"

LaMar read the complete sentence, made the comment That doesn't make sense, then repeated the phrase to sell. He then backed up and read, donkey to and said, Oh yeah as if it now made sense to him. Because this is how he left the sentence, he has actually abandoned the correct response town to sell. We have therefore lost syntactic structure and meaning.

While he was reading this sentence, I helped him adjust his clip-on microphone to be sure he was being picked up by the tape recorder. I must have made some indication to him that he needed to direct his voice toward the microphone, hence his side comment, I know. His other side comment, Oh yeah, is in the transcription in the margin, but with everything else going on in the markings, I just ran out of room to try to put it over the sentence. The line underneath the phrase to sell shows us how far he read before backing up. The *R* in the circle stands for "Repetition." The caret symbol (^) shows us his side comment, where he is talking, not reading (see p. 226). Side comments are put in quotation marks. The line that shows us the second regression all the way back to donkey is lower than the line for the repetition to sell, indicating that it happened later. The *AC* in the circle stands for "Abandons the Correct response," meaning that LaMar read what was in the text, then made a miscue, the omission of town to sell.

2. They had not gone far when they saw some girls at the well.	They had not gone far when they saw some girls at a well.	They had not gone far when they saw some the girls at a well.

He substituted the/a, he left it uncorrected, and there was no significant change in meaning.
A substitution is written over the word in the text.

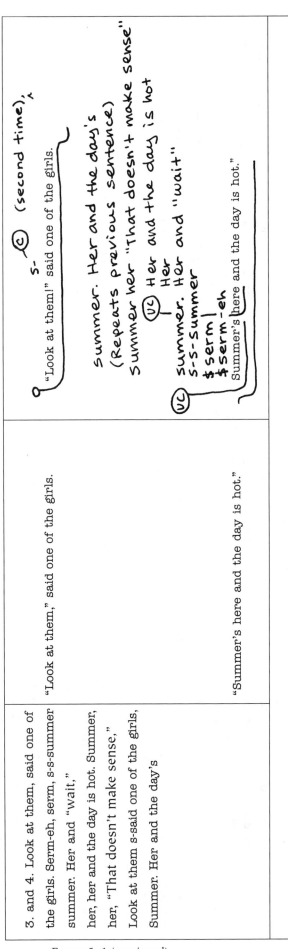

3. and 4. Look at them, said one of the girls. Serm-eh, serm, s-s-summer summer. Her and "wait," her, her and the day is hot. Summer, her, "That doesn't make sense," Look at them s-said one of the girls, Summer. Her and the day's	"Look at them," said one of the girls. "Summer's here and the day is hot."	s- Ⓒ (second time), "Look at them!" said one of the girls. summer. Her and the day's (Repeats previous sentence) Summer her "That doesn't make sense" ⓋⒸ Her and the day is hot Her ⓋⒸ summer. Her and "wait" s-s-summer $serm $serm-eh Summer's here and the day is hot."

We really have to look at both Sentences 3 and 4 together. He was having a little trouble entering into this text right at the beginning. If we think about it, the syntactic structure is unusual, and not really the style of language an eight-year-old would use. He'd probably say, Man, it's hot out here instead of Summer's here and the day is hot.

He was very concerned with this making sense, as shown by his side comments, Wait and That doesn't make sense but even with a great deal of effort, he isn't able to get this to work for him. He went all the way back (with a big sigh) to the beginning of Sentence 3 (I think to get a running start), and even uses intonation that indicates he might have thought Summer was a girl's name, but it still wasn't sounding right to him. He left the sentence incomplete, abandoned all his attempts, and moved on. However, from here on in the story, it seems he figured out the author's syntactic style, or the "storybook language," and rolled right along.

I've made an effort to mark these sentences accurately, but on the typescript with double or triple spacing, there isn't room to do this much marking. Realistically, this is an example of a spot in the text where there is so much miscue activity that it is best to transcribe what the reader has said in the margin. When we come back to the typescript some time later, this transcription is much more informative than trying to decipher the actual markings, even though they may be correct. Sometimes we simply don't have enough room to mark everything, and even if we do manage to, it is so cumbersome, it's difficult to know what the reader said. In this instance, because there were many different attempts, and the typescript has limited space, I decided to only provide a verbatim transcription.

The dollar sign ($) is used to indicate a nonword. The curved little hook at the end of the line underneath the text shows us that the regression flows across the line in the typescript. The open circle at the end of the line shows us that more than one thing is going on in the regression. Some things were fixed, but some things are still left uncorrected.

FIGURE 5–1 (continued)

<table>
<tr><td>5. And those two walk when they,
two walk when they might ride.</td><td>And those two walk when they might ride.</td><td>Ⓡ
And those two walk when they might ride.</td></tr>
<tr><td colspan="3">I think LaMar's regression on the phrase, two walk when they is a checking-up move, as if he were asking, Did I say that right? Again, he was trying to figure out the unusual structure of the language and perhaps might have been more familiar with something like, Those two people are walking when they could be riding.
Also, LaMar was probably more used to the meaning of might being the connotation that something is conditional or tentative—we might go to the movies. In this sentence, the author used a different meaning of the word might, as in would be able to.
The line under the text indicates how far he read before he regressed and reread. The R in the circle indicates a "Repetition."</td></tr>
<tr><td>6. What fools they are!</td><td>What fools they are!</td><td>What fools they are!</td></tr>
<tr><td colspan="3">No miscues</td></tr>
<tr><td>7. All the girls laughed at the, this.</td><td>All the girls laughed at this.</td><td>Ⓒ the
All the girls laughed at this.</td></tr>
<tr><td colspan="3">LaMar miscued the/this, then self-corrected. The at that point in the sentence was a great prediction! We can think of a sentence with that structure that would make sense, for example, All the girls laughed at the donkey. But LaMar caught the miscue and self-corrected, probably getting cues from two things: the period after this, and the lack of a noun or noun phrase following what he thought was the in the sentence. Because he is a proficient language user, he has a tacit understanding that a determiner signals that a noun or noun phrase will be next, and when there wasn't one, his syntactic cueing system told him he didn't have an acceptable sentence structure.
The C in the circle stands for "Corrected." The line underneath shows that he didn't go any further than the word this.</td></tr>
<tr><td>8. The old man heard the,
them laugh.</td><td>The old man heard them laugh.</td><td>Ⓒ the
The old man heard them laugh.</td></tr>
<tr><td colspan="3">LaMar predicted a noun here, maybe something like The old man heard the girls, but again, he caught the miscue and self-corrected. This is a miscue similar to the one in Sentence 7 and is marked the same way, as a corrected substitution.</td></tr>
</table>

FIGURE 5–1 (continued)

<table>
<tr><td>9. “Get up a, and ride,” h-, he said to his son.</td><td>“Get up and ride,” he said to his son.</td><td>“Get up and ride,” he said to his son.</td></tr>
<tr><td colspan="3">LaMar miscued a/and then self-corrected. The possible reason for this miscue is not as clear syntactically. It’s possible that a sentence could have that structure (Get up a), but it wouldn’t be common. For instance, someone might tell the conductor of an old train to Get up a head of steam. Perhaps he saw the first letter of and, said a, then his prediction was not confirmed by having a noun or noun phrase follow after the determiner a.
He said a partial word, h–/he, then self-corrected.
The partial is indicated by a dash after the sound we hear (h–, he).</td></tr>
<tr><td>10. So the son got on the donkey—s back.</td><td>So the son got on the donkey’s back.</td><td>So the son got on the donkey’s back.</td></tr>
<tr><td colspan="3">LaMar hesitated in the middle of the word donkey’s, creating a split syllable, but this did not create a change in meaning. I think we have to remember there is much more going on in the head of the reader during reading than we are privy to, and in an instance like this, the reader gets enough linguistic information to leap to meaning and doesn’t do us the courtesy of saying the word again. I believe, in his head, he was making sense.
Maybe he paused mid-word because he was looking ahead to the word back and running through possible meanings. (I had a weak back about a week back from sitting in back of the saddle, so I took back the new running shoes.) I think he realizes it is the noun back, and continues reading.
The vertical line through the word shows where he hesitated.</td></tr>
<tr><td>11. The old man walked.</td><td>The old man walked.</td><td>The old man walked.</td></tr>
<tr><td colspan="3">No miscues</td></tr>
<tr><td>12. Soon they came to some men in a field.</td><td>Soon they came to some men in a field.</td><td>Soon they came to some men in a field.</td></tr>
<tr><td colspan="3">No miscues</td></tr>
</table>

Figure 5–1 (continued)

<table>
<tr><td>13. “Look at that!” one of the men shuh-aw, shouted.</td><td>“Look at that!” one of the men shouted.</td><td>Ⓒ shuh-aw
“Look at that!” one of the men shouted.</td></tr>
<tr><td colspan="3">Using the “sound-it-out” strategy, LaMar gets enough information to decode this word. I marked it as a corrected substitution, writing the shuh-aw over the word shouted.</td></tr>
<tr><td>14. “That big boy rides well. His, his poor old father must walk.”</td><td>“That big boy rides while his poor old father must walk.”</td><td>well Ⓡ
“That big boy rides while. His poor old father must walk.”</td></tr>
<tr><td colspan="3">Lamar and his parents own horses, and it’s interesting to consider the influence his background experience may have had on this miscue. Perhaps he had heard someone say, That big boy rides well. Once he had made the miscue well/while, he created an appropriate place for the sentence to end, and his voice dropped to indicate the period. He then repeated his at the beginning of the “next” sentence, as if he needed to regain his linguistic footing.
To show where LaMar indicated an inserted period, we use a caret marking. I used a capital letter when I wrote His, to show that it is the beginning of LaMar’s new sentence, based on his intonation.</td></tr>
<tr><td>15. The old man heard the, their word, words.</td><td>The old man heard their words.</td><td>Ⓒ the Ⓒ word
The old man heard their words.</td></tr>
<tr><td colspan="3">This is an interesting set of miscues. It’s hard to speculate what might have been going on for LaMar, but I’d guess one thing would be the high graphic similarity: the word the is the first part of the word their. On his miscue word/words I think he was just reading too quickly, that is, sometimes our mouth works faster than our brain. He did correct both of these miscues.
The lines underneath the text indicate for us that the/their was corrected before he went on to say word and then to correct to words.</td></tr>
</table>

Figure 5–1 (continued)

16. "Get right down," he said to his son.	"Get right down," he said to his son.	"Get right down," he said to his son.
No miscues		
17. and 18. "I will ride the, I will ride." The son got down, and the old man got on the donkey's back.	"I will ride." The son got down, and the old man got on the donkey's back.	C "I will ride." The son got down, and the old man got on the donkey's back.
Again, we need to consider these two sentences together, as LaMar omitted the period in Sentence 17 and moved us across the sentence boundary into Sentence 18. Think about what he may have been predicting. The man could have been saying, I will ride the donkey. Also we can think about syntactic structures that would be familiar to LaMar, as in hearing his father say, Today I will ride the gelding. But we hear LaMar back up and read with a different intonation that clearly indicated the end of a sentence, I will ride. Then he read Sentence 18 with no other miscues. To show the omission of the period, we circle it, as we would a word or phrase that was left out. The line underneath the text shows he went into Sentence 18 and said The before returning to the beginning of Sentence 17. This is a good example of miscue activity in which there were no changes and corrections in the words in the text per se, but there are differences in phrasing and intonation that give us insight into the reader's construction of meaning.		
19. 20. and 21. "It feeled, It f—eels good to ride," the old man, the old farmer said, "It isn't right for me to walk, son." Son, Soon they came to a woman and her child walking on the road.	"It feels good to ride," the old farmer said. "It wasn't right for me to walk." Soon they came to a woman and her children walking on the road.	C f/eels $feeled C man isn't "It feels good to ride," the old farmer said. "It wasn't C son, Son. right for me to walk." Soon they came to a woman and child her children walking on the road.

FIGURE 5–1 (continued)

Here we need to examine three sentences together because he has omitted the periods on Sentences 20 and 21.

In Sentence 19, when LaMar first miscued the nonword $feeled/feels, he might have been trying to create a past tense form of feel, then he realized it was incorrect and tried again. This is a common thing for young children to do, when they overgeneralize the rules for constructing past tense forms, but LaMar had "outgrown" this usage and regressed to self-correct.

Here again we see the use of the *sound-it-out* strategy. In trying to correct, he split the one syllable feel into the onset and rime f—eels and made no further attempts. I give LaMar the benefit of the doubt that in his head he "created" the word feels as a complete, meaningful word, even though he didn't say it out loud in one chunk, similar to the donkey—s example in Sentence 10.

When he corrected man/farmer he also omitted the period of Sentence 19 and then the period of Sentence 20, creating the meaningful sentence, The old man said, "It isn't right for me to walk, son." If we look back through the beginning of the story, we can clearly see why LaMar made the miscue man/farmer. In Sentence 1, the author referred to this character as, An old farmer, but in the title and Sentences 8, 11, 15, and 18, he is referred to as The old man. This is a great example of a miscue that indicates the reader is constructing meaning, and although LaMar caught this miscue and self-corrected, it would have been syntactically and semantically acceptable to leave this miscue uncorrected. The split syllable is indicated by a vertical line through the word where the reader paused. The line under the text shows us he backed up to It to make another attempt on feels, and in the second instance, the line underneath shows us that he regressed to the word the and said, the old man, the old farmer.

As he moves into Sentence 20, we hear a soft whisper, or subvocalization, as he is trying to figure out wasn't. He left the miscue isn't/wasn't uncorrected, which just changed the verb tense. If we look back through the text he's read so far, the tense changes repeatedly. A narrator is telling us the story in the past tense, using verb forms such as were taking, had not gone, saw, got, walked. Then, interspersed with these usages, the text moves to first person, and the tense moves to present tense, during the dialogue and interactions between the son, the father, the girls at the well, and the men in the field. For example, we have the verb forms look, walk, get up, rides, must walk. So we are not at all surprised that LaMar changed the verb tense isn't/wasn't and left it uncorrected. In my mind, there was no change in meaning.

While he doesn't back up into Sentence 20 and "correct" the omission of the period by rereading with a different intonation, his second attempt on soon (son/soon) and subsequent correction essentially accomplished the same thing by establishing a definite beginning to Sentence 21. When I marked the two attempts and correction on soon, I used the period and comma, and made a note to myself in the margin to remember how these were different in intonation (son./soon)(son,/soon).

Later he miscues child/children and leaves it uncorrected. This results in a partial meaning change because, as the author wrote the story, the woman had more than one child. Again, we can speculate on the influence of his own experiences as an only child that may have caused this miscue.

22. "Well, well you look at him!" the old, the woman said.	"Will you look at him!" the woman said.	(d) (uc) well Well (c) old "Will you look at him!" the woman said.

FIGURE 5–1 (continued)

<table>
<tr><td colspan="3">I consider LaMar's miscue well/will to be a dialect usage. Here in eastern Oregon, this would be a common thing to say for someone raised here. I can just imagine that in this small, rural town, LaMar might have heard someone saying, Well, (if) you look at him, he's got his work done. So I didn't consider this a change in meaning, as I think it sounds like the language used "in these parts."
If we think about the references to the man so far in the story, it has always been with the adjective old as in old man and old farmer. So we can understand why LaMar said old woman. He did, however, correct this miscue.
The UC in the circle indicates an "Unsuccessful Attempt to Correct" because LaMar never did say will. We indicate the insertion of old using the caret symbol. The line underneath the text goes through the caret symbol to show that LaMar didn't say woman before he backed up to correct.</td></tr>
<tr><td>23. "That man rides well. His poor little son must walk."</td><td>"That man rides while his poor little son must walk."</td><td>"That man rides while his poor little son must walk." [handwritten above "while his": RM well, with a caret and a capital H over "his"]</td></tr>
<tr><td colspan="3">Here we have the same structure and patterns of miscues we saw in Sentence 14. LaMar has created a "parallel text" where he is making sense, but he has partially changed the author's intended meaning. His miscue well/while created a sentence that ends there, and then he read the rest of the author's sentence as a "new" sentence. This miscue partially changed the meaning, because the author intended a statement in which one thing is happening (the man is riding) while this other thing is happening (the boy is walking).
The RM over the miscue well/while indicates a "Repeated Miscue," that is, an exact match between a previous miscue and related text item.</td></tr>
<tr><td>24. The old man heard the woman.</td><td>The old man heard her words.</td><td>The old man heard her words. [handwritten over "her words," in a bracket: the woman]</td></tr>
<tr><td colspan="3">Here is a complex miscue, where LaMar substituted a phrase the woman for a phrase in the text her words. In my view, there is no change in the meaning. I have had students argue that there is a partial change in meaning, because to say he heard the woman does not necessarily imply he heard the woman's words, that is, heard her talking. Perhaps the woman was crying or shouting, for instance. But this may be a case of being overly analytical, which can happen. I ask myself, Does he realize which character the man hears? I think he does. We use a bracket around the phrase to show that we cannot assume a one-to-one correspondence between this complex miscue and the text.</td></tr>
<tr><td>25. "Get up here with me," he said to his son.</td><td>"Get up here with me," he said to his son.</td><td>"Get up here with me," he said to his son.</td></tr>
<tr><td colspan="3">No miscues</td></tr>
</table>

FIGURE 5–1 (continued)

26. The son got up on the donkey in, donkey in, in back of his father.	The son got up on the donkey in back of his father.	The son got up on the donkey in back of his father. [Ⓡ Ⓡ]
There are two regressions in this sentence, the first being a repetition of the phrase donkey in. Then LaMar continued reading, in back of so we hear a repetition of in. Perhaps he is having difficulty because of the close proximity of these two prepositional phrases, on the donkey and in back of his father. The first time he paused, he might have been working with the phrase on the donkey in which wasn't making sense for him. Then he regrouped the words and restarted with in back of his father. The lines underneath the text indicate not only how far the student read, but also the chronological order of reading events, moving down away from the printed text.		
27. Soon they saw a man and his wife standing by their house.	Soon they saw a man and his wife standing by their house.	Soon they saw a man and his wife standing by their house.
No miscues		
28. "It, It's, Is that your donkey?" the man asked the old man.	"Is that your donkey?" the man asked the old man.	[Ⓒ It's It] "Is that your donkey?" the man asked the old man.
LaMar made two attempts on the word Is and then self-corrected.		
29. "Yes, it is," said the old man.	"Yes, it is," said the old man.	"Yes, it is," said the old man.
No miscues		
30. "How can you be s-, be so mean?" asked the wife.	"How can you be so mean?" asked the wife.	[Ⓒ s-] "How can you be so mean?" asked the wife.

FIGURE 5–1 (continued)

LaMar said a partial word s–/so, then backed up and said the phrase be so correctly.

31. "The two of, The two of, The two of, 'wait,' The two, The two of you up there one on, on one poor little donkey!"	"The two of you up there on one poor little donkey!"	(R) (C) "wait" "The two of you up there on one poor little donkey!"

I think the unusual structure of this sentence is the reason for these particular repetitions. While typical of "storybook language," it may not have been too familiar to LaMar. He probably would have said, Both of you up there on one poor little donkey! So he's trying to predict what might make sense and come after the phrase the two of. He said wait, then repeated the two, and continued on through the sentence.

He reversed the phrase on one but then self-corrected.

When marking repetitions, there is always one less line underneath the text than the number of times we actually hear the phrase spoken. This is another instance where it is extremely helpful to transcribe verbatim what the reader said. It makes it more clear to us how to mark the miscue. We heard the two of three times, represented by the first two lines underneath the text. The first time he is *reading*, then the second time we hear the phrase it is a "repetition," and the third time is also a "repetition," hence the two lines. Then we heard the two, which is indicated by the shorter line under this phrase. Then there are no more lines underneath because LaMar is now continuing to read on through the text.

32. Then she went on to say, "Two big people like you couldn't carry him."	Then she went on to say, "Two big people like like you could carry him."	couldn't Then she went on to say, "Two big people like you could carry him."

Again, I have to consider LaMar's experience and how it probably influenced this miscue. LaMar's father is a teacher, but he is also a farrier. From a young age, LaMar helped his father work with horses, donkeys, and mules. He knows it is unreasonable to think that a boy and a man could pick up a donkey. The uncorrected substitution is written over the text item. This miscue results in a change in the author's meaning, which is critical to the end of the story.

33. "Very well," said the old man, "Very well," said the old man, "w-, we'll try that."	"Very well," said the old man, "we'll try that."	(R) (C) w- "Very well," said the old man, "we'll try that."

FIGURE 5–1 (continued)

Intonation is often a strong indication of a reader's comprehension, as we saw in Sentence 17. In Sentence 33, LaMar reads, "Very well," said the old man in a monotone voice. He realizes this is dialogue, then he backs up and rereads it with a rising intonation and slight stretching of well. Clearly he was speaking as the old man might have spoken.

He self-corrects his partial w–/we'll.

I made a note to myself in the margin to remind me of this important change in intonation.

34. and 35. The old man and his son got off the donkey and tried to pick him up. The old man picked up two leg, the, and tried to pick him up. The old man picked up two legs, and said, "Son, pick up the other two legs."	The old man and his son got off the donkey and tried to pick him up. The old man picked up two legs, and his son picked up the other two legs.	The old man and his son got off the donkey (C) leg and tried to pick him up. The old man picked up two legs, the said, "Son, pick " and his son picked up the other two legs.

While there are no miscues in Sentence 34, we see the line from Sentence 35 indicating a regression in which LaMar came back to and tried to pick him up. When he miscues leg/legs, he realizes he needs to go back and check where he got off track. We can put a "C" in the circle showing this regression because both miscues are corrected. He corrected leg/legs and the/and but then turns the remainder of the sentence into a request from the father to the son, . . . and said, Son, pick up the other two legs. For me, there is no significant change in meaning when LaMar changed the statement to a command. The implied end result is the same. LaMar's father often calls him son and probably many times has used this intonation and sentence structure, as in Son, pick up that rasp and hand it to me.

There is a bracket around the entire phrase his son picked to indicate a complex miscue. And because in my judgment he has created a dialogue statement, I have added quotation marks at the end of the sentence.

36. But just then, some poor people came by.	But just then, some more people came by.	poor But just then, some more people came by.

Now he's locked into fable language so well, he miscues poor/more, which is understandable. Earlier in the text, we had his poor old father, his poor little son, one poor little donkey so we can see why LaMar said poor people came by. He leaves this miscue uncorrected because, to him, it makes sense.

Figure 5–1 (continued)

37. And when they saw the old man and the, his son, they all started laughing.	And when they saw the old farmer and his son, they all started laughing.	RM man ⓒ the And when they saw the old farmer and his son, they all started laughing.
Just as he did in Sentence 19, LaMar substituted man/farmer, but this time he left it uncorrected, with no meaning change. He self-corrected the/his.		
38. "Ha, ha, ha, ha, ha!" they laughed.	"Oh, oh, oh!" they laughed.	UC Ha Ha Ha Ha Ha "Oh, oh, (oh)" they laughed.
What do we usually use to indicate a character's laughter? "Ha, ha, ha!" This is a great example of a reader's miscues actually improving the text! I marked the third Oh as an omission because of LaMar's clear grouping of the Ha, Ha and the Ha, ha, ha. The *UC* indicates he made more than one attempt, his two groupings, but never did say the text item, Oh. The bracket indicates a complex miscue.		
39. "Look!	"Look!	"Look!"
No miscue		
40. The fools are carrying the donkey!"	The fools are carrying the donkey!"	The fools are carrying the donkey!"
No miscues		
41. The donkey didn't like the noise and he didn't like to be carried.	The donkey didn't like the noise and he didn't like to be carried.	The donkey didn't like the noise and he didn't like to be carried.
No miscues		

FIGURE 5–1 (continued)

42. So he pulled l—oose and ran out into the fields.	So he pulled loose and ran out into the fields.	So he pulled l|oose and ran out into the fields.
This is one more example of LaMar's use of a split syllable when he's a little unsure of a word, but he doesn't go back and restate the word as a whole. Again, I assumed he knew the word and was making sense. This can be marked using the vertical line to show the mid-word hesitation, or it can be marked by writing it out, as I did with f—eels above. Either way is fine.		
43. The old man and the son tried to tie and, tired and tired but they couldn't catch, tried and tried to, tried and tried but they couldn't catch up, they couldn't catch up him, "Shouldn't there be a 'with' right there, 'with him'?" they couldn't catch up him, they couldn't catch him, "Oh," catch him.	The old man and the son tried and tried, but they couldn't catch him.	The old man and the son Ⓡ "Oh" catch him Ⓒ they couldn't catch him Ⓤⓒ they couldn't catch up him "Shouldn't there be a 'with' right there, 'with him'?" Ⓒ they couldn't catch up him Ⓡ tried and tried but they couldn't catch up Ⓒ Ⓒ ⒶⒸ tried and tried to ⒶⒸ Ⓒ Ⓤⓒ Ⓒ tired and tired but they couldn't catch to tie and tried and tried, but they couldn't catch him.
Look at his first attempt, tried to tie. I believe this is again coming out of his background experiences being around horses; that is, LaMar was thinking that the man and his son tried to tie up the donkey. His second attempt changes tried and tried to tired and tired (which they would have been after carrying a donkey!), but then he corrects this to tried and tried. LaMar has predicted that the text will read they couldn't catch up with him, which we see in his further attempts and his side comment, Shouldn't there be a 'with' right there, 'with him'? Because this is a Procedure III, I do not enter in to a conversation with him about this, as I would in an Over the Shoulder setting. I just respond with a "hmmmm," which is a tacit invitation to keep reading, which he does. This is another place in this reading that we have very complex miscue activity and subvocalized attempts to figure out the text (tired and tired/tried and tried). When the miscues are this involved, generally I will listen to the tape repeatedly and transcribe verbatim what the reader has said. I am more concerned with what the miscues were and how I can interpret them, than I am with struggling to squeeze in all the markings between the lines. And in a case like this, I simply can't, so I made a note to myself on the typescript to "see margin" off to the side. I also reminded myself with a *C* inside a circle at the beginning of the line that all miscues were ultimately corrected. On this chart, however, I have marked them, just to demonstrate the complexity involved.		

FIGURE 5–1 (continued)

<table>
<tr><td>44. So now they had no donkey to sell.</td><td>So now they had no donkey to sell.</td><td>So now they had no donkey to sell.</td></tr>
<tr><td colspan="3">No miscues</td></tr>
<tr><td>45. At last, the old man turned to his son.</td><td>At last, the old man turned to his son.</td><td>At last, the old man turned to his son.</td></tr>
<tr><td colspan="3">No miscues</td></tr>
<tr><td>46. So, Son, he said, “You cannot ple-please, you cannot please very, very, everyone.</td><td>“Son,” he said, “You cannot please everyone.</td><td>(C) so “Son,” he said, (R) “You cannot (C) ple- please (C) very very everyone.</td></tr>
<tr><td colspan="3">Here again the miscue activity gets somewhat involved, but the markings are doable. While they are correct, the transcription in the margin is most helpful in really remembering precisely what the reader said.
We might wonder if he inserted so at the beginning of the sentence, or if so/son is a corrected substitution. Listening to the online reading, we clearly hear his intonation indicate it is indeed a self-correction.
Perhaps his false start and correction on ple-/please may be due to the fact that he may have been more familiar with this word as “the magic word” when asking for something, rather than a verb as it is in you cannot please everyone.
He miscues very/everyone twice and then self-corrects. We can speculate that the high graphic similarity here may have been part of the cause for this miscue.</td></tr>
<tr><td>47. If you try, you only make a donkey of yourself.</td><td>If you try, you only make a donkey of yourself.</td><td>If you try, you only make a donkey of yourself.</td></tr>
<tr><td colspan="3">No miscues.</td></tr>
</table>

FIGURE 5–1 (continued)

Coding the Sentences

Now that we have LaMar's reading accurately marked on the typescript, we're ready to code each complete sentence. I used all 47 sentences in this brief folk tale, but if you were using a passage from a chapter book that had 114 sentences, generally you would only need to code about 50 of them. This number gives us a lot of information about the patterns of meaning construction indicated by the sentence codings.

Sentences that have no miscues are coded YYN. For the other sentences, we look at all the corrections and unsuccessful attempts to correct, and read the sentence aloud *as the reader left it*. Then, for each sentence, based on a consideration of the reader's dialect and the context of the story, we ask the following three questions (Y. Goodman, Watson, and Burke 1987):

- Does it sound like language? Is it syntactically acceptable? (Yes, No),
- Does it make sense? Is it semantically acceptable? (Yes, No),
  If we answer *No* to the first question, we must answer *No* to this question. If we don't have syntactic structure, we don't have the framework of language to scaffold the meaning. *If it isn't language, it can't make sense.*
- Did it change the author's intended meaning? (Yes, No, Partially)
  We can only ask this question if we answer *Yes* to both the first and second question. We are glad when the answer to this question is *No*, as in our YYN coding. We can also make the determination that the miscue partially changed the author's meaning. The *dash* (–) indicates we weren't able to ask this question.

Possible sentence codings are:

YYN (what we want to see!) YYP YYY YN– NN–

Use the chart in Figure 5–2 to examine the process for coding sentences. In the left column, we first consider the sentence as LaMar left it, after all corrections and regressions. The sentence coding is in the center column, and a discussion of my rationale for each coding is in the right column.

Tallying the Miscues

In the original Procedure III (Y. Goodman, Watson, and Burke 1987), it is suggested that one-word substitution miscues be examined for graphic similarity and an *H*, *S*, or *N* be placed above each miscue or in the typescript margin (for High, Some, or No graphic similarity). However, I have found that the typescript becomes too full of other information (sentence numbers, miscue markings, sentence codings, transcriptions, and notes in the margin).

The Sentence as LaMar *Left It* (After all attempts and corrections)	Sentence Codings			Discussion
	Does this sound like language?	Does this make sense?	Did this change the author's intended meaning?	
1. An old farmer and his son were taking their donkey to	1. N	N	–	On his regression, the sentence was left incomplete, and therefore we have lost syntactic structure. It doesn't sound like language. Once we have answered "No" to the first question, we know we can't have semantic acceptability, so we have to answer "No" to the second question, and we can't even ask the third question.
2. They had not gone far when they saw some girls at the well.	2. Y	Y	N	The uncorrected miscue the/a doesn't change meaning.
3. and 4. Look at them said one of the girls, summer. Her and the day's . . .	3. Y 4. N	Y N	N –	No miscues in Sentence 3. After many attempts, he left Sentence 4 incomplete.

FIGURE 5–2 LaMar's Procedure III Sentence Codings

5. And those two walk when they might ride.	5. Y	Y	N	There were only repetitions in this sentence, which don't affect meaning.
6. What fools they are!	6. Y	Y	N	No miscues.
7. All the girls laughed at this.	7. Y	Y	N	Miscue was corrected.
8. The old man heard them laugh.	8. Y	Y	N	Miscue was corrected.
9. "Get up and ride," he said to his son.	9. Y	Y	N	Both miscues were corrected.
10. So the son got on the donkey—s back.	10. Y	Y	N	He leaves donkey's as a split syllable, but I believe there is no loss of meaning.
11. The old man walked.	11. Y	Y	N	No miscues.
12. Soon they came to some men in a field.	12. Y	Y	N	No miscues.
13. "Look at that!" one of the men shouted.	13. Y	Y	N	Miscue was corrected.
14. "That big boy rides well. His poor old father must walk."	14. Y	Y	P	He has changed this to two sentences, which partially changes the meaning because the idea has been lost that one thing was going on *while* another thing was going on.
15. The old man heard their words.	15. Y	Y	N	Both miscues were corrected.
16. "Get right down," he said to his son.	16. Y	Y	N	No miscues.

FIGURE 5–2 (continued)

17. and 18. "I will ride." The son got down, and the old man got on the donkey's back.	17. Y 18. Y	Y Y	N N	Omission of period was corrected.
19. "It f—eels good to ride," the old farmer said.	19. Y	Y	N	He leaves a split syllable, and I think there is no loss of meaning.
20. and 21. "It isn't right for me to walk." Soon they came to a woman and her child walking on the road.	20. Y 21. Y	Y Y	N P	He changes the tense from present to past, with no loss of meaning. However, he changes the text from the woman having more than one child, to one child, so there is a partial meaning change.
22. "Well, you look at him!" the woman said.	22. Y	Y	N	His dialect usage does not result in a change in meaning.
23. "That man rides well. His poor little son must walk."	23. Y	Y	P	Same changes as in Sentence 14, resulting in a partial meaning change.
24. The old man heard the woman.	24. Y	Y	N	There is a complex miscue that is left uncorrected, with no change in meaning.
25. "Get up here with me," he said to his son.	25. Y	Y	N	No miscues.
26. The son got up on the donkey in back of his father.	26. Y	Y	N	Just repetitions.
27. Soon they saw a man and his wife standing by their house.	27. Y	Y	N	No miscues.

FIGURE 5–2 (continued)

28. "Is that your donkey?" the man asked the old man.	28. Y	Y	N	Miscue corrected.
29. "Yes, it is," said the old man.	29. Y	Y	N	No miscues.
30. "How can you be so mean?" asked the wife.	30. Y	Y	N	Miscue corrected.
31. "The two of you up there on one poor little donkey!"	31. Y	Y	N	Repetitions and a corrected miscue.
32. Then she went on to say, "Two big people like you couldn't carry him."	32. Y	Y	Y	There is a change in meaning because of the uncorrected miscue couldn't/could.
33. "Very well," said the old man, "we'll try that."	33. Y	Y	N	Just a repetition, with lots more expression!
34. and 35. The old man and his son got off the donkey and tried to pick him up. The old man picked up two legs, and said, "Son, pick up the other two legs."	34. Y 35. Y	Y Y	N N	His uncorrected miscues change the statement to a request. I think the resulting meaning is not significantly changed.
36. But just then, some poor people came by.	36. Y	Y	P	His uncorrected miscue poor/more results in a partial meaning change.
37. And when they saw the old man and his son, they all started laughing.	37. Y	Y	N	The miscue man/farmer is left uncorrected but does not change meaning. The other miscue the/his was corrected.
38. "Ha, ha, ha!" they laughed.	38. Y	Y	N	Changing oh to ha was an improvement!

FIGURE 5–2 (continued)

39. "Look!	39. Y	Y	N	No miscues.
40. The fools are carrying the donkey!"	40. Y	Y	N	No miscues.
41. The donkey didn't like the noise and he didn't like to be carried.	41. Y	Y	N	No miscues.
42. So he pulled l—oose and ran out into the fields.	42. Y	Y	N	The split syllable is left uncorrected, with no change in meaning.
43. The old man and the son tried and tried but they couldn't catch him.	43. Y	Y	N	Even with all this miscue activity, everything is ultimately corrected.
44. So now they had no donkey to sell.	44. Y	Y	N	No miscues.
45. At last, the old man turned to his son.	45. Y	Y	N	No miscues.
46. Son, he said, "You cannot please everyone.	46. Y	Y	N	All miscues are corrected.
47. If you try, you only make a donkey of yourself."	47. Y	Y	N	No miscues.

FIGURE 5–2 (continued)

I prefer to use a separate sheet to tally the miscues. It gives me a more orderly way to isolate the miscues and observe what I know about them in terms of correction, meaning change, and graphic similarity. It also makes it easier to see patterns of miscue activity and to get a count of each type of category (self-corrected, uncorrected with meaning change, and so on). When I shared this form with the Goodmans, Yetta said this was an example of "the adaptability of the system" (Y. Goodman 2000). I explained my rationale, and we discussed my process of constructing the form with careful consideration of the theory and reading process model on which miscue analysis is based.

In the original Procedure III, you would write *H*, *S*, or *N* above each one-word substitution miscue (or in the margin beside the miscue). You would include the following at the bottom of each typescript (Y. Goodman, Watson, and Burke 1987):

Question 1:	No. of Y	____ ____	%;	No. of N	____ ____ %
Question 2:	No. of Y	____ ____	%;	No. of N	____ ____ %
Question 3:	No. of Y	____ ____	%;	No. of P	____ ____ %;
	No. of N	____ ____	%		
Question 4:	(How much does the miscue look like the text item?)				
	No. of H	____ ____	%;	No. of S	____ ____ %;
	No. of N	____ ____	%		

LaMar has a little bit of trouble right at the beginning of this particular text; it takes him a couple of paragraphs to become comfortable with the author's style and language structure. Because of this, I chose to start tallying the miscues in Sentence 7, then continued consecutively from there on throughout the passage. Because this is a short story, I used all 31 miscues. Regardless of whether the student reads a whole picture book or four pages from a chapter book, it is only necessary to use 30 to 40 consecutive miscues to examine patterns in graphic similarity (see Appendix B for the miscue tally form from LaMar's reading).

In the first column, it is helpful to write down the sentence number in which the miscue occurs, particularly if we are going to come back and discuss the reading with a student and family members, or talk about the reading with colleagues. If there is more than one miscue in a sentence, I write the page number only once, as I did for Sentence 35, for example.

In the next two columns, we write down what the reader said on his first attempt, and what the text said. We use the same marking conventions, like the dollar sign ($) for nonwords and a dash (–) after partials. I also maintain the same *capitals and punctuation* as the text because these are relevant to our interpretation of the miscues.

For *complex miscues*, we write the phrase in the *Reader Said* column, and we put the cluster of words from the text that were bracketed on the typescript in the *Text Said* column. For *omissions*, we write a dash in the *Reader Said* column and the related text item in the *Text Said* column. For *insertions*, we reverse that, and put a dash in the *Text Said* and the inserted word or phrase in the *Reader Said* column.

The next four boxes between the bold lines allow us to examine the relationships between corrections and the reader's ability to maintain meaning. If the miscue is *Self-Corrected*, we put a check in the first box. An example is `the/this` in Sentence 7. If the miscue is left uncorrected, the three columns that follow allow us to record our judgment regarding the effect it had on the meaning of the sentence. Miscues that are determined to be *No Meaning Change* are called high-quality miscues. An example is the miscue `Ha, ha/Oh, oh, oh` in Sentence 38. Miscues with a *Partial Meaning Change* alter the text in some way, but not significantly, when considered in the context of the entire story. An example is the miscue `child/children` in Sentence 21. And finally, there are miscues with Meaning Change, such as the miscue `couldn't/could` in Sentence 32.

In the last three columns, we determine the graphic similarity of one-word substitutions by comparing the letters in the miscue to those in the related text item. To decide how much two words look alike, we divide the words into three parts: beginning, middle, and end. Then we determine the graphic similarity to be one of the following:

- *High*: If two of the three parts of the miscue look like two of the three parts in the text item and they are in the same location within both words, then there is a High degree of graphic similarity (beginning–middle, middle–end, beginning–end).
- *Some*: If the miscue and text item have one or more letters in common, there is Some degree of graphic similarity.
- *None*: There are No letters in common.

At the bottom of the miscue tally form is a reminder of those miscues we cannot code for graphic similarity: complex miscues, omissions, insertions, and partials. For these miscues, we draw a line through the three boxes for graphic similarity, because we either have too much or too little linguistic information to make this judgment. There are some miscues I *don't write down* on the form, including:

- *Repetitions*: When a reader repeats one or more words, and there are no miscues within the repeated phrase (`donkey in, donkey in`).
- *Split syllables*: LaMar left uncorrected three split syllables (`f—eels, donkey—s, l—oose`). I gave him the benefit of the doubt that these were *sounded out* sufficiently until he knew what they were; that is, I believe he corrected `f—eels` to `feels` in his head, and that he did not think these split syllables were *real* words.
- *Punctuation miscues:* Sometimes there were miscues that were indicated by LaMar's phrasing and intonation, but the words in the text weren't changed, such as the omission of the period in Sentence 17 (`I will ride`

the/I will ride. The). LaMar backs up and says I will ride. with the definite inflection that says, I am finished with this sentence!

- *Repeated miscues*: When a reader makes the same miscue more than once, as LaMar did on well/while and man/farmer, I just write the miscue on the form one time. If it happens repeatedly, I make note of it in some way, such as by making tally marks in the margin. This is common for name changes; often readers will give a character a different name, then use that new name throughout the story.

Most often I complete two tally forms when I am doing a Procedure III. Sometimes there are fewer miscues, like on LaMar's, but usually I don't write down many more. Two pages of miscues gives us plenty to look at in terms of what the reader is doing. I total each column, then bring the two pages' numbers together for overall totals. Later I transfer this information to a reader profile.

Completing the Retelling Guide

When my students are first learning how to conduct miscue analysis, I ask them to make a transcription of the conversation during the retelling. This gives them the opportunity to closely observe the reader's language and comprehension of the story, and it gives them a way of examining their own support to the reader in discussing the text. However, it is *not necessary* to transcribe the retelling each time you conduct a Procedure III. You can listen to the tape repeatedly, as you complete the retelling guide, until you are confident you have represented all the information the student said during the retelling on the form.

In the conversation LaMar and I had after his reading (see Appendix D), you will notice that, as he is talking, there are a number of false starts and incomplete sentences. I think this is a clear example of "exploratory talk," through which learners talk their way to understanding (Barnes, Britton, and Rosen 1969). I think his retelling also gives us evidence of a reader who is not only able to understand the story, but one who can recall it in great detail. He shows his ability to make inferences from the actions of the characters throughout the story, and he demonstrates that he understands the meaning of donkey here, as he moves from You cannot please everyone. If you try, you only make a donkey of yourself (the lines in the text), to If you try to please all the people, you're making a fool of yourself (his summary, or a *gist* statement).

If I have the retelling guide ahead of time, it helps me offer supporting cues to the reader as they are trying to recall important information from the text. If I don't, I flip back through the text to help me recall points I want to discuss with the reader (see Appendix E for LaMar's completed retelling guide). As I go back through the tape, or in this case, the transcription of the retelling conversation, I check off characters and events LaMar mentioned and often make note of his wording. I give a half a point for some items—for example, when he said poor people for more people.

While a lot of things were working well for LaMar in comprehending this story, there are a couple of places where he doesn't quite get the meaning the author intended. Let's compare his miscues on Sentences 14 and 23 to some excerpts from his retelling that reflect these misunderstandings.

14

"That big boy rides while his poor old father must walk."

LaMar read this as:

"That big boy rides well. His, his poor old father must walk."

23

"That man rides while his poor little son must walk."

LaMar read this as:

"That man rides well. His poor little son must walk."

In his retelling conversation, LaMar said:

And then they met some other people and they were walking because, um, wait, and they said, "Your s-" and then they met some men and they shouted, "Um, your s-, your son is re-, is a very good rider and, but um, but poor, but his poor fath-, father isn't very, isn't very good." They said all that he did was walk . . .

And then they met some other people and they said, um, the, the other way around, they said that the, the man, the old man was a pretty good rider and the son was a not very, that the poor son just walked.

When we look at the structure of the story, these conversations were important. When the father and the son spoke with the men in the field and the woman on the road, there were *turning points* in the story, that is, these were two of the three events where the father and son were trying to please everyone else. So after careful consideration, I decided that while LaMar understood there was a conversation and there was something to do with the father and son riding or walking, it becomes apparent in his retelling that he didn't understand the particular nuances the author intended.

I then added up the points within each area and transferred this number to the list of totals at the bottom. Adding all the points, I got 86/100, which translates to 86 percent comprehension. I think this is a pretty accurate representation of how well LaMar understood this story. This is one of the great lessons we learn from him: A reader can make a lot of miscues and still comprehend the text.

Running the Numbers and Completing the Reader Profile

Now it is time to pull together all the information we have about LaMar as a reader and complete the reader profile (see Appendix F). We use the data from these documents:

- The typescript (miscues and sentence codings)
- The retelling guide (comprehension score)
- The miscue tally form (corrections and graphic similarity)

Information from the Typescript

Looking down the right side of the typescript, we count the number of each type of sentence coding (number of sentences with coding of YYN, YYP, and so on). On the reader profile, we fill in the raw numbers on the first line, then calculate the percentage for each by dividing by the total number of sentences coded (47), then multiplying by 100.

40	85%	YYN
4	9%	YYP

For example, there were 40 sentences with the coding of YYN. If we divide 40 by 47, we get 0.851. To multiply by 100, we move the decimal point over to the right two places, and we have 85.1, which we round to 85 percent. There were 4 sentences with the coding of YYP. If we divide 4 by 47, we get 0.0851; when we move the decimal point over two places, we have 8.5, which we round up to 9 percent.

$\frac{40}{47} = 0.851$ $\quad 0.851 \times 100 = 85.1 \quad$ 85% YYN

$\frac{4}{47} = 0.085$ $\quad 0.085 \times 100 = 8.5 \quad$ 9% YYP

We continue this process for all five types of sentence codings. The left column (raw numbers) should add up to 47, and the right column (percentages) should add up to 100. If we are off on the percentages (sometimes I end up with 99), we go back and check the rounding up or down process.

In the next reader profile section, we are looking at syntactic acceptability: Did LaMar's reading sound like language? YES! We look at all the sentences that have Y as the first coding, like these:

40	85%	Y	Y	N
4	9%	Y	Y	P
1	2%	Y	Y	Y
0	0%	Y	N	–
2	4%	N	N	–

We get a total of 45 sentences that were coded syntactically acceptable. We write this number on the first line, then calculate the percentage by dividing by 47 and multiplying by 100. We get 96 percent acceptability, which is excellent! We follow the same process for the sentences (2) that were not syntactically acceptable.

SYNTACTIC ACCEPTABILITY

45	96%	Acceptable
2	4%	Unacceptable

In the next section, we are looking at semantic acceptability, that is, Did LaMar's reading make sense? We look down our list of sentence codings for the second question, and see that only two of his sentences did not make sense.

40	85%	Y	Y	N
4	9%	Y	Y	P
1	2%	Y	Y	Y
0	0%	Y	N	–
2	4%	N	N	–

Pretty amazing, considering all the miscue activity throughout his reading! We see his ability to monitor his reading for meaning through his side comments (That doesn't make sense), his uncorrected high-quality miscues (man/farmer), and his self-corrections (71%).

SEMANTIC ACCEPTABILITY

45	96%	Acceptable
2	4%	Unacceptable

Next we consider the third question in our sentence coding: Did LaMar's miscues result in a change in the author's intended meaning? We look at the last letter (or dash) of our sentence codings and see how many sentences were coded *N*, No Meaning Change; how many were coded *P*, a Partial Meaning Change; and then we count up together all the sentences that were coded either *Y* or –, indicating With Meaning Change. The dash indicates that we couldn't even ask the question (Did it change the author's meaning?) because we did not answer *Yes* to both the first two questions.

40	85%	Y	Y	N
4	9%	Y	Y	P
1	2%	Y	Y	Y
0	0%	Y	N	–
2	4%	N	N	–

We see that we have 40 sentences that were coded *N*, four that were coded *P*, and three that were coded either *Y* or –. We calculate the percentages in the same way as described before.

MEANING CHANGE

40	85%	No Meaning Change (N)
4	9%	Partial Meaning Change (P)
3	6%	With Meaning Change (Y, –)

Information from the Retelling Guide

We take the comprehension score we calculated on the retelling guide and transfer it to the reader profile form. I determined LaMar understood 86 percent of this story.

Information from the Miscue Tally Form

There are two separate sets of calculations here. First, look at the corrections LaMar made, or didn't make, during his reading. We take the column totals off the two pages of the miscue tally form, add them together, then write the total in the left column of the following chart. Based on the *total number of miscues* (31), we determine the percentages as described before. For example, there were 22 self-corrections of the 31 miscues. Divide 22 by 31 to get 0.709, move the decimal point two places (multiply by 100), and get 70.9, which we round to 71, or 71 percent self-corrections.

CORRECTIONS (TOTAL NUMBER OF MISCUES TALLIED): 31

22	71%	Self-Corrected
5	16%	Uncorrected—No Meaning Change
3	10%	Uncorrected—Partial Meaning Change
1	3%	Uncorrected—With Meaning Change

Finally, look at graphic similarity. We base our calculations here on a different number: the *total number ofmiscues coded for graphic similarity* (20). The reason this number is different from the total number of miscues tallied is that we can only code one-word substitution miscues for graphic similarity. We cannot code complex miscues, partials, omissions, or insertions.

GRAPHIC SIMILARITY (TOTAL NUMBER OF MISCUES CODED FOR GRAPHIC SIMILARITY): 20

15	75%	High
4	20%	Some
1	5%	None

We take the column totals from the two pages of the miscue tally form and see that we have 15 miscues coded *H,* four coded *S* and one coded *N*. We calculate the percentages in the same manner as described before. We see that the graphophonic cueing system is working well for LaMar, as 19 out of 20 miscues had either High or Some graphic similarity to the related text items.

Identifying Strengths and Areas of Concern

Now that we have gathered all the information we know about LaMar together onto the reader profile, we can reflect on what we see to determine what's working well for him and where to offer support.

Strengths

From the various sources of information, we observe that this is a reader who:

- Self-corrects 71 percent of his miscues
- Makes miscues that don't change meaning 16 percent of the time
- Makes appropriate predictions, then self-corrects when these predictions are not confirmed
- Asks questions as he is reading
- Draws on his background knowledge
- Comprehends during the reading 85 percent of the time
- Maintains the author's intended meaning 85 percent of the time (number of sentences coded YYN)
- Comprehends 86 percent of the story (after the reading)
- Makes his reading sound like language 96 percent of the time (syntactic acceptability)
- Makes his reading make sense 96 percent of the time (semantic acceptability)
- Gives a detailed retelling and is able to make a summary statement
- Makes miscues that have High or Some graphic similarity to the text items 95 percent of the time
- Has the language cueing systems well in balance

Areas of Concern

From each experience reading with a student, I try to select one strategy to work on, or as we'll see in Chapter 6, one teaching point during the teaching conversation. Suggestions that could be given to LaMar after this reading include the following:

- Try the "think about what would make sense here" strategy before the "sound it out" strategy when an unfamiliar word is encountered.
- When you do sound out a word, blend it together to see if it is indeed the word you thought it was, and to check to see if it makes sense there.

- Use graphic information from the beginning and end of a word, not just from the beginning of the word. (LaMar's miscues with High or Some graphic similarity had most of the letters in common at the beginning in these instances, indicating he could attend more to graphic cues in the rest of the word as well.)

Bringing It All Together: LaMar as a Reader

I was able to share with LaMar and his parents that I saw a very capable reader. He was developing many good strategies, such as making appropriate self-corrections and monitoring his comprehension (shown by his side comments, e.g., `That doesn't make sense`). He doesn't accept nonwords, although he did neglect to restate his sounded-out words that ended up as split syllables. He knows story structure and is able to follow the events in this folk tale and retell them in the right order with a surprising amount of detail. He makes good predictions as he reads, indicating he's constructing meaning and knows his reading should sound like language. He's diligent in working on a section of text that is difficult for him and can usually work his way to meaning.

He draws on appropriate background, even when this happens to work against him! In the story two people carried a donkey, but from his experiences working with horses, LaMar knew this wasn't possible. He read (and retold!) with expression, particularly during dialogue, which is another clear indication of his understanding of the text. He has all the language cueing systems working in balance for him, and he understands and recalls the text both at the detail level and at the summary level. What we see here is a very proficient reader!

Now that we've taken an in-depth look at this taped miscue analysis procedure, let's investigate procedures that can be conducted in a shorter period of time, without making a tape recording, in the context of the busy school day: Over the Shoulder miscue analysis and Procedure IV.

6

How Do I Conduct an Over the Shoulder Miscue Analysis Procedure and a Procedure IV?

Miscue analysis enabled us to see reading behaviors differently because we now had new understandings about what these behaviors meant. Whereas previously we would see a deviation from the text as an error leading to a prescription to eliminate that error, now we saw the very same phenomenon as a miscue, providing insights into what the students were attempting to do. This allowed us to increase our understandings about the reading process, and to provide true support for readers.

—Brummett and Maras (1995, 25)

Making Miscue Analysis Workable

After learning about the more in-depth miscue analysis procedures (Y. Goodman, Watson, and Burke 1987), and looking at an example of a Procedure III with LaMar, you may be saying, No way I'd have time to do that! I've got twenty-seven students! and, in fact, right now you may not have time to do a Procedure III with each of your students. But you *do* need to get to know your twenty-seven students as readers. And, perhaps more important, students need to *know themselves* as readers!

Many teachers are "seeing reading behaviors differently" and taking the best of the *thinking* behind miscue analysis, listening carefully to their readers at every opportunity, and developing modifications of different miscue analysis methods that become workable in their busy classrooms. They are using what they know about the active nature of the reading process and how language works to interpret in new ways what they hear students doing as they read aloud (Flurkey 1995; Martens 1995).

Brummett and Maras (1995) discuss an informal adaptation of Procedure III they use in the classroom with all students. Each student will have his or her reading taped several times throughout the year. As each student reads during a reading conference, a tape recording is made. After the conference, the teacher borrows the student's text to make a photocopy. If necessary, the image is enlarged a bit to provide enough space for writing between the lines. This copy is used to write down, or mark, the student's miscues, then the teacher conducts the rest of the Procedure III steps.

This use of miscue analysis is very informative and our best-case scenario, but it also takes many after-school or evening hours for listening to the tape, marking the miscues, coding the sentences, and analyzing the details of the student's reading. Ideal, but for some, perhaps not yet doable to that extent. This is where the *untaped* miscue analysis procedures are so beneficial. These can be done with every student, reading any text, as often as you like, and they do not require the second copy or typescript of the text the student reads.

The two main untaped procedures are Over the Shoulder miscue analysis (OTS) (Davenport 1998) and Procedure IV (Y. Goodman, Watson, and Burke 1987). Either assessment could take place during a one-on-one conference with a student. Both procedures bring to the conscious level, for both the teacher and the student, what is going on during reading. Both methods provide documentation about the reading process that can be shared with students, who in turn, share this information about themselves as readers with their parents.

The main difference between the two procedures is that the OTS is conducted by listening to and writing down information about ways the reader is constructing meaning through the lens of *individual miscues*, viewed within the context of the sentence as a whole and the overall story. Procedure IV focuses the teacher's ear on ways the reader is making meaning relative to the *sentence as a whole* (see Figure 6–1).

How Do I Conduct an OTS?

An OTS session takes place during a one-on-one conference. A teacher and student sit together; the student reads aloud; the teacher takes notes on the OTS form; and then there is a discussion about what was read, called the *teaching conversation.* Let's examine the classroom context that allows us to hold these reading conferences and the documentation we use to record what we hear: the cover page, the miscue page, and the insights page.

The Invitation

To create a cozy space in my classroom for reading conferences, I had a couple of chairs side by side in a corner. My students and I were accustomed to reading and talking together in this comfortable setting. When a student was invited to come to a conference, she understood she could bring any text she was currently reading. It could be a chapter book for literature study, a book from the science center, or a picture book. To begin, generally, there was a brief moment of conversation and catching up, maybe about something going on at home. Then I would ask her to bring me up to date on what was going on in the book, if it was a chapter book; or I'd ask her about what she had selected to read, if it was an information book or a picture book.

	Over the Shoulder	Procedure IV
Setting	Reading conference	Reading conference
Time to conduct	10–15 minutes	10–15 minutes
Area of focus	Within the context of the story, did individual miscues make sense?	Within the context of the story, did each sentence make sense?
Students for whom most appropriate	Ongoing documentation for all students	Ongoing documentation for all students, especially for highly proficient readers for whom you have no concerns
Information about a reader	• Is she understanding the text? • Does her reading make sense? • Does she self-correct miscues? • Does she make miscues that don't change the meaning? • Does she leave miscues uncorrected that do change the meaning? • Is there graphic similarity between the miscues and the text items? • Percentage of self-corrected miscues • Percentage of high-quality miscues that don't change meaning • Percentage of miscues that do change meaning • Percentage of miscues with High, Some, or No graphic similarity to the text item • General sense of comprehension	• Is he understanding the text? • Does his reading make sense? • Comprehending score percentage • General sense of comprehension The teacher may notice the following, but there is no record, per se, of these on the form: • Does he self-correct miscues? • Does he make miscues that don't change the meaning? • Does he leave miscues uncorrected that do change the meaning?

FIGURE 6–1 Comparisons Between OTS and Procedure IV

Before she began reading, I would often go through the three pages of the OTS form and remind her what I would be listening for. I explained the columns on the' miscue page frequently so that students *were repeatedly reminded that I was not writing down their "mistakes."* After the reading, I always came back to this form and talked about what we both heard during the reading and what patterns we saw in the columns on the miscue page. For every student, every reading, every time, I ended my invitation to read with OK, you can go ahead and read now and I'll just be making some notes about your good reading. I made sure the students knew that when my pencil was moving, they had not made a *mistake,* but rather, I was keeping track of what they were *doing right* and gathering information that would guide me in helping them become better readers.

Generally I didn't interrupt students in the flow of their reading, unless they clearly were not understanding what they read. This is a different setting than that described for Procedure III, in which we do not interrupt the reader along the way to talk about the text. The OTS conference is a *teaching setting,* during which I might ask a student to stop and talk a minute if any of the following occurred:

- The passage had a particularly high concept load, confusing sequence of events, or unusual twist of plot.
- She miscued repeatedly on a word that was critical to the story.
- She made quite a few miscues that changed the author's intended meaning, and I had a sense she wasn't understanding important information.

To determine the length of the text to be read during an OTS session, I considered the type of reading material the student brought to the conference. If a student was reading a chapter book, she could read two to four pages during the conference; usually two to four pages in an information book, depending on the concept load; and if reading a picture book, she usually was able to read the whole book. This, of course, depended on the length of the book and the pace of her reading. Our sessions usually lasted ten to fifteen minutes, so I had students read for five to seven minutes and saved the rest of the time for us to talk about what they read.

The Cover Page

There are three pages of the form for the untaped OTS: the *cover page,* the *miscue page* and the *insights page.* The information on the cover page includes the student's name, the date, and the text he is reading (see Appendices I and J). I keep track of the type of book, and if it is not a chapter book, I make a few notes about the length of the book, and the size and amount of print. This information puts my assessment in perspective when I'm looking at the OTS form later. For example, if a student read four pages of a chapter book and only had eight miscues, two of which changed meaning, I know a lot of things are working well for this reader, at least on the surface. If I am going to appropriately interpret numbers from the OTS, I need to be able to situate the reading within this larger context. When I saw "25 percent With Meaning Change," I would be able to understand that the number represents two out of eight miscues.

That's a very different situation from a student who reads a short picture book and makes thirty-two miscues, eight of which change meaning. Knowing the context of this particular instance of reading, I can see that this reader is making a high number of miscues while reading a single, relatively brief text. Comparatively, 25 percent of this reader's miscues are "With Meaning Change," but knowing the volume of text read, I have a different perspective on what that means.

The rest of the cover page gives me a place to write down as much as I can about what the reader said after the reading, during the teaching conversation. I use a shorthand with lots of abbreviations and capture as much as possible of the talking that goes on. I realize it is not a verbatim transcription of every word, but it is sufficient for me to consider the extent of the student's understanding.

It is important to remember that the teaching conversation is not scripted, but more like the conversation that would take place between two people who had just read the same book. Also, each conversation will be unique because of the reader, the text, and the appropriate teaching point for that reader at the moment. While not exhaustive, the following list of suggestions on the cover page offers possible directions for the teaching conversation:

- Tell me about what you just read—Anything you'd like to add?
- Do you remember what happened when . . . (if something significant was omitted)
- Does this remind you of anything?
- Do you have any questions?
- Discuss the miscue page: What patterns do you notice? What do the patterns mean?
- Go back to individual miscues: What were you thinking when you said . . . ? How did you get this?
- Go back and clarify concepts or words where meaning may have been lost
- Select a brief teaching point
  Model or remind student of a strategy
- End with a celebration point—what the student is doing well

The purposes of the cover page are: to capture and highlight the talking that takes place after the reading; to value the teacher's insights about the reader and decisions about the teaching points; and most important, to convey the message:

> *I am most interested in the insights gained from listening to this reader. I view reading as a process of constructing meaning, not just saying all the words. By writing down information about individual miscues, I am* not *prioritizing the word level as a stance for observing the reader. This form is not about writing down all the "mistakes" I hear a reader make.*

It is critical that students and teachers understand this point.

The Miscue Page

After a student joined me in the conferencing corner, I completed the top of the cover page while we were visiting, and I then asked her to begin reading. I became *focused on listening* as she read aloud, while I was literally *looking over her shoulder* at the text. Students knew I would be doing this and would situate themselves beside me where I could see their book.

I found it easiest if I had the form on a clipboard I could hold in my lap. Because no tape recording or typescript was used, I did my best to catch as many miscues as possible. *During the reading,* for each miscue, I wrote down three things:

- What the reader said
- What the text said
- Whether the miscue was corrected

I came back to the form *later* to:

- Examine graphic similarity
- Total each column and calculate the percentage for each column based on the total number of miscues in this instance of reading
- Examine the patterns of miscues
- Determine my insights about this reader, his comprehension and his strategies

Let's take a look at the three types of information we write down on the miscue page *during* the reading.

What the Reader Said

When a miscue occurred, 1 wrote down the student's first attempt at a word. It is certainly fine to write down other attempts if you catch them and have time. I find if I can write down a word or two around the miscue, this helps me when I am considering the reading later. For example, on a simple *substitution,* if I only put one word (Reader Said) for one word (Text Said), it is often difficult to remember a meaningful context for the miscue within the overall sentence. It is also difficult to remember how I made the judgment that, for instance, omitting a word could result in no change of meaning. If I just have an extra word or two, I can remember these things more clearly when discussing the information on the form with students, colleagues, or parents.

Please accept the fact that *you will miss some miscues.* Just get your ear ready for the next one. You'll get better at this with practice and you'll be surprised at how many you *do* catch!

Some miscue activity will be quite *complex,* and we won't be able to get all the information written down on the miscue page, as we would if we were able to listen to the reading repeatedly on a tape recording. When writing down notes about the reading *in the moment*, we only get one chance, and when a reader is making multiple attempts on an unfamiliar word, we usually cannot catch them all. When there is a great deal of miscue activity, like a number of regressions with different attempts, or several types of miscues within a phrase (omissions, multiple attempts, reversals, insertions), I make some notation to remind me of that complexity, such as jotting the text phrase in the margin with some of the attempts. I realize that I cannot get down the shorthand representation of the precise reading on the miscue page, but I can make note if the cluster of miscues is *ultimately corrected* or if collectively there is no change in meaning.

Some complex miscues are the substitution of one phrase for another. Here is an example of a complex miscue from second-grader Josh:

Text: So did I . . . because I am thankful for Clifford, and he is thankful for me.

Josh: So did I . . . because I am thinking of Clifford, and he was thinking for, of me.

On Josh's miscue page (see Appendix I), you can see how I write down this complex miscue. I put the *AC* to remind me he said for, which is in the text, then abandoned that and said of so that the rest of his sentence would make sense. It is interesting to note that this is a case of a reader making one miscue, then *needing* another one later in the sentence in order to keep the structure and meaning (albeit slightly changed).

This is also an example of a reader moving to a *parallel text*; that is, one in which the meaning he is personally constructing is maintained, but there is little correspondence to the graphic information available (Watson 1989). There is a difference of meaning between thinking of and thankful for, but if one considers the context of the entire story and the strong picture clues, Josh is making sense of this text.

A couple of pages earlier, there was a picture of the character Emily Elizabeth having Thanksgiving dinner with her grandmother. There is a thought bubble above her head in which there is a picture of her dog Clifford, who also has a thought bubble above his head showing he is thinking of Emily Elizabeth. Josh was able to infer the layers of meaning conveyed by this picture, shown by his side comment, That's funny, because she's thinking about Clifford thinking about her.

I believe this idea that both Clifford and Emily Elizabeth were missing each other and thinking of each other influenced this complex miscue. It was also the last line in the story, and his complex miscue has sort of a *bringing to closure* or *wrapping up* quality about it and does capture a big point in the story.

I did not write down simple *repetitions* of a word or two on the miscue page, if there were no other miscues in the sentence. If I noticed a reader doing this a great deal, I would note it and talk with her about strategies for reading more fluently.

When a student *changed a name*, like saying Shelley for Sally, I wrote this substitution down on the miscue page and put a *P* in the "Uncorrected—No Meaning Change" column. This indicated that the student had partially changed the meaning by using a different name than the one the author had chosen. If the reader used this other name all the way through a text, I didn't keep writing it down on the form, but instead, I made tally marks in the margin to indicate the reader was making this repeated miscue. I believe a reader is constructing meaning when this happens, so I don't keep counting it as a miscue per se. For examples of the system I used for *insertions* and *omissions*, see Figure 6–2.

The first miscue is an insertion, so I put was in the first column and a dash in the second column (the text said nothing!). Because this miscue was uncorrected, we have lost syntactic structure, and therefore we have lost meaning. If we don't have the framework of language, we can't have meaning.

Text: But it only made his stomach hurt more.

Casey: But it was only made his stomach hurt more.

Reader Said	Text Said	Self - Corrected	Uncorrected - No Meaning Change	Uncorrected - With Meaning Change	Graphic Similarity			Self-Corrected During Conversation
					High	Some	None	
was	—			✓		—		
—	front	✓				—		

FIGURE 6–2 Insertions and Omissions

The second miscue in Figure 6–2 is an omission of front and then the reader self-corrected. The dash (–) goes in the first column to show that the reader said nothing, and front goes in the second column, indicating what the text said.

Text: . . . up the front hall, just as usual . . .

Cydni: . . . up the hall, up the front hall, just as usual . . .

What the Text Said

This can be one word or it can be a phrase. I try to write down an extra word or two around the miscue, even if it is a one-word substitution. This just helps me remember more about the miscue when I come back to the form later. Sometimes I make other notations, such as tally marks in the margin for repeated miscues or brackets to show complex miscues.

Here is an example from Audra:

Text: "Mom, come and help me find him!"

Audra: Mom came and helped me find him.

Audra's omission of the comma, as indicated by her phrasing and intonation, and her first miscue, came/come, changed the syntactic structure from a request to a statement of what happened. To keep an appropriate past tense structure, Audra then changed help to helped. Neither miscue was corrected and the "Uncorrected—No Meaning Change" column was checked for both because she was making sense.

These miscues were bracketed on the miscue page to show that we cannot consider them in isolation (see Figure 6–3). I wrote down the first miscue, not knowing there were more to come that would be related! I only knew to bracket the miscues after the fact. Doing so calls my attention to the level of considering

Reader Said	Text Said	Self - Corrected	Uncorrected - No Meaning Change	Uncorrected - With Meaning Change	Graphic Similarity: High	Graphic Similarity: Some	Graphic Similarity: None	Self-Corrected During Conversation
{ came	come }		} ✓			—		
{ helped	help }					—		
seem	smell		P		✓			✓
garage	garden		P		✓			

Mom came and helped me / "Mom, come and help me"

Figure 6–3 Audra's Miscue Page

Reader Said	Text Said	Self - Corrected	Uncorrected - No Meaning Change	Uncorrected - With Meaning Change	Graphic Similarity			Self-Corrected During Conversation
					High	Some	None	

FIGURE 6–4 Miscue Page Showing Corrections Columns

a miscue in relation to the other miscues in the same sentence. It also helps me appreciate what a fine grammarian Audra is, because she is able, as a result of the second miscue, to maintain the sentence's appropriate syntactic structure.

Whether the Miscue Was Corrected

We make this determination as quickly as possible *during the reading* and then make a check mark in *one* of the columns between the bold lines on the miscue page (see Figure 6–4). We decide if the miscue is (1) Self-Corrected; (2) Uncorrected—No Meaning Change; or (3) Uncorrected—With Meaning Change.

We don't usually have time to make a finer judgment gradation (Partial Meaning Change) like we do in Procedure III. When I *am* able to make this determination, however, I mark a *P* in the "Uncorrected—No Meaning Change" column.

Another example from Audra shows how we make this judgment call. She was reading a book about a cat who ran away because he didn't like his family's new house. In one passage, the little girl is trying to find her lost cat.

Text: It did not look like his old house, and it did not smell like his old house.

Audra: It did not look like his old house, and it did not seem like his old house.

While seem/smell is a miscue, let's take a look at it in terms of the meaning that Audra was constructing and what she was doing with language. First, syntactically, the miscue (seem) is the substitution of a present tense verb for a present tense verb (smell), so the surface structure of the sentence remains intact. Second, if we think about the meaning of her sentence within the context of the story, we realize the cat isn't happy with his new home because it looks and smells different, that is, it didn't "seem" like home. Perhaps this is the use of this word and the meaning Audra was predicting when she said, it did not seem like his old house. Finally, there is high graphic similarity between seem and smell, the letters s – e – m. Based on my consideration of the syntactic and semantic acceptability of the word within the sentence and the story, I decided this miscue was "Uncorrected—No Meaning Change."

But later, when discussing this miscue with my colleague Debbie Mills, she said she would consider this a miscue "Uncorrected—With Meaning Change," because, to her, it was significant to the story. She thought the cat's strong sense of smell was important at this point, as the author was conveying one of the ways the cat knew this was not his old house. We agreed that a *P* (for Partial Meaning Change) in the "Uncorrected—No Meaning Change" column was perhaps most appropriate. Yes, it did change the author's intended meaning, but *not significantly*.

In the same story, the cat has run away and the girl is looking everywhere for him. Audra made the following miscue:

Text: They looked in the garden, and they looked up and down the road, but Tiger was gone.

Audra: They looked in the garage, and they looked up and down the road, but Tiger was gone.

It is interesting to note how Audra is constructing meaning here. The garage is certainly a logical place to look for a lost cat, and there was a picture of an open garage on the page (and no picture of a garden!). Audra didn't stop to fix this miscue because she was making sense as she read. To some, this miscue could have been marked "Uncorrected—With Meaning Change," but I considered it within the context of the entire story and decided this one detail was relatively unimportant. I considered it a Partial Meaning Change and put a *P* in the "Uncorrected—No Meaning Change" column.

Often, after the reading, I ask the student to take me back to any spot in the text that caused some difficulty, or I take a student back to a specific miscue and ask him what he was thinking when he read a particular passage. Usually the student remembers the miscue, often he can talk about what strategies he was using, and sometimes he corrects it as we are talking, which, incidentally, Audra did on the seem/smell miscue.

I am always fascinated by students' thinking in these instances because this is the kind of metacognitive thought we'd love to have going on all the time during reading (Harvey and Goudvis 2000; Wilhelm 2001). When the student corrects a miscue on his own during the talking that takes place as we revisit a miscue, I put a check mark in the last column on the miscue page, "Self-Corrected During Conversation." I might also make some notation in the margin to remind me how the student was able to get this word the second time around, such as Josh noticing a letter he hadn't seen before. When I revisited the text with fifth-grader Selina, I asked her how she corrected a miscue; she told me, It just came out!

Sometimes during the reading, the student makes side comments, such as second-grader Claire's Oops, I mean, before she made a self-correction. This kind of talk gives us further insights into students' thinking processes. At other times, the student and I stop and talk to clarify something: for example, when Selina and I were talking about the idea of a tipi having a section of thatch on it. I jot notes about these exchanges in the margin of the miscue page and sometimes ask the student to explain a particular comment.

In that same text, Selina was reading about outlaws playing cards and she read the line, . . . he sat down at the faro table. She didn't miscue, but I asked her about that passage later and she said she thought it was like that guy in Egypt, thinking of the word pharaoh. I asked her to reread the line and to reconsider a meaning for faro that would make more sense there based on what was going on in the story. I told her I didn't know the word faro either, but that I could make a guess. She thought a minute and then said she thought faro was probably some kind of card game.

I also use the margins to jot down words or concepts I want to return to in the teaching conversation. When Selina made an attempt at benefactor and then self-corrected, I asked her if she knew what that meant. She said the word was like benefit so it was probably the guy in the story who gave Eli a lot of money. In another example, I wrote brandishing in the margin when fifth-grader Lacy read brandishing a sword without blinking an eye. I wanted to remember to check with her about this idea. When I asked her if she knew what brandishing meant, she showed me with gestures that she knew exactly what it meant!

The Insights Page

Using the OTS, I am looking for global patterns in the actions of the reader. In general terms, the reader is either:

- Making sense of the text, monitoring meaning, making self-corrections, and using effective decoding strategies
- Making a high number of miscues that change meaning and using ineffective strategies for decoding unfamiliar words

On the insights page (see Appendix I), we summarize the reader's actions, which usually fall into one of these two main patterns of miscues. There is also a place where the teacher can total each column from the miscue page and, for each category of information, calculate a percentage of the total number of miscues in this reading. From all this information, the teacher can determine what readers are doing well and where they need to improve.

Before calling over the next student to read with me, I usually made a few additional anecdotal notes of strategies or characteristics of the reader I just observed during the reading. For example, after Skyler read two pages in *Shiloh*

(Naylor 1991), I wrote: able to make inferences—Judd's character and work on intonation and talk about accepting nonwords. These key points help me remember teaching points for future conferences with Skyler and a point to celebrate in this session.

In our teaching conversation, I talked with him about his comment, Judd's looking like he might break his promise and nothing's good enough. He thought Judd would go back on his word to let Marty keep Shiloh and that he wouldn't be satisfied with the work Marty was doing in exchange for the dog. I asked Skyler why he thought so and he said: [Judd] kills deer out of season; he's the biggest redneck in town, and earlier he had mentioned that Judd abuses his dogs. While not explicitly stated in the text, Skyler was able to predict that someone who did these things might be the type of person who would break a promise—an inference he was able to make based on a synthesis of various descriptions of this character's actions. I brought this ability to make inferences to Skyler's attention so that he could become more aware of his strengths. We also talked about strategies that would be helpful for him, such as listening for nonwords and fixing miscues that don't make sense for him.

To summarize, here are the details about the OTS documents:

BEFORE THE READING:

- Complete the top part of the cover page with information about the student and the book

DURING THE READING:

- Write down information about each miscue on the miscue page
  - What the reader said
  - What the text said
  - Whether the miscue was corrected, and if not, if it changed the meaning
- Make notes in the margin of any conversations or side comments that occurred during the reading

AFTER THE READING:

- On the cover page, scribe as much of the teaching conversation as possible
- On the insights page, total each column from the miscue page and record your observations about this reader

Like learning anything else, it will take practice to become proficient at listening with "miscue ears" during these reading conferences and to develop a system of writing down what you hear.

I encourage you to take ownership of the form and to come up with a shorthand that works for you to record your comments, or other ways to make it easier to keep track of what you observe about students, miscues, or reading strategies.

The Teaching Conversation

The talking that takes place after the reading is a critical part of OTS. The purpose of the teaching conversation is to allow you and the student to embark together on a shared exploration of the reading process and the student's comprehension and reading strategies. One of the main goals is to help students—*all students*—understand that they're doing a lot of things right as readers, discover what those things are, and consider ways they can continue to improve.

When talking with Yetta Goodman about the teaching conversations that take place in a reading conference, she said she thought these needed "to be put into an inquiry mode . . . so that the questions are constantly being fed back to the student: 'What do you think about this? Why did this happen? What was going on when you were doing this? Let's look at this together' . . . we have to start talking about inquiry conversations" (Y. Goodman 2000).

Paulo Freire (1985) believes that inquirers need to be more than just problem solvers. They also need to be problem posers (Short and Harste, with Burke 1996). Ultimately, my goal in teaching conversations is to have the reader pose her own questions and to share her own observations of her reading process. I also have questions, such as What did you notice about your reading? and What patterns do you see on the form? or Based on our observations, what do you think you could do differently?

Teaching conversations are *not scripted* and the teacher does not know ahead of time where the discussion will go. Each conversation will be unique, based on the selection read, the strengths of the reader, the miscues that changed meaning, and the areas in which the reader needs to improve. Teaching conversations might consist of the following:

- Discussing, in a conversational manner, what was just read
- Discussing the student's understanding
- Discussing the patterns of miscues
- Selecting brief teaching points
- Discussing specific miscues, particularly those that changed meaning
- Celebrating something the student is doing well

Let's examine each of these areas of talk that could occur during a teaching conversation.

Discussing What Was Just Read

If I ask students in a conversational manner to retell for me what you just read, I often get stares that imply, You just sat there and listened to me read that. Why do you need me to retell it? Weren't you listening?. It seems the invitation—Let's talk about what you just read—gets students off to a better start in responding. With this kind of opening, I tend not to get formulaic detail-by-detail retellings because students respond in a more conversational manner. They are offering their own responses to the reading and discussing their understanding of the gist, or the important information in the passage, and they tend to respond in a more authentic manner, as they would in a literature study group discussion. In fact, with this invitation, I often get more mature responses, much like an adult would give through a global summary. I also hear students who are able to move to a broader synthesis as well, weaving in information from the text, the world, and their lives into a cohesive, meaningful whole.

As the student is discussing the passage, I scribe as much of the talk as possible on the cover page, using the back of the page if necessary. I write down the main points discussed, and make a judgment about the student's overall comprehension of the book or passage. Finally, I make note of my decisions under the "Global Observations" section on the insights page. I am not coming up with a *comprehension score* from the OTS, that is not the purpose. The purpose is to know each student well through:

- *Qualitative* information from the teaching conversation (comprehension, connections, inferences, predictions, responses to text, questions)
- *Quantitative* information from the column totals on the miscue page (percentages of self-corrections, miscues with no meaning change, and so on)
- *Linguistic* information on the miscue page (types of miscues, balance of cueing systems)

I think it is fine to let the student look back through the book as he's discussing the story. We get interesting insights into how he uses picture cues (if they are available) and how he organizes or sequences information. We really have to ask ourselves some hard questions regarding the *retelling* after reading. I struggle with this question when I am trying to determine a reader's comprehension: Am I assessing what the student *committed to memory* or am I interested in what the student *understood during the reading*?

I think it is the latter. Remember, in OTS, there is *no retelling guide*, as in Procedure III; you are just looking back through the text with the student and talking about what was read, keeping in mind the characters, setting, and main events in the passage. We stay focused on the big picture of the reader's overall understanding of the passage rather than becoming overly concerned about minute story details and expecting the reader to tell us everything.

Discussing the Student's Understanding

During the talk after the reading, it is helpful to clarify words or concepts that may have been confusing, and to return to and discuss one or two miscues. This type of discussion can also occur *during* the reading. In these instances, I am interested in seeing if students are able to go below the surface structure and share their understanding of meaning in the deep structure, including inferences and connections to personal background.

Discussing Patterns of Miscues

I invite the student to take a look at the miscue page with me to see what patterns they notice. Over time, students become better able to identify and explain patterns that emerge on the form relative to self-corrections and the types of miscues made frequently. They realize checkmarks in the "Self-Corrected" column are a signal that they're monitoring their comprehension and using smart fix-up strategies when needed. They see that uncorrected nonwords result in a meaning change. They recognize that some miscues can be left uncorrected and not affect their understanding of the story. Again, this is a good opportunity to remind students that *this is not a list of their mistakes*. I tell them repeatedly that all readers change the text, and that not all those changes are *bad*.

Selecting Brief Teaching Points

As we listen to a student read, we make notes on the miscue page to remind us of words, concepts, or strategies that might serve as teaching points. How do we choose the one or two we'll spend a few minutes on? Here are some considerations for our choices and examples of how they guide our talking:

- *Is there a word or phrase the reader may not have understood?*—I asked Skyler if he knew what the author meant when she said that the dog feeds our spirit, and he thought it meant Shiloh made them happy.
- *Is there a reading strategy this student is currently using that is helpful and appropriate?*—I pointed out to a student that there were several omissions of words that didn't change the meaning. I was showing her that she was monitoring meaning, and since those miscues didn't change meaning, she didn't have to correct them.
- *Is there a reading strategy that this student needs right now?*—When Josh encountered the names of Clifford's sisters, Bonnie and Claudia, he first paused for a while, then miscued Bone/Bonnie (see Chapter 7). We talked about the capital letter, and he realized it would be someone's name. I also pointed out that there was a comma after his sisters, so the author was letting us know that he's going to give us the names. We talked about a strategy he could use when he comes to a word that he knows is a name, but he's not sure what it is.

The focus of my thinking during these conferences was on how well the student was constructing meaning, what strategies would be helpful, and whether the language cueing systems were in balance for this reader. Yetta Goodman refers to this on-the-spot decision making that teachers do during a reading conference as "critical moment teaching" (2000), and I believe this is what is going on in teaching conversations. In the moment, we make a decision about a strategy the reader needs, or we select specific miscues, particularly those that changed meaning, to return to and discuss. This *lesson* does not need to be lengthy, and it is almost given in the spirit of an "FYI."

Discussing Specific Miscues

To discuss particular miscues, I often take a student back into the text and ask, `Let's go back right here, do you remember what you said here?` and `Do you remember what you were thinking when you said that?` When a student begins to share her thinking relative to a particular difficulty, she often has something completely different in mind from what I might have been considering as a possible reason for that miscue. If the teacher continues to model his own thinking during reading and encourages his students to hold onto their thoughts when they're reading, students will continue to improve in their ability to become aware of and articulate their own thinking processes as they read (Wilhelm 2001).

Celebrating Something the Student Does Well

To bring our conversation to a close, I point out something the student is doing well and congratulate her on all the smart things she is already doing as a reader. Sometimes I'll ask students how it feels to know all these things about themselves as readers. I get answers like `Holy Cow!` and `It's neat—I don't think people really take the time to think about what kind of readers they are.` Students walk away feeling great about themselves as readers. They have something to think about next time they read (perhaps using a new strategy), and they're more aware of the particular engagements during reading that help them understand the text.

The Follow-Up

Later in the day, perhaps after school, I returned to the two or three forms I had started that morning during reading workshop. To complete the insights page, I would do the things discussed in the following sections.

Run the Numbers

Total each column and calculate the percentage of this type of miscue based on the total number of miscues from this reading. To get the percentage, divide the number of miscues in a particular column by the total number of miscues, then multiply by 100.

For example, if a student made a total of eight miscues in this instance of reading and five of those were self-corrected, I would calculate the percentage of self-corrected miscues this way:

$$\frac{\text{Number of miscues in a column}}{\text{Total number of miscues}} \times 100 = \text{Percent for that column}$$

$$\frac{5}{8} \times 100 = 62.5\% \text{ Self-Corrections}$$

Make Notations About Graphic Similarity

In order to determine how the student is using the graphophonic cueing system, I examine the graphic similarity between the miscues and the related text items. These determinations are made in this way:

- High—Most letters in common between the text item and the miscue
- Some—At least one letter in common
- None—No graphic similarity

Certain types of miscues cannot be coded for graphic similarity—insertions, omissions, partials, and complex miscues. For insertions and omissions, we only have one half of the miscue/text item pair. For partials, we don't have enough linguistic information to make a judgment about graphic similarity. For complex miscues, we are not able to make a one-to-one correspondence between the phrase substituted and the words in the text.

Figure 6–5 lists some examples of miscues that have been coded "High," "Some," and "None" for graphic similarity, and some miscues that cannot be coded. A dollar sign ($) is used to designate a nonword. When writing out the nonword on the miscue page, we retain as much as possible of the spelling from the word in the text for which it is substituted.

Reader Said	Text Said	Self - Corrected	Uncorrected - No Meaning Change	Uncorrected - With Meaning Change	Graphic Similarity: High	Graphic Similarity: Some	Graphic Similarity: None	Self-Corrected During Conversation
huddled	huddling	✓			✓			
kicks	kicked	✓			✓			
$jügilation	jubilation	✓			✓			
grabbed	gathered		✓			✓		
pumpkin	cucumber			✓		✓		
in	on		✓		✓			
to	dry	✓					✓	
Calvin	he	✓					✓	
the	as	✓					✓	
—	him		✓			—	—	
quite	—		✓			—	—	
the ground	his garden		✓			—	—	

FIGURE 6–5 Miscure Page Showing Graphic Similarity

This information is helpful in determining if the graphophonic system is working *in balance* with semantics and syntax for this student. If so, we will see a lot of miscues that have High or Some graphic similarity to the text items while the reader is still constructing meaning (like grabbed/gathered).

If these language cueing systems are *out of balance*, we will see miscues that have High or Some graphic similarity, but change the meaning of the text (like house/horse). In other words, in this case the reader is overattending to the letters on the page and calling out words rather than being concerned with whether the text makes sense.

File the OTS Form

Use whatever system works best for you. I found it least cumbersome to keep my anecdotal records and OTS forms in a three-ring binder with a divider for each student. At the end of each school day, I put the OTS forms in the appropriate spot in my binder, making them readily accessible for conferences when needed.

As part of my recordkeeping, I do the following about once every two to three weeks for each student:

- Complete at least one OTS conference
- Make decisions about instruction for small groups with similar needs

Once a quarter I complete a Holistic Evaluation of Reader form for each student (see Appendix L), which helps me to observe:

- The students' strengths and areas of concern
- The students' use of the language cueing systems and patterns of miscues
- How students were constructing or disrupting meaning
- How students were drawing on their background knowledge
- How well students were able to discuss what they had just read

This recordkeeping helps me feel confident that I know all my students as readers and also provides a wealth of information to share with parents. Because I go over the information from the OTS forms with students at the end of each reading conference, they know themselves well as readers too! When it is time for parent conferences, students are proud to share the strategies they use and they are clear about areas in which they need improvement. As they talk with their parents about the information on the forms, they demonstrate developing knowledge about the reading process and astute awareness of their own abilities as readers. Clearly, students are empowered readers in charge of their own learning.

Why Do I Conduct OTS Evaluations?

When I was a classroom teacher sometimes I would wake up at 4:00 AM and gasp, Oh m' gosh, do I really know Melissa as a reader!? I occasionally panicked at one of the daunting tasks teachers manage every day: knowing all my students—knowing them as people, mathematicians, scientists, writers, thinkers, and readers. Once I developed and consistently used the OTS, I no longer had to be so concerned. I did know my students as readers.

The primary purpose of an OTS is to provide ongoing reading assessment of all students. It is a method for making notations about a student's miscues during oral reading, a *means of sharing* what we know about students with students and a source of insights into each student's strategies as a reader. In the life of a busy classroom, teachers are finding time to meet individually with students, to listen to them read, and to use OTS to get to know their own Melissas as readers.

One of the most important purposes of OTS is to *provide a platform for talking* with students about their reading. The OTS form provides evidence for students that allows them to observe what they are doing as readers, and with these metacognitive skills, they are able to take ownership of their own reading process. If students become more aware of the nature of reading, the strategies good readers use, and their own actions as readers, they can take important steps in becoming better readers (Harvey and Goudvis 2000; Wilhelm 2001).

The reading conferences in which the OTS miscue analysis takes place are not only assessment settings, but also an *opportunity for teaching*. We reap surprising benefits from these brief interactions with students. These focused, short teaching conversations can greatly impact a student's awareness of herself and her reading strategies. The information we gain through the reading conferences informs our instruction, in the moment with that particular student, and it also helps us identify strategies that would be helpful to the entire group.

Another purpose of the OTS is to *provide information about a reader's strengths* (e.g., correcting nonwords) and *areas of concern* (e.g., overrelying on the "sound-it-out" strategy). This assessment is more focused on a *holistic evaluation* in an authentic setting than on number crunching. Sitting beside a student as he reads, we gain important insights about the reader's strategies by examining individual miscues, determining where meaning was lost, and looking at patterns of self-correction. We know a great deal about how well the student comprehended through the discussion during the teaching conversation after the reading. We are not interested in generating numbers, such as accuracy rates, words per minute, or percent comprehension scores, with this assessment. If you need those numbers for other reasons, such as qualifying a student for special services, you will need to use other assessments to generate them.

Not only can the OTS form serve as a reading *work sample*, as it does in my state of Oregon, but it also *provides documentation* about the reading process for teachers, students, and parents. It is a powerful moment when students confidently say, as they sit beside their parents in quarterly conferences: Mom, Dad, let me tell you about myself as a reader. Parents have a sense that their child is doing particular things well and also working on developing specific strategies that will help him improve. Teachers have evidence to guide instructional planning and the assigning of grades if needed.

Finally, a purpose of OTS is *engaging* students *in reflective thinking* needed in some high-stakes testing. If we talk with students about their reading on a regular basis, when the time comes for them to take the state or national reading tests (as much as we abhor them and are opposed to them), they are more capable of engaging in the reading and retelling tasks, and they are better prepared to articulate what they are doing as readers. They become comfortable examining their thinking and are better able to meet the state goals for reading.

An Invitation: Try an OTS with LaMar

I now invite you to try the OTS while listening to LaMar. Here's how you can get set up for your practice run:

- Use Appendix M, the text for "The Old Man, His Son, and the Donkey," to *look over* LaMar's shoulder as you listen to him read.
- Use the blank OTS form in Appendix J (or make a copy). See Figure 6–6 for LaMar's OTS form and my summary of our teaching conversation. (I used two miscue pages.) Please keep in mind this is an "idealized" OTS, that is, I did not complete the form during LaMar's reading. It has been provided for you here to serve as a model for those miscues you do catch as you listen to LaMar's reading online or have a friend read from Figure 5–1.
- Listen to LaMar's reading online, or ask a friend to read the first column in Figure 5–1 ("What We Hear LaMar say").

Now let's look at the other untaped method for analyzing reading, Procedure IV.

How Do I Conduct a Procedure IV?

The main difference between Procedure IV and the OTS miscue analysis is that the focus here is on ways the reader is constructing meaning at the *sentence level*. The teacher listens closely to the semantic acceptability of each sentence and to the reader's self-corrections.

During a Procedure IV, we are listening as the reader finishes each sentence; noticing how she left it, with any uncorrected miscues; and asking one question: Does the sentence, as the reader left it, make sense within the context of the selection?

We simply make a tally mark beside *Yes* for those sentences that are fully semantically acceptable, and a tally mark beside *No* for those sentences that are partially acceptable or unacceptable. This procedure allows the teacher to focus "on the most important questions used in miscue analysis: semantic acceptability and correction" (Y. Goodman, Watson, and Burke 1987, 125). After the reading, the teacher talks with the student about what has been read and about any problems she may have had, such as not understanding particular words. Notes are made about this discussion.

Over the Shoulder Miscue Analysis
Cover Page

Student LaMar **Grade** 2nd **Date** October 12

Selection Read The Old Man, His Son, & the Donkey **Type of Text** Folk Tale

Amount Read Whole story **Comments on Text** Read from typescript, not book

Notes from Teaching Conversation – Scribe as much as possible – Continue on back if needed
These are **suggestions** for the conversation, which **may** include **any or all** of the following (**or other discussion**):

- *Tell me about what you just read – Anything you'd like to add? – Do you remember what happened here?* (if something significant was omitted) – *Does this remind you of anything? – Do you have any questions about this?*
- Take back to OTS form – Discuss patterns of miscues – Go back to individual miscues (teacher-selected or student-selected) - *What were you thinking when you said...? How did you get that?*
- Go back and clarify concepts or words where meaning may have been lost
- Select a brief Teaching Point – Model or remind student of a strategy – Suggest something to work on
- End with a Celebration Point – Point out what the student is doing well

say every word no
old man - son - going to sell
donkey - both walking - girls
laughed - son, get on - met
people - said son a good rider -
father isn't - all he did was
walk - met other people - man
said get down - met other
people - said old man good
rider - met man & wife - that's
mean - both up there - I bet you

can't carry the donkey -
OK we will - tried to pick
him up - couldn't - met
some poor people - they
laughed - donkey didn't
like sound or being
carried - ran off - couldn't
catch - had to go to town
w/out donkey - didn't have
anything to sell - moral:
Try to please all the
people, you're making
a fool out of yourself

Figure 6–6a Over the Shoulder Miscue Analysis Cover Page

Over the Shoulder Miscue Analysis
Miscue Page

Student LaMar **Date** Oct. 12 **Selection Read** The Old Man, His Son & the Donkey

Page 1

Reader Said	Text Said	Self - Corrected	Uncorrected - No Meaning Change	Uncorrected - With Meaning Change	Graphic Similarity: High	Graphic Similarity: Some	Graphic Similarity: None	Self-Corrected During Conversation	
—	town to sell			✓		—			
the	a		✓				✓		
$serm-eh	Summer's			✓		✓			– multiple attempts leaves unc. "Summer's here and the day is hot" unusual syntax
the	this	✓			✓				
the	them	✓			✓				
a	and	✓			✓				
h-	he	✓				—			
don/key's	donkey's		✓		✓				
shuh-ah	shouted	✓				—			
well ; His	while his		P			—			– That big boy rides well. His poor old father...
the	their	✓			✓				
word	words	✓			✓				
$feeled	feels	✓			✓				
man	farmer	✓				✓			
isn't	wasn't		✓		✓				
son	soon	✓			✓				
child	children		P		✓				
well	will		d		✓				
Total Miscues this page	18	10	6	2	10	4	1	0	– I didn't take him back to any miscues

FIGURE 6–6b Over the Shoulder Miscue Analysis Miscue Page 1

Over the Shoulder Miscue Analysis
Miscue Page

Student LaMar **Date** Oct. 12 **Selection Read** The Old Man, His Son & The Donkey

Page 2

Reader Said	Text Said	Self - Corrected	Uncorrected -No Meaning Change	Uncorrected - With Meaning Change	Graphic Similarity: High	Graphic Similarity: Some	Graphic Similarity: None	Self-Corrected During Conversation
old	—	✓				—	—	
the woman	her words		✓			—	—	
It	Is	✓			✓			
s-	so	✓				—	—	
one on	on one	✓				—	—	
couldn't	could			✓	✓			
w-	we'll	✓				—	—	
leg the	legs, and	✓				—	—	
Said, "Son pick	his son picked		✓			—	—	
poor	more		P			✓		
man	farmer		✓			✓		← Repeated miscue (could be omitted)
the	his	✓				✓		
Ha Ha	Oh Oh Oh		✓			—	—	
l/oose	loose		✓		✓			
tried to tie	tried and tried	✓				—	—	
so	son	✓			✓			
ple-	please	✓				—	—	
very	everyone	✓			✓			
Total Miscues this page	18	11	6	1	5	3	0	0

Figure 6–6c Over the Shoulder Miscue Analysis Miscue Page 2

Over the Shoulder Miscue Analysis Insights Page

La Mar		SC	Unc No Chg	Unc With Chg	H	S	N	SC During Conv.
Overall Totals	36 miscues	21	12	3	15	7	1	
Percentages		59	33	8	66	30	4	

Cannot code for graphic similarity: Complex miscues, omissions, insertions, partials

Number of miscues coded for graphic similarity 23

Observations about Comprehension During this Reading (Not all will be observed during each reading)

Mentions important information very thorough - details in sequence

Able to summarize, gets the gist after I explained what a "moral" is - he restated in own words

Able to synthesize text information – Gains a new perspective – Combines ideas - und. "making a donkey of yourself"

Able to extend understanding through connections to self exp. w/ horses to the world can't carry a donkey to other texts (or movies)

Refers to making visual images of the text during reading

Able to analyze the author's craft (interesting words, metaphors, similes, colorful images) (storybook language difficult at first)

Asks questions "shouldn't there be a 'with' right there?" Makes inferences and predictions inference about donkey not liking sound of laughter or being carried

Global Observations

X **Reader is self-monitoring his/her reading and constructing meaning**
High number of self-corrections, uncorrected miscues don't change meaning (*it's* for *it is*, *Mother* for *Mom*)

___ **Reader needs to be more concerned with the construction of meaning**
High number of uncorrected miscues that change meaning, accepts nonwords

___ **Reader is over-relying on print – Sounding out is strategy most commonly used**
Graphic similarity is high on miscues that change meaning (*house* for *horse*)

Additional Insights about this Reader and Suggestions for Instruction

- 92% of miscues were sc or unc. - no meaning change
  reads for meaning - understood what he read
- Makes high quality miscues
- Reads with expression

FIGURE 6–6d Over the Shoulder Miscue Analysis Insights Page

The Procedure IV Form

The form for the Procedure IV is quite simple (see Appendix K). To complete the form, at the top of the page write down information about the reader and the text he has selected. The next section is for making the tally marks for each sentence: *Yes,* it made sense, or *No,* it didn't make sense. In this section, we also calculate the comprehending score. The remaining two boxes are for writing down comments from the student's retelling and for making anecdotal records and recommendations for instruction.

The Follow-Up

The numbers obtained from the Procedure IV form provide the teacher and a student with a good sense of how well she is able to construct meaning during reading. It also allows the teacher to calculate a comprehending score, which is found by dividing the total number of *Yes* marks by the total number of sentences. For example, Claire had 48 of 62 sentences that were semantically acceptable (see Figure 7–2, p. 183).

$$\frac{48}{62} = 0.774 \qquad 0.774 \text{ X } 100 = 77.4 \text{ — } 77\% \text{ Comprehending Score}$$

Why Do I Conduct a Procedure IV?

The main purpose of Procedure IV is to determine if the reader is constructing meaning at the sentence level. We listen carefully to how the reader left the whole sentence, and if there were miscues or self-corrections, we decide if it still makes sense. We also make notes about the reader's retelling, write down our comments related to the reader's strengths, and make suggestions for instruction. Procedure IV is often sufficient documentation for those very proficient readers for whom we have no concerns. According to Y. Goodman, Watson, and Burke (1987, 125):

> Procedure IV provides a vehicle for those very familiar with miscue analysis to do a quick evaluation of a student's reading. It is especially helpful for the classroom teacher during an individual reading conference or for an initial evaluation by a reading specialist or special education teacher.

The Choice: Which Untaped Procedure Should I Use?

An important question to ask here is, When do I use OTS and when do I use Procedure IV? Great question!

USE OTS WHEN:

- You listen to students read individually in reading conferences during reading workshop (see Chapter 8). For most of your students who are rolling along as readers, the OTS offers frequent snapshots of their current abilities as readers.
- You listen to students read any time of the day, any type of text.
- You want information about an individual's miscues and comprehension.
- You are providing an opportunity for students to examine their own reading and become aware of how well they're doing as readers.
- You are gathering information for conferences with students and their families and you want some evidence to share about each student as a reader.
- You want information about how the reader is constructing meaning and you want to examine individual miscues.

USE PROCEDURE IV WHEN:

- You have a proficient student for whom you have no concerns as a reader, but you'd like some evidence of his success.
- You want information about how the reader is constructing meaning at the sentence level.

The Steps: Summaries of OTS and Procedure IV

To summarize, an OTS consists of the following:

WITH THE STUDENT:

- *Invite* a student to bring any book she is currently reading and join you in a one-on-one conferencing setting.
- *Complete* the information on the cover page.
- *Listen* to the student read aloud while looking over her shoulder at the text—No tape recording or typescript is needed.
- *Fill in* the miscue page as the student is reading aloud. For each miscue write down:
  –What the reader said
  –What the text said
  For each miscue check the appropriate column to indicate:
  –If the miscue was corrected
  –If the miscue was left uncorrected, and if so, if it changed meaning
- *Ask* the student to talk about what was just read—Anecdotal notes are made about comprehension. There is no retelling guide.
- *Choose a teaching point* and discuss the student's understanding, clarifying words or concepts that may have been confusing; return to and discuss miscues; review the use of particular reading strategies, and suggest alternative strategies.

- *Discuss* the miscue page with the student and point out patterns that emerge relative to self-corrections and the types of miscues frequently made.
- *Celebrate* something the reader is doing well.

AFTER THE STUDENT LEAVES THE CONFERENCE SETTING:

- *Make* anecdotal records about the conference and the reading.
- *Calculate* the percentage of each column.
- *Examine* graphic similarity between miscues and text items.
- *Determine* insights about this reader.
- *File* the OTS form in the student's portfolio.

A Procedure IV consists of the following.

WITH THE STUDENT:

- *Invite* a student to bring any book he is currently reading and join you in a one-on-one conferencing setting.
- *Listen* to a student read aloud while looking over his shoulder at the text—NO tape recording or typescript is needed.
- *Evaluate* each sentence for semantic acceptability and ask, "Does the sentence, as the reader left it, make sense within the context of the selection?"
- *Tally* the sentences as the student is reading as either:

  –*Yes*
    - This sentence makes sense; it is semantically acceptable
    - This was partially acceptable, but it was corrected
    - This was unacceptable, but it was corrected

  or

  –*No*
    - This sentence doesn't make sense; it is semantically unacceptable
    - This was unacceptable and was not corrected
- *Ask* the student for a brief retelling of the selection—Make anecdotal notes. There is no retelling guide.
- *Discuss* the reading with the student. Clarify misunderstandings and discuss strategies or miscues.

AFTER THE STUDENT LEAVES THE CONFERENCE SETTING:

- *Make* additional anecdotal notes about the student and the retelling.
- *Calculate* the comprehending score.

Bringing It All Together: Holistic Evaluation of Readers

When using both the OTS and Procedure IV, the focus is more on the teacher's holistic insights about the reader than on the numbers per se. The expectation is that, with practice, the teacher will be able to take the numbers and percentages of each category of information and discern various patterns from the OTS form and to interpret narrative and numerical information from the Procedure IV form. These kinds of insights inform instruction and help the teacher plan for groups of students with similar areas of concern.

In Chapter 7 we will look at complete examples of OTS and Procedure IV, including the interpretation of the information gained.

7

OTS and Procedure IV—Examples with Readers

I use miscue analysis now in several ways. First I use the entire analysis for extreme problems. Those students that I cannot seem to help through in-class work. I use Davenport's idea of an Over the Shoulder miscue analysis monthly if not more with my seventh graders. This is done during their reading workshop time. I sit with them; listen to them read; and dialogue with each student about what I am seeing, what they are seeing, or about any reading concerns or pleasures. I keep careful notes of these conferences to share with parents and other teachers.

—Jennifer Wilson, Seventh-Grade Language Arts

Now that we've seen how the untaped procedures are conducted, let's walk through an Over the Shoulder (OTS) session with second-grader Josh and a Procedure IV session with second-grader Claire. To give us further insights into possibilities for the teaching conversations, we'll also *listen in* to a session with sixth-grader Ceci.

The Invitation: The Cover Page

When he came to work with me, second-grader Josh brought with him *Clifford's Thanksgiving* (Bridwell 1993). I told him I'd like to have him read to me, then we'd talk about what he had read. I explained that when we read aloud, everyone changes the text in some way. I showed him the columns on the miscue page and told him I'd be listening for his changes in the text, when he corrected those himself, or when he left changes uncorrected. I asked if he had any questions for me, and he said, No. I had him sit beside me so that I could see his book, then he began reading.

While Josh and I were talking, I filled in the top of the cover page (see Appendix I). This information helps me remember the type and difficulty of the book and puts the reading in context. I returned to the bottom of this page, after he finished reading, to scribe his retelling and to make notes about our teaching conversation.

The Notation: The Miscue Pages

As Josh began to read, I turned to the miscue page and got my ear ready to listen for any changes in the text that might occur during his oral reading. At this time, for each miscue, I was only writing down what Josh said, what the text said, and whether the miscue was corrected. I came back later to examine graphic similarity. Sometimes one miscue page is sufficient to record a reader's miscues within a brief reading conference. Usually I don't complete more than two miscue pages because the time I have for one-on-one visits with students is limited. Keeping to two pages reminds me to stay within a time frame of about ten to fifteen minutes per conference. With that much information about the reading, I have plenty to discuss with the student.

Generally, I don't number the miscues on the miscue page, but for our purposes here, I have done so to facilitate examination of Josh's actions as a reader. If there is more than one miscue in a sentence, I list them all before I discuss them. Let's talk through his miscues together.

1. lots of/a lot of: Uncorrected—No Meaning Change

Text: My dog Clifford and I have a lot of fun on Halloween.

Josh: My dog Clifford and I have lots of fun on Halloween.

This is an uncorrected complex miscue that does not change meaning.

2. on our next/our: Self-corrected

Text: Our neighbors took care of him.

Josh: On our next, our, our next door neighbors took care of him.

There was a lot going on in this complex miscue right at the beginning of the sentence. Miscues at this level of complexity sometimes slip by me in the OTS setting, and if so, I jot myself a note, something like: complex—Our neighbors, then I get ready for the next miscue. In this case, I realized Josh was making several attempts at reading this phrase, and rather than trying to write them all on the miscue page, I got down some notation about the first one, then listened carefully to *how Josh finally left the sentence.* Was there ultimately any change in meaning? This is *most important in an untaped procedure.*

Our intent on the miscue page is not to represent the level of complexity we achieve on the Procedure III typescript, for which we can listen repeatedly to the tape recording and strive for a precise representation of what the reader said. The goal during the OTS is to make the most accurate notes we can of what Josh has done as a reader: Here he has made a complex miscue involving several attempts on the phrase Our neighbors, and he left a meaningful sentence that did not change the author's intention.

When Josh was trying to read this sentence, he kept looking at the picture of two people in front of the house next door to Clifford's house, and he was getting stuck on his attempt to say, Our next door neighbors. Looking closely, we see he first corrected his miscue on our next/our, he repeated our, and then he inserted next door. So ultimately the way Josh left it is: Our next door neighbors took care of him, which resulted in no change in meaning.

3. he/his: Corrected
4. is/his: Corrected
5. sister/sisters: Uncorrected—With Meaning Change
6. Bone/Bonnie: Uncorrected—With Meaning Change
7. Nor/Nero: Uncorrected—With Meaning Change

Text: He thought about his own family—his father, his sisters, Bonnie and Claudia, his brother, Nero.

Josh: He thought about his own family—he, his father, is, his sister, Bone, Bone, Boney—and . . . [*he paused for a long time—we discuss naming strategy*] . . . his brother Nor.

Shortly into the text, the author says Clifford was lonely when he was staying with the neighbors, and was thinking fondly of his own family members. When Josh came to the names of Clifford's sisters, Bonnie and Claudia, he first used a "sound-it-out" strategy and came up with a long "o" sound. He said, Bone, Bone, Boney/Bonnie, then he paused for a long time. 1 saw this as an opportunity to talk with Josh about the strategies he was trying and to introduce the naming strategy. When he finished the sentence, he actually omitted Claudia and left the miscue Nor/Nero uncorrected.

I considered these two substitutions (Bone/Bonnie and Nor/Nero) miscues that resulted in a change in meaning. If he had substituted Betty/Bonnie or Nick/Nero, I would have considered that a partial change in meaning because he was using other names. But Bone and Nor are not generally names, even for dogs (at least not the dogs I've known!). Here is the conversation we had when he paused after saying Bone, Bone, Boney/Bonnie:

R: What are you thinking about Josh?

J: I'm thinking about that word

R: You're thinking about that word, uh-huh. What do you know about that word since it's got this right here [*capital letter?*] What is that—little letter or big letter?

J: Big

R: Big letter, OK, so it might be somebody's . . .

J: Name

R: Name, yeah, see, it says, "his sisters" and then there's a comma, so the author is letting you know he's going to list the names of the sisters

J: Oh

R: There's a name, and there's a name [*I point to the words* Bonnie *and* Claudia]

J: Bone-y and . . . um . . .

R: You know, if you don't know a name, what's a strategy that you can do Josh?

J: Skip it

R: You could skip it, or you could call it "Miss C." and keep going

J: Oh [*He continues reading*]

Here is an important distinction between the Procedure III and the OTS: We can enter into a teaching conversation at any appropriate point *during the reading.* Although I don't interrupt the reader at every miscue, if there is obvious confusion or loss of meaning, I ask him to stop and talk about what's going on in his head. If he is just making repetitions, self-corrections, or high-quality miscues, he's most likely making meaning and can just keep rolling through the text. If he read through a passage with several meaning-change miscues and didn't pause or go back on his own, I would let him finish a few sentences, take him back to one or two miscues, and discuss his understanding and his strategies.

If there is an inordinate number of miscues, particularly those that change meaning, I would also reconsider the book selection. Since Josh selected this book himself, if he had been having a lot of trouble with this text, I would have had an opportunity to talk with him about how he picks a book. If I were his classroom teacher and I had picked the book for that conference, and if Josh had a great deal of difficulty, then I would need to reevaluate my current understanding of which books were appropriate for him right now at his developmental level as a reader.

When Josh paused for a long time, I stopped to consider some of the things that could have meant: He might have been thinking through the unfamiliar word and trying different options, like sounding it out or looking for parts of the word he knew. He might have been rereading the previous sentence to get another running start. He might have been reading ahead to try and get additional cues to meaning. He might have tried a strategy and given up. He might have been thinking about something else, like what he had for lunch or soccer practice after school.

I consider a long pause a good time to ask, What are you thinking? and to try to get a sense of the reader's process of constructing meaning. While this type of metacognitive talk can be difficult for very young readers, with practice, most students become able to access their thoughts and let me in on what's going on in their heads to some degree. Then we discuss possible strategies to get past a point of difficulty in the text. This is the inquiry: a *shared exploration* of the reading process.

There are actually two teaching points briefly stated in my conversation with Josh: the convention of using a comma to indicate clarification or elaboration is to follow (his sisters, Bonnie and Claudia), and the use of a naming strategy for difficult names (watch for the capital letter, then you'll know it's a name and call it "Miss C." and keep going). If Josh were a student in my class, I would keep an eye on his use of the naming strategy during future reading conferences.

After I told him the two names and suggested the naming strategy, he did two things that told me he either hadn't really understood me, or this brief FYI introduction wasn't sufficient for Josh to take ownership of this strategy. First, he said Boney again, so I could have continued talking with him about the name Bonnie right then, but I didn't. I came back to it later in our conversation after his retelling of the second part of the story and discovered it was a name he hadn't heard before. Second, he used the word Nor for Clifford's brother Nero, which is an unusual name, rather than immediately putting to use the strategy I suggested, that is, call him "Mr. N." and keep going. I think Josh was just trying to move along through the text and used Nor as a placeholder, without really considering whether it was a name he'd heard before and without trying the naming strategy I had just mentioned.

8. dis-decided: Uncorrected—With Meaning Change

Text: He decided to spend Thanksgiving with her.

Josh: He dis-, di-, to spend Thanksgiving with her.

Josh makes two attempts at this word (dis-, di-) but leaves the second partial uncorrected. I just wrote the first attempt on the miscue page. Whenever you can catch multiple attempts at a word, it is fine to write them down; whether you can depend on how fast the student is reading. The same applies to writing down punctuation on the miscue page. If you can catch a miscue involving punctuation, such as an omitted or inserted period, that's great. You'll have more to think about when you're interpreting the miscues later, but generally I don't write these down unless it becomes a prevalent pattern.

An example of this is Josh's miscue where he was./Where was his (see miscue 22 later in this chapter).

Text: Nothing looked familiar. Where was his mom?

Josh: Nothing looked familiar where he was. Where his mom,
Where was his mom?

I was able to write down Josh's complex miscue and the period. This helped me remember the structure of the sentences and how the omission of the author's period and Josh's inserted end punctuation were important as I considered what he was doing with language.

Following is an example of a miscue I misheard. Josh's miscue was actually start/started.

9. set/started: Uncorrected—No Meaning Change

10. to/—: Uncorrected—With Meaning Change

Text: Early Thanksgiving morning, Clifford started out.

Josh: Early Thanksgiving morning, Clifford set out to.

In a classroom situation, I wouldn't be making a tape recording, and probably never would have known about this mistake on my part. However, this session was conducted during research in which I was working with readers from kindergarten through college age. My colleague Carol Lauritzen and I were comparing the data gained through an OTS and a Procedure III conducted on the same instance of reading (Davenport and Lauritzen, 2002), so I had a tape of his reading. When listening to it again, I discovered that Josh actually said: Early Thanksgiving morning, Clifford start out to.

So, on the OTS form, this would have been most appropriately considered as a complex miscue: start out to/started out: Uncorrected—With Meaning Change.

However, I wrote these out as two separate miscues, a substitution and an insertion. Originally, I accidentally wrote his insertion (to/—) as an omission (—/to)—that is, I wrote the dash in the wrong column. Then I caught myself, and rather than erase or cross out and try again, I just put a little double arrow between the columns to remind me that the notations were reversed. I encourage you to develop this kind of personal shorthand—anything that will help you know what the reader said or to remind you of something about the miscue you'd like to remember.

It's best to capture as much of your thinking as possible, either by writing down an extra word or two around the miscue in the "Reader Said" and "Text Said" columns of the miscue page, or by writing down observations or other notes about your interaction with the reader in the margin of the miscue page. For example, when I was working with a first grader, the only decoding strategy I observed was "sounding-it-out." I gave her some other options, and after our conference, I wrote the following in the margin of her OTS miscue page: I turned the book over and asked her to stop trying to sound out the word and to just talk to me about what would make sense there. She instantly got it. After a few more times of me turning the book over, she started doing it herself when she got stuck.

11. Er-/Everybody: Self-Corrected

12. smiled/seemed: Self-Corrected

13. —/see: Uncorrected—No Meaning Change

Text: Everybody seemed to be going to see their moms.

Josh: Er—, Everybody smiled to be going to, seemed to be going to their moms.

Josh self-corrected his partial at the beginning of the sentence Er-/Everybody and then self-corrected his substitution smiled/seemed after saying the phrase smiled to be going to, which didn't make sense. When Josh omits see, I think the sentence he is constructing in his head is Everybody seemed to be going to their mom's (houses).

14. beeped/bumped: Self-Corrected

Text: They bumped into Clifford and honked at him.

Josh: They beeped, they bumped into Clifford and honked at him.

The picture on this page showed a crowded freeway with the words Beep, Beep, Beep written above the cars. Josh said Beep, Beep, Beep several times as an aside, and there is High graphic similarity between these words, so it is understandable why he made the miscue beeped/bumped. He caught his miscue and self-corrected.

15. was/were: Uncorrected—Dialect Usage

Text: There were no cars on it.

Josh: There was no cars on it.

I gave Josh the benefit of the doubt and considered this his "kid dialect" or an immature use of the singular verb form rather than the plural. I believe he was making meaning here.

16. wanted way/wondered why: Uncorrected—With Meaning Change

Text: Clifford wondered why.

Josh: Clifford wanted way.

In this complex miscue, I think the graphophonic cueing system was a greater influence for Josh than the semantic or syntactic systems. While we cannot assume one-to-one correspondence in complex miscues, we do see similar word structures and a lot of letters in common. Josh makes no attempts at correcting this miscue and he loses meaning. Although we talked about other miscues, this certainly would have been a miscue I could have come back to later in the teaching conversation.

17. —/drawbridge: Uncorrected—With Meaning Change

Text: It was a drawbridge.

Josh: It was a —.

While Josh makes no attempt at saying drawbridge, when he first turned to this page and saw that Clifford fell off the opening drawbridge into the water, he said, Uh-oh, this can't be good. When we returned to this miscue in our conversation, at first when I asked if he knew what kind of bridge it was, he said, No. I asked him if he saw two words inside that word, then he was able to say drawbridge, and he knew what it meant. I think when he first read it, he was having trouble decoding this long word and because he had enough information from the picture to understand what was going on, he skipped it and kept reading.

After the next few sentences, he again made predictions during his side comments. In the picture, he saw that Clifford has gone down a subway tunnel, and we have the following conversation:

J: Oh no, he's gonna get stuck

R: Good prediction

J: He's either going to get stuck or get hit by a train

R: Another good guess

This type of comment indicates a very engaged reader who is revealing his active process of constructing meaning by anticipating what might happen next!

18. road/roar: Uncorrected—With Meaning Change

Text: Suddenly there was a roar and a bright light in Clifford's eyes.

Josh: Suddenly there was a road and a bright light in Clifford's eyes.

Josh's miscue road/roar is syntactically acceptable and could make sense, but it is not what the author intended. Perhaps he was thinking of the scene on the freeway where the cars were bumping into Clifford, and his "road" schema was still active. For a child his age, the word roar is probably more commonly used as the sound of a lion than the sound of a train. He probably just picked up a few visual cues (r-o-a), said the word road and didn't reconsider his miscue.

19. there/the: Uncorrected—With Meaning Change

I wrote this down on the miscue page, but when I listened again to the tape, I couldn't hear it. So this is a *phantom miscue*—it didn't really occur. I've talked with my students in miscue analysis classes about this phenomenon and third-grade teacher Heather Johnson said she had a similar experience, which she attributed to making miscues herself as she's listening to a reader. This reminds us that language is not perfectible, nor is the use of this or any other reading assessment. There is always a human factor; that is, we will miss some miscues and not get them written down, and we will *mis*hear others. In these untaped procedures, we accept that as part of the process of *listening* to readers *in-the-moment*. This happens when using any untaped reading assessment, but occurs infrequently enough that it doesn't diminish the value of a procedure. We glean a wealth of valuable information from the miscues we do correctly catch and write down.

We should consider the reading event as a whole, based on linguistic, numerical, and qualitative information we gather. We also need to take into account social factors, such as the quickly-established rapport between Josh and myself as we walked from his classroom and chatted before he read, the background he brought with him about what takes place in a reading conference, the predictions he made about what kind of interaction he might have with me during his reading, and his understanding of what I expected of him when he finished reading. Any or all of these factors could have been an influence on Josh's interactions with me or his *style* of discussing the story. We have to consider what Josh has been taught about talking about books, and what counts as a retelling within the culture of his classroom (Bloome 1985).

At this point I asked Josh to retell the first part of the story. He seemed to be getting a little distracted, and I thought talking about the text would help him get refocused. Here's his retelling of the first part:

R: You want to talk to me about what you've read so far?

J: He wanted to spend Thanksgiving with his mom

R: So what did he do?

J: So he set off to find her—and he bumped into a lot of cars

R: Ok, good

J: He fell into the ocean

R: You're doing great. What happened after he got out of the water?

J: He went into a tunnel and he got hit by a train—Boom! Ow!

R: Who was he staying with at the beginning?

J: He was staying with the next door neighbors

R: Anything else you want to tell me about that part? [*Long pause*] You did a pretty good job Josh [*He doesn't make any comment*] Do you want to go ahead and finish the story? [*He finishes reading*]

This is another distinction between the OTS and Procedure III: The conversations and the reading become part of a recursive cycle as the teacher and student talk through the text together (Davenport 1993). For my notes from this first retelling, see the bottom of Josh's cover page in Appendix I.

This brief exchange was a sufficient *check in* with Josh to let me know he was understanding the story so far and to help him redirect his attention back to the book. Let's continue looking at Josh's miscues as he read the second part of the story.

20. so/to: Self-Corrected

Text: He couldn't turn around, so he pushed the train back to the station.

Josh: He couldn't turn around, so he pushed the train back so, back to the station.

This miscue was an appropriate prediction that was semantically and syntactically acceptable, as if he were thinking the text was going to say something like . . . he pushed the train back so he could get out. He caught this miscue and self-corrected.

21. the/a: Self-Corrected

Text: He was in a strange neighborhood.

Josh: He was in the strange neighborhood.

Sometimes readers can interchange the determiners a and the and there is little change in meaning. But here it seems that, to Josh, there was a difference between his miscue in the strange neighborhood (a specific neighborhood that was "strange") and the text in a strange neighborhood (any neighborhood that had characteristics that were "strange"). Though a slight difference, he went back and self-corrected.

22. where he was./Where was his: Self-Corrected

Text: Nothing looked familiar. Where was his mom?

Josh: Nothing looked familiar where he was. Where his mom, Where was his mom?

In this complex miscue, Josh was predicting a meaningful sentence based on what had happened in the story so far. Clifford is a long way from home on a trip to see his mom, and it would be natural for the narrator to say, Nothing looked familiar where he was. However, Josh regresses to rethink this, perhaps after attending to the period and the question mark. He tried again, and left it corrected.

23. always/usually: Uncorrected—Partial Meaning Change

24. —/to: Uncorrected—With Meaning Change

Text: Clifford usually like parades . . . but he was in a hurry to get to his mom.

Josh: Clifford always likes parades . . . but he was in a hurry so he, to get his mom.

This is an example of how writing down just an extra word or two on the miscue page can help you think about the context more clearly. If we just saw the substitution always/usually, we'd say there's a pretty big difference between what these words mean. But if we look at the context of the sentence and the story, we see that Josh has used always to mean every time he comes to a parade, he likes it and the author has used usually in this context to mean his regular pattern of behavior is to enjoy parades when he sees them. This distinction, within the context of this story, doesn't result in much of a meaning change, if any.

Josh often made side comments during his reading. On one page, the illustrator had a little bit of fun with the picture; he included a balloon of Clifford in the parade! We only see half the balloon in the picture, and Josh said, Oh! There's a balloon of him! Josh made another side comment shortly thereafter when Clifford started playing in a football game in the park: Ah, get it, get it! Look at all of them. I responded that it looks like they're having a good game. After the author's line, Clifford didn't mean to but he wound up in the game, Josh made noises and voices like the children in the park playing football, then said, Touchdown! Look, Clifford-down, making a great play on words! When Clifford finally arrived at his mom's house, Josh noted repeatedly, Man, his mom's tiny. All these side comments give us evidence of Josh's connections to this text and his active process of constructing meaning.

25. he/she: Uncorrected—With Meaning Change

Text: She was happy to see her little boy.

Josh: He was happy to see her little boy.

While this miscue is syntactically acceptable, the meaning is changed. We see High graphic similarity, so maybe Josh was just reading too quickly and wasn't monitoring his understanding closely enough to keep the pronoun referent in his mind, and therefore he didn't catch the miscue.

26. to see/too: Self-Corrected

Text: Her owner was happy too.

Josh: Her owner was happy to see, happy too.

Here's another great prediction! The author has built up anticipation of the reunion between Clifford and his mother. Finally, they meet, she's very happy to see him, and Josh used the context of the story to predict the text would read, Her owner was happy to see Clifford too. But he caught his miscue and self-corrected.

Josh makes a great inference from the picture on the next page. It shows Emily Elizabeth, Clifford's owner, eating Thanksgiving dinner with her grandmother. There is a thought bubble above her head, and inside it there is a picture of Clifford. Coming out of his head is a thought bubble, and inside it there is a picture of Emily Elizabeth. Josh says, That's funny, because she's thinking about Clifford thinking about her. I responded, Good for you Josh, that's complicated, you figured that out. The text that followed confirmed his inference: I was having fun at grandma's house, but I kept thinking about Clifford. I wondered if he was thinking of me.

27. worried/wondered: Self-Corrected

Text: I wondered if he was thinking of me.

Josh: I worried, wa-, wondered if he was thinking of me.

Here we have more evidence of Josh's ability to make great predictions based on all the language cueing systems. In his miscue, worried/wondered, we have a past tense verb (syntax is working), High graphic similarity (graphophonics is working), and an appropriate possibility; that is, there is a certain poignant tension in their missing each other that could involve worry (pragmatics and semantics are working). However, he corrected this substitution.

28. called/could: Abandons the Correct Response

Text: He loves his mom, but as soon as he could, he hurried home.

Josh: He loves his mom, but as soon as he could, as soon as he called, he hurried home.

I'm always fascinated by this type of miscue. To me it indicates that there is something the reader is bringing to the text—a memory, an association, a mental image, or a feeling—that is so compelling that it overrides what is on the page. Perhaps in Josh's background there was an association between making a phone call and going home after a trip (as if to say, We're on our way home!).

29. thinking of/thankful for: Uncorrected—Partial Meaning Change

Text: So did I . . . because I am thankful for Clifford, and he is thankful for me.

Josh: So did I . . . because I am thinking of Clifford, and he is thinking for, of me.

We can understand why Josh made this miscue, following closely after his careful attention to the layers of meaning depicted in the previous picture. While at the story level, the author's closing sentence is important (this was, after all, a

Thanksgiving story), to me Josh's complex miscue resulted in a partial change in meaning. I had to give Josh credit because he was doing an excellent job of constructing meaning here.

Also, I think he was paying close attention to the picture on this page. Clifford is arriving home, while looking in the distance at an airplane landing. At this point in the text, Emily Elizabeth is saying that Clifford hurried home and So did I. Again, it is clearly conveyed in the text and the picture that they are thinking of each other. Josh's side comment here was They're there at the same time. So I believe he was thinking about what is going on right now for these two characters (they're thinking of each other) rather than referring to the more general, well-established affection for one another (they're thankful for each other).

The Reflective Talking: The Teaching Conversation

When Josh finished reading, we began talking again. Let's take a look at each section of the teaching conversation (remember that they flow seamlessly from one to the other).

Invitation to Retell

I helped Josh remember the point at which we stopped on his retelling of the first part of the book. He makes brief statements, then I ask him to tell me more. Even though I gave Josh some wait time after each comment, he wasn't offering any elaboration, so I asked follow-up questions. While not as conversational as I like, our interaction shows clearly that Josh understood what he read.

R: What was that last part about? We stopped where he was just getting out of the tunnel. He just got hit by the train, he just got out of the tunnel, and then what happened? [*Actually, Clifford pushed the train out of the tunnel—*Getting hit by the train *was Josh's original prediction, and I repeated that here*]

J: He jumped out onto the street

R: OK, then what?

J: There was a town he didn't recognize

R: OK, good, what else?

J: And then he climbed a bunch of buildings and he saw his mom's house and he walked there and he got involved in a football game on the way

R: OK, you're doing great. After the football game, what did he do?

J: He found his mom's house and he, then he went home

R: What did he do while he was at his mom's house?

J: He ate dinner—and then he went home and he saw Emily Elizabeth 'cause they got home at the same time

R: OK, good for you, what a great reader you are Josh!

Discuss Patterns of Miscues

Now I take Josh back to the miscue page to help him see what patterns of miscues emerged. This is one of the *most important purposes* of the form: It provides a platform for talking with students about their reading. When I was a classroom teacher, my students looked forward to this exchange after their reading. They knew I *wouldn't keep any secrets* from them; what I knew about them, I shared with them. They also knew that I was interested in their own observations and insights into their reading, and they came to observe in themselves characteristics of good readers.

Clarify Words or Concepts

Next, we go back and discuss whether his miscue sister/sisters resulted in a significant meaning change.

R: OK, let me show you this. You're such a great reader [*showing columns on the miscue page*]. OK, remember this one is where you fixed it yourself, look how many times you did that [*I run my pencil down the "Self-Corrected" column*]. That means you were really listening carefully as you were reading. And here you said "sister" for "sisters." That's a little bit of a change because the "s" on the end means what? What's the difference between "sister" and "sisters"—when we have the "s" on the end?

J: If you didn't have the "s" on the end it would be "sister" instead of "sisters"

R: Right, what's the difference between those two?

J: "Sisters" means you have, t-, "sisters" means you have um, two, more than one, and "sister" means you have one

Here's an important observation point that emerged from our conversation: Josh understands the use of the "s" to form a plural noun. As his classroom teacher, this would have been a valuable anecdotal record, and something I would watch for in Josh's writing.

Select a Brief Teaching Point

There were two points I wanted to revisit with Josh. First, I chose to return to our discussion of the names of Clifford's sisters and brother. Once I found out he'd never heard the name Bonnie before, I moved on to calling his attention to other miscues I'd written on the form. Second, I took him back to his omission of drawbridge.

R: Exactly, and then we talked about that naming strategy, look here, you had a couple places where you were having trouble with that name, that's "Bonnie"—His sister's name is Bonnie, have you ever heard that name before?

J: Bonnie?

R: Bonnie, have you ever heard that name? [*He shakes his head no*] OK, and then there was the brother's name, and this one, you just, you just made a little attempt [*an uncorrected partial*] and then you just kind of gave up on that one, that was OK, you just kept reading—And this one didn't change the meaning, and this one you fixed, this one you fixed, this one didn't change, this one you fixed—And this one was just a different way of saying something, a grammar change [*his dialect miscue*]—And this one changed the meaning, and so did this one—Look at this one again [drawbridge—*We look at the picture*]—Do you know what kind of bridge that is?

J: No

R: Let's look at this word again where it tells you—Do you see two words inside that word?

J: Braaww [*He starts sounding it out with a "b" sound*]

R: It starts with a "d"

J: Drawbridge [*He just says it*]

R: Drawbridge—Have you ever heard of a drawbridge before?

J: Yep

R: OK, what does a drawbridge do?

End with a Celebration Point

Here Josh got a little silly but I just kept going and took him right back to the miscue page. I could tell he was getting a little tired, so I wrapped things up by celebrating things I had observed he was doing well.

J: It opens when a boat comes, so no cars go, and it breaks and it lands on the boat and the boat sinks and everybody drowns and then it closed

R: And then this one you fixed, and then look at all these, fixed it, fixed it, fixed it

J: Holy cow!

R: Yeah, aren't you a good reader? All those times you fixed it yourself! Isn't that great? [*I show him where I scribed his retelling*] And this is what you told me when you retold the story and you remembered the whole story. You're so smart!

J: Yeah!

The Follow-Up: The Insights Page

To complete our OTS, we need to determine graphic similarity between the miscues and the related text items on the miscue pages. We do this in the same manner as we did on the Procedure III miscue tally form (see Appendix C).

On the insights page, we bring forward the totals from the columns on each miscue page. We now turn these numbers into percentages to enable us to identify the reader's strengths and areas of concern. We also begin thinking about comments from the discussion and retelling and make notes as appropriate. Finally, we reflect on our experience with this reader, review all the numbers, make some general observations, and conclude with recommendations for instruction.

Determining Graphic Similarity

On the miscue page, divide the miscues and the text items into three parts. If there are two parts that are graphically similar—that is, they have most of the letters in common—there is High graphic similarity. If there is at least one letter in common, there is Some graphic similarity. We just look at graphic similarity for one-word substitution miscues, and for some of these miscue/text pairs, there is None.

Totaling the Miscues and Calculating the Percentages

At the bottom of each of the miscue pages, total each column. Then bring these totals to the insights page for Grand Totals.

Now, calculate the percentages: Take each column total, divide by the total number of miscues, and multiply by 100. Remember, these numbers are based on the miscues we were able to write down in this instance of reading. These numbers are always considered in conjunction with other linguistic and qualitative information about each reader.

Observations About Comprehension

Look back through the notes you made on the cover page as the reader was retelling and discussing the story. Also look at any notes you made in the margin of the miscue pages during the reading. While considering the developmental level of the readers, look at the following as possible questions to consider when observing comprehension. I'll respond to each based on Josh's reading and retellings:

- *How much and what kind of information did the reader mention?* He made brief statements of the main events, he listed details in the right sequence, and he was able to follow up when given this type of prompt: `Then what happened?`
- *Did the reader hit the highlights and talk about the most important ideas?* Yes, he only omitted two big ideas: Emily Elizabeth went to her grandmother's house, and on the way to his mom's, Clifford saw a parade. He also thought Clifford was hit by the train, when actually he pushed it out of the tunnel.

- *Did the reader give a detail-by-detail type of retelling, or "get the gist" and give summarizing statements, or both?* His responses were given in a detail-by-detail manner without elaboration.
- *Was the reader able to synthesize text information?* Synthesis is a hard thing for some younger readers to do, but for older readers, we can consider the reader's ability to move beyond the text, to combine knowledge of the world with information from the text, and move to a new perspective. Josh didn't do this, but I don't think I would expect a reader his age who reads this particular text to do so.
- *Was the reader able to make connections within the text, across texts, between the text and themselves, and between the text and the world?* I think Josh's active engagement with this text was demonstrated through his many side comments. He showed within-the-text connections when he said, `Uh-oh, this can't be good`, implying things so far had gone fine for Clifford on his journey, but now there might be trouble. He showed connections between the text and his own background when he narrated the football game and when he made the joke, `Clifford-down`. He was able to draw on his knowledge of the world when he interpreted the picture and understood what was happening with the drawbridge.
- *Did the reader mention any sensory images while reading, like getting a picture in his or her head?* There was sort of a visceral connection between Josh and this text, again revealed through his noises and comments. He said, `Beep, beep, beep` when reading about the cars on the freeway; he said, `Boom! Ow!` when he thought Clifford got hit by the train, and he commented several times about how tiny Clifford's mom was. All these connections show clear mental images of the dog's experiences.
- *Did the reader make any comments about the writing style of the author, or about the illustrations?* Josh said, `That's funny` about the picture with the thought bubble above Emily Elizabeth's head, which had a picture of Clifford in it, who also had a thought bubble above his head. He also noticed the illustrator put a Clifford balloon in the parade.
- *Did the reader ask questions, make inferences, or make predictions?* Josh made several clear predictions when Clifford went down the subway tunnel. He thought he might get stuck or get hit by a train. He also made an inference about Clifford and Emily Elizabeth missing each other and thinking of each other when he saw the thought bubble picture and at the end when they arrived home at the same time.

Global Observations

At this point in conducting an OTS, we know a lot about our readers. We have the following:

- *Numerical information*—the percentages from each column on the miscue pages

- *Linguistic information*—by examining:
  Syntax—the relationships between the miscues and the text item: Are they the same part of speech? Did the reader substitute a past tense verb for a noun, or for a past tense verb?
  Semantics—the reader's ability to construct meaning: Did the reader lose meaning, leave uncorrected a high-quality miscue that didn't change meaning, or self-correct?
  Graphophonics—the reader's knowledge of symbol–sound relationships: Are most of the letters the same in the miscue and the text item?
- *Qualitative information*—by considering whether this reader is monitoring his reading and is actively involved in the process of constructing meaning or whether he needs to be more concerned with making meaning. We can also think about other observations, such as expression, fluency, personal connections, as shown through side comments, questions, and whether the reader is enjoying the story.

From all these sources of information, we can determine strategies the reader needs to know and make recommendations for further instruction.

Insights About Josh

The next sections summarize what we know about Josh from this one instance of reading.

Numerical Information

It is interesting that Josh had the same percentage of self-corrections as he did miscues that changed meaning. However, if we add together the self-corrections and the high-quality miscues that didn't change meaning, we see that 59 percent of the time he was making sense of the text. If this was all we had to go on, we might say he was a struggling reader or that this text was too hard for him. But if we consider the amount of information he was able to recall, and his very active engagement during the reading (shown by his predictions and side comments), we get a different view of Josh as a reader. We note he was able to use picture cues to compensate for the miscues that resulted in a loss of meaning.

We can see from close examination of his meaning change miscues that each individual miscue was indeed different from what the author intended; however, taken collectively, they did not interrupt his construction of global meaning—Josh was still able to understand the gist of the story. This is why we interpret the numbers from an OTS cautiously. They are *never the sole source* of our reflections about the reader. We must also consider the linguistic and qualitative information we have gained.

Linguistic Information

Here we want to examine how Josh is using the language cueing systems. Let's first consider the syntactic cueing system, and look at the syntactic acceptability of his one-word substitutions (see Figure 7–1).

Josh said	Text said	Syntactically acceptable prediction at the point in the sentence (Up to and including the miscue)	How Josh Left It
He	His	Yes	Corrected
Is	His	Yes	Corrected
Sister	Sisters	Yes	Uncorrected
Bone	Bonnie	No	Uncorrected
Nor	Nero	No	Uncorrected
Set	Started	Yes	Uncorrected
Smiled	Seemed	Yes	Corrected
Beeped	Bumped	Yes	Corrected
Was	Were	Yes	Uncorrected (dialect usage)
Road	Roar	Yes	Uncorrected
So	To	Yes	Corrected
The	A	Yes	Corrected
He	She	Yes	Corrected
Worried	Wondered	Yes	Corrected
Called	Could	Yes	Uncorrected

FIGURE 7–1 Josh's Syntax Chart

Clearly Josh understands reading should sound like language. He didn't make any nonword miscues and all but two of his fifteen one-word substitutions were syntactically acceptable predictions. *You do not need to make a chart* like this every time you conduct an OTS, but you should go through a similar thought process. I've just done one to demonstrate my thinking when considering the question, Did Josh's reading sound like language?

Considering the semantic cueing system, we ask the question, Did Josh's reading make sense? Here we see the interesting pattern of 41 percent self-corrections and 18 percent high-quality miscues—those that were left uncorrected but did not change meaning. While we are not calculating a comprehension score, these numbers do tell us that Josh is monitoring his reading for meaning 59 percent of the time.

However, 41 percent of Josh's miscues do change the meaning. I found it appropriate to check both places on my Global Observations to indicate that Josh had a concern for meaning, but that he could still have a greater concern for meaning. This tells me he is a reader who has a lot of good strategies working for him, but being a young reader, he has room for improvement in this area.

Considering the graphophonic cueing system, we see that of the seventeen miscues we could code, 94 percent had either High or Some graphic similarity.

Therefore, there is no reason to worry about Josh's knowledge of symbol—sound relationships.

Qualitative Information

Now, after all this, what do we know about Josh from this one reading? What's working well for him?

- Josh understood this text. While he didn't give a summary statement (which I didn't ask for), he was able to talk about the main points of the story. He gave accurate details in the proper sequence.
- A real strength for Josh is his use of picture cues to help him make sense of what he's reading, which is appropriate for a reader his age. I think this book was a good choice for him, but without picture cues to support his construction of meaning, he may have found it a little challenging.
- Josh is actively engaged in constructing meaning. He demonstrates his involvement in the text, his monitoring of meaning, his predictions, and his personal connections through his many side comments.
- Josh makes appropriate predictions, both at the word level and at the story level. This again demonstrates his involvement with the text, his comprehending ability, and his use of the syntactic and semantic cueing systems.
- Josh makes sophisticated inferences based on both the text and the pictures—for example, his interpretation of the thought bubble picture and his final line about Clifford and Emily Elizabeth thinking of each other.
- Josh's use of the language cueing systems is well-balanced. His reading sounds like language (syntax), it makes sense (semantics), and he does not overrely on the "sound-it-out" strategy (graphophonics).
- Josh's reading has buoyancy and expression, which says, I'm having fun here!

Recommendations for Instruction

If I were continuing to work with Josh, I would come back to his use of the naming strategy, and I would ask him to more closely monitor his miscues that do result in a change of meaning. I would work with him on continually asking himself two all-important questions for readers: Does this sound like the way we talk? Does this make sense? Also, I would continue to model my own thinking during reading to help Josh become more aware of the strategies proficient readers use and to help him see that he is already using many of them. I think, overall, we could say that Josh is well on his way to becoming a proficient reader.

Teaching Conversation with Ceci

As another example of the types of talking that can take place during a teaching conversation, let's "listen in" on my conference with Ceci, a sixth grader who had just read three pages from *The Westing Game* (Raskin 1997). Ceci considers herself a good reader, and indeed, she was. After she retold the section that she read, we discuss the inferences she made, I take her back to a couple of points she didn't mention in the retelling, and we look at her patterns on the miscue page. We discuss several of her miscues, and in a few instances, she demonstrates that even though she wasn't able to say the word, she knew what it meant. On others, she hadn't ever heard the words before, couldn't pronounce them, and didn't know what they meant. This conversation gives us an example of the clarifying talking and teaching that helps readers construct meaning.

R: That's wonderful Ceci, you are a great reader. OK, first thing I want you to do is just retell the story for me, just things that happened during the story that you can remember and I'll help you out if you get stuck. Just at first, just pretend like I'm somebody who wasn't listening to you read, like I was just a friend that you wanted to share all those exciting details with, OK?

C: OK, um, what happened is there's um, the Sunset Towers, and a lot of people have moved in to there and there's Doug Hoo, Turtle, and Theo Theodorkas and they were told about a house up on the hill by, I think the doorman, and how kids would bet each other a dollar for every five minutes they stayed in there and one of them came out running right after he went through the doors and didn't stop screaming until he hit the rocks at the bottom of the cliff and his hands had been dripping with warm red blood and ever since he came out he always said—the only two words that he'd ever said after that was "purple waves" and I think that maybe Theo and Doug, they probably don't think it's true

R: Hmmm, why not?

C: 'Cause they just exchanged winks and they were probably—they probably just don't believe in all that stuff—but Turtle did

R: Oh, how do you know?

C: She acted like it because she shivered more than most and she seemed kind of scared of that and that's about it for that chapter

R: OK, great job Ceci, let's go back now and let's see if there's anything else . . . it says "delivery boy" but he's an older man, right?

C: Yeah, 62

R: Sixty-two years old, but they keep calling him the "delivery boy" so that was the doorman right? [*I had a misunderstanding; they're actually two different people.*] Tell me about Mr. Hoo and the restaurant

C: Mr. Hoo I think runs the restaurant

R: What kind of a restaurant is it?

C: Breakfast, lunch, and dinner

R: OK, gosh, you really remembered a lot. Who were they talking about who used to live in that house on the hill? Do you remember who that is?

C: Huh-uh (no)

R: Old man Westing. What were they saying about him?

C: That he, some say that he had his own private island that he lived on, you know, down in the south seas, but some, most of 'em, people say that he was dead and his body was sprawled out on a really fancy rug

R: OK, good. It was kind of gruesome when they were describing that, wasn't it? OK, anything else you want to tell me there? You did a great job Ceci—you really remembered a lot—anything else?

C: No

R: That's all right. Let's go back and take a look then at what your miscues were. Remember what this one is, when we see it in this column—what does that mean?

C: I self-corrected

R: You fixed it yourself. Yeah, and I missed this one—you made a miscue there and I didn't quite catch it there [*I wrote down the miscue but not the text item*], so I'll just let that one go and let's go back and look at this one right here [*I'm reading*], ". . . specializing . . ." —can you read that for me?

C: ". . . in authentic Chinese casoon"

R: Yeah, do you know what this word means [*cuisine*]?

C: No

R: OK, what do you think it might mean?

C: Ummm . . .

R: If we know the restaurant is serving "authentic Chinese . . ."

C: Probably some Chinese food

R: Yeah, Chinese food, so "cuisine" is the way we say that and I think it's from French origin and it means the food of that region or the food of that group of people, so Mexican cuisine, or French cuisine, or Chinese cuisine would be the food eaten by those people. So you're right, it's Chinese food. OK, so it's a fancy word for "food"—all Chinese cuisine. Had you ever heard that word before?

C: Huh-uh (no)

R: OK, so if you've never heard a word before, it's hard to know how to say it, isn't it? But you knew what it meant, that's good. Look at all these [*miscues*] that you fixed [*I go through them*] and then let's look down at this one. They're standing there, "they face North . . .

C: ". . . gaping like statues cast in the moment of discovery" [*Pronounces* gaping *correctly—she had miscued* gapping]

R: What does that mean? You got it

C: Gaping, uh, they had their mouths open and they were just staring real hard at it

R: Good for you. That's exactly what "gaping" means—your mouth is open and you're staring. Good for you Ceci. Why do you think you said "gapping" the first time? Do you remember what you were thinking?

C: No

R: OK, that's fine—all right, let's go on now [*I go through miscues that didn't change meaning, listing them*] and then, "he's usually a cheery fellow" and you said "a cherry fellow" and you kept going, and that was not a huge deal, but it did change the meaning; that doesn't mean the same thing. And then I think you might have just mispronounced this one Ceci, where you say "in the autumn hair" [*air*] and you meant "autumn air." Do you remember that one?

C: Yeah

R: ". . . the smoke was going to write the answer in the autumn air." He's waiting for the smoke [*I'm looking through the text*] might have been back a page—"waiting for the smoke to write the answer in the autumn air." Here and you said "autumn hair."

C: Uh-huh (yes)

R: Yeah and you said "she" for "he"—whoever this track star is, you said "she" right there—"she couldn't chance" and maybe, do you know why you might have said that? she?

C: Probably just hurrying

R: Yeah, and look at the sentence right before it—who are they talking about?

C: Turtle

R: Uh-huh, who's a girl

C: Uh-huh

R: Right, so they're saying "Turtle's" and then you said "*her* precious braids . . ." and "*she'll* kick you in the shins" and then, so you're thinking girl, girl, girl, and then you came to that and you said "she"—OK, so just switching characters then to the track star [*who was a boy*]—and yeah, probably in a hurry, good thinking. Let's look at this one right here, "Otis Amber said a 'sshhh' with a shudder that sent the loose straps of his leather 'something' [*I use this as a placeholder for her miscue*] helmet swinging about his long thin face." What kind of a helmet is that? A leather helmet—have you ever seen that word before, Ceci? [*aviator*]

C: I don't think so

R: It's "aviator." Do know who an aviator is?

C: Huh-uh (No)

R: Have you ever heard that word?

C: No

R: It's a pilot, somebody who flies

C: Oh

R: Have you ever seen those?

C: Yeah

R: Sometimes motorcycle guys will wear those leather caps that just fit right over and they have the straps down and that's an aviator's helmet from like WW II so that's what this guy Otis is wearing and he's going "horrible, horrible" and this strap is flapping around like this, on his aviator's helmet—those that fit real snug to the head—so, again, if you've never heard the word before, then it's hard to know how to say it. OK, good for you.

Procedure IV with Claire

If we have conducted several OTS sessions with a student and have confidence she is doing well, we may want to conduct a Procedure IV (see Appendix K for a blank form). In this procedure, we are listening to each entire sentence and making a decision about whether it made sense, as Claire left it, within the context of the story (see Figure 7–2). We make tally marks either by "Yes" or "No" on the form. We count the totals, and then calculate a comprehending score by dividing the total number of sentences that were coded "Yes" by the total number of sentences. We multiply by 100; this gives us our percentage score (Y. Goodman, Watson, and Burke 1987; Rhodes and Shanklin 1990).

As the reader is discussing the story, we scribe as much as possible in the Retelling Information box on the form. In the Comments box, we make a summative statement about our observations of this reader. Claire's score of 77 percent is reflected in her thorough retelling of *Amazing Grace* (Hoffman 1991).

Reader *Claire* Date *9·10*

Teacher *Dr. D.* Age/Grade *7/2nd*

Selection *Amazing Grace*

Does the sentence, as the reader left it, make sense within the context of the story?

Yes *卌 卌 卌 卌 卌 卌 卌 卌 卌 ///* Total *48*

No *卌 卌 ////* Total *14*

Number of Sentences *62* Comprehending Score *77%*

Divide the total Yes by the Total Number of Sentences for Comprehending Score

Retelling Information

Grace loved stories - read to her - told by her Nana - likes to act them out - she was a - and a pirate - gets Ma & Nana to act out with her - teacher says they'll do play of Peter Pan - she wants to be P.P. - boy says she can't - she's a girl - Natalie says she can't b/c she is black. Nana takes her to see ballet - Knows she can be anything she wants to be - acts out being Juliet - gets to be P.P. - she liked to pretend and have imagination

Comments

Got main idea and gist of story - lots of details in sequence - lacked some detail on things Grace liked to act out - work on catching nonwords

Figure 7–2 Miscue Analysis Form, Claire's Procedure IV

Bringing It All Together: What Do We Learn from an OTS and Procedure IV?

LaMar, Josh, Ceci, and Claire are great teachers. They've shown us that reading is an active process of constructing personal meaning, not just *saying all the words* on the page. Through these procedures we've seen evidence that informs our teaching.

These readers helped us see that we need to discuss strategies to help them monitor understanding when we observe the following:

- A high number of miscues that change meaning
- A high number of miscues that change meaning at the same time we see a high number of miscues with little or no graphic similarity
- A number of uncorrected nonwords
- Few self-corrections
- Difficulty discussing what was read

These readers also helped us see:

- How readers use picture cues
- How delightful side comments tell us a reader is actively constructing meaning
- How we can assess reading using qualitative, numerical, and linguistic information
- How readers use an expressive voice to convey their understanding
- How well readers do at their selection of a book to read
- How readers are able to monitor their reading to make sure it sounds like language and makes sense
- How readers can make astute predictions and inferences from what they read
- How readers can make many types of connections between the text and their own lives, other texts, and their background knowledge
- How a reader uses strategies flexibly to decode print and construct meaning
- How readers' retellings and discussions provide evidence of their comprehension
- How we can interpret readers' actions based on the language cueing systems
- How we can engage in a teaching conversation to help readers become aware of what they're doing well and to do some clarification teaching
- How we can value readers' miscues as important information to us as teachers

Let's now turn our attention to how we can use these miscue analysis procedures in classrooms on a daily basis.

8

Now What?

Teachers are like artists as they construct classrooms that are innovative and conducive to learning. Artists bring to their work knowledge of perspective, color, line, form, space, and theme, as well as techniques implemented with a variety of tools. Outstanding teachers bring to reading instruction a strong knowledge base of language, learning, and teaching, and they know the cultural background and experiential differences of their students.

—Y. Goodman, Watson, and Burke (1996, vii)

Now that we can bring to our work knowledge about three miscue analysis procedures, we need to turn to the question of finding time in the busy school day to allow the insights they provide to become an integral part of our daily lives with students. Let's look closely at the following:

- One teacher's use of miscue analysis
- The foundational characteristics of an overall reading program
- The daily ebb and flow of a classroom's reading workshop
- The moment-to-moment conversational setting of reading conferences
- The evidence we have from conducting an Over the Shoulder (OTS) miscue analysis
- The ways miscue analysis informs our teaching
- The use of OTS with speakers of other languages
- The ways we can talk with parents about miscue analysis
- The ways miscue analysis helps readers be self-reflective

One Teacher's Practice

Miscue analysis is an essential part of the daily rhythm of Mary Diener's third-grade classroom (2001). She has taught her students to listen with "miscue ears" as their peers read, to mark miscues on a typescript, to ask the questions from Procedure III, and to conduct OTS miscue analysis.

When her students arrive in the morning, they do their "office work," which includes sharpening pencils, taking care of morning responsibilities, and getting their lunch tickets. Students then join her for an opening class meeting at which she provides time for "kid talk." This includes sharing everything from what happened last night at the soccer game to questioning news events around the corner or around the world. The rest of her morning is spent in "reader-writer workshop" (Serafini 2001; Atwell 1998; Allen and Gonzalez 1998; Hindley 1996; Hagerty 1992).

Three mornings a week, the workshop consists of students meeting in small groups for literature circles. Children are in groups of four to five students, each of whom has read the same book (Peterson and Eeds 1990). Two mornings a week, Mary uses this time to teach reading strategies in whole-group lessons, which she selects based on her observations during the literature circles (see Figure 8–1).

Early in the school year, Mary has all her students complete a Burke Reading Interview (see Appendix H) in writing (Y. Goodman, Watson, and Burke 1987). During the school year, she has them complete the interview four times, giving her valuable information over time about their understanding of the reading process, strategies good readers use, and themselves as readers. She uses these interviews to inform her teaching and to provide evidence for parents of children's development as readers.

"Fishbowl": Making Reading Visible

To teach her students how to conduct Procedure III, Mary uses a "fishbowl" setting during which someone volunteers to read in front of the class (Scherer 1997). Before Mary asks students to *be fishbowled*, she models this process many times with herself or the reading specialist as the reader. She shows students how to listen without interrupting the reader at every miscue, to recognize different types of miscues, to mark simple miscues on the typescript used for Procedure III, and to speculate on possible reasons for miscues. In a process parallel to teachers learning miscue analysis, young learners can develop miscue ears and analysis eyes to help them interpret what they hear when listening to another reader.

In Mary's room, there is a very strong sense of community, which she cultivates daily in her morning class meetings. She begins conducting the fishbowl sessions *after* she has created an environment in which students feel comfortable taking this huge risk as readers. She helps students get lots of practice receiving comments from others in a safe setting because Mary realizes "it takes a lot of courage for somebody to read out loud in front of twenty-one other children and have everybody marking them" (Diener 2001). Even in this supportive setting, there are usually a few students who opt out of reading in front of the whole class, which is fine. Generally, after students become more familiar with miscue analysis themselves and have the chance to observe other students in this setting, they come to understand its value, they learn to trust that their peers will be respectful and helpful, and they eventually volunteer.

For her fishbowl readings, Mary makes copies of the brief text the student is going to read so that each child in the class is able to read along with a reader. If the "fishbowler" is reading a picture book, Mary combines the brief text from each page and creates a one-page typescript for her students. For chapter books, she copies two or three pages and enlarges the image to provide space between the lines for marking miscues. There is a tape recorder running during the reading so that everyone can listen again while marking the typescript. While it is difficult for some students to be able to do the markings quickly, all students gain a new awareness of the miscues readers make. Because young readers usually do not read too fast, some students become adept at marking miscues along the way. For complex miscues, everyone listens to the tape as a group and makes a verbatim transcription in the margin of their typescript.

After the reader is finished and the group has listened to the tape enough to mark the miscues, remarkable conversations ensue. In a respectful manner, students and the teacher conduct a group inquiry with the reader into the reading that just occurred. The reader begins by sharing his own observations, then the students ask the reader questions; share their observations; and offer suggestions to the reader by combining ideas from previous strategy lessons, coming up with new strategies, or sharing what they've done themselves as readers.

As a follow-up to the reading and discussion, Mary invites students to compare themselves to the fishbowler. She uses questions such as What are some things she did well? Do you do those things too? How many of you think you're a good reader because you do this? In this way, Mary can see the strategies students value, and she can discern the students' awareness of their own actions as readers. She completes the experience by asking all students to write a positive note to the fishbowler. Sometimes she finds that the notes have to do with observations of reading strategies, and at other times the notes convey a message to the reader, such as You were so brave to sit up there and read that book with us. She loves the way this reading experience gives kids a way to shine at something; whereas "they may not be good at sports or drawing people, they are skillful readers" (Diener 2001). The fishbowl makes their capabilities visible and they can feel great about themselves as readers.

This fishbowl experience that Mary provides for her students has many of the characteristics of the Retrospective Miscue Analysis (RMA) (Y. Goodman and Marek, 1996). The purpose of the fishbowl process is to revalue the reader, point out what he is doing well, examine individual miscues, talk about why he may have made them, discuss his comprehension, and suggest strategies that will move him forward as a reader. The reading and conversations after a fishbowl not only provide assessment data, but they also inform Mary's choice of strategy lessons to teach to the whole group.

"A Talking Tool": A Shared Inquiry into Reading

In addition to teaching students how to conduct Procedure III, Mary does many demonstrations of OTS as well. She finds "teaching kids to do OTS is really easy!" She invites the reading specialist to be the reader, and in a fishbowl situation, Mary shows the miscue page on an overhead transparency, explains the

	Monday	Tuesday	Wednesday	Thursday	Friday
READING WORKSHOP	Office Work				
	Opening Class Meeting				
	Literature Study **IN GROUPS** • Responding to and reflecting on a text • Sharing a significant passage • Mary conducts OTS with a few students **IN PAIRS** • Buddy reading • Conducting OTS with a peer **INDIVIDUALLY** • Reading silently for next meeting • Writing in a reflection journal • Creating an artistic response • Mary conferences with students with whom she did OTS	Whole-Group Lessons Strategies	Literature Study	Whole-Group Lessons Fishbowl	Literature Study
	Closing Class Meeting				

FIGURE 8–1 Mary Diener's Morning Schedule

purpose of each column, and demonstrates how she makes notes during the reading. She talks through her thinking and decision-making process as she works, and after the adult is finished, Mary goes back through the form to debrief the reading and discuss her notes. She invites students to help her decide about meaning change and graphic similarity. She finds her students can enter into "some heated discussions about whether the miscue changes meaning . . . when they really believe something, they don't want to give it up . . . and they have a great justification for it." Sometimes she and her students simply have to agree to disagree. She recalls similar discussions in our university class when she learned how to conduct miscue analysis!

Sometimes Mary is amazed at how long these discussions with her third graders can continue, as OTS becomes a "talking tool" and students thoughtfully examine each miscue they observe. Because they have learned and practiced Procedure III first, they think about information from the language cueing systems and are therefore able to consider possible reasons why the reader made the miscues. For example, when discussing Tess's miscue house/horse, Beth offered, I think you might have made that miscue because it has high graphic similarity. Mary tells her students that through such discussions and investigations of their peers' reading, they're being researchers, which they think is "so cool." This kind of dialogue is part of her process of building community and developing a sense of trust between herself and the students, and also between peers. Mary models this process many times, which she and her students call their "practices," to ensure that they understand how and why we do an OTS.

Although some students are a bit reluctant to try at first, Mary wants all her third graders to learn how to conduct an OTS. She offers several options to help students become comfortable with the process before doing one with a peer. She invites students to conduct an OTS with her or the reading specialist as the reader, or to do one at home with a parent or sibling. She finds that usually after several times in a different setting, students are ready to try an OTS at school with a peer. As with every engagement we offer students, there will be differing levels of proficiency. Some students at this age are still developing the metacognitive and fine-motor writing skills needed for these tasks. Often young students are more capable of talking about their observations than they are of writing them down.

"No Secrets": OTS in Practice

After several whole-group introductions to the process, language, and forms for the OTS miscue analysis, Mary conducts sessions with individual students during literature circles. Her students know what she's listening for and what her notes mean. In a literature circle, students first have a period of responding to and reflecting on the text read that day. Then Mary invites students to share a passage from the book that they "really found significant." Students may read a few sentences or a few paragraphs aloud, and if a student tells her he's going to read several paragraphs, Mary will choose to conduct an OTS with him rather than with a student who is only going to read a few lines.

Mary is sensitive to the students' comfort level in this setting, and to diminish their nervousness as much as possible, she does her best to create a caring, trusting community; to completely explain what she'll be doing; and to consistently share her observations with students. She tries to keep them as comfortable as possible because she believes "when kids get nervous like that, then I don't think it makes their miscues 'authentic'" (Diener 2001).

Mary also helps students feel at ease with the OTS process by teaching them the language of miscue analysis. They say *miscue* rather than *mistake* or *error* and understand that it means they've said something different from the text. They know that high-quality miscues don't change the meaning, and they know they'll always have the opportunity to revisit the text they just read and discuss what they did as a reader. They understand there will be no secrets kept from them. What the teacher knows, she'll share with them. Most important, they realize the focus of the OTS session is *not on the list of miscues,* but on how the *patterns of those miscues* and the discussion during the conference *provide evidence of their skills* as readers and whether they understood what they read.

When Mary meets with her students, she first discusses the things they're doing well as readers, then offers suggestions for strategies they need to work on. She asks them, Now that we know this about you as a reader, what would you like to do about this? These OTS conferences give students ownership of their learning and the opportunity to say, I think *this* is important to discuss about my reading. This is the problem-posing opportunity we want to keep at the heart of our teaching conversation (Short et al. 1996; Short and Harste, with Burke 1996). Helping students understand the *nature of the reading process* is our starting point in teaching them how to do miscue analysis.

After the discussion and reading time in literature circle, the students disperse to work on their reading for the next meeting, to write a reflection in their literature journal, or to create an artistic response project. During this time, Mary holds individual conferences to share the OTS forms with the students who just read aloud with her, "so they're not in front of two or three of their peers to hear all that [discussion and feedback]." Later in the year, Mary moves to conducting the OTS with longer passages after students become more comfortable with the process. She feels these early sessions, using brief texts, give her a lot of information about each student as a reader and a baseline to work from in planning her instruction.

Mary also "loves" conducting OTS conferences during the content-area inquiry workshop in the afternoon. Usually her students are reading nonfiction books during this time, and she finds they often use different strategies and "a totally different vocabulary." She can then compare a student's OTS form from reading a narrative text to one completed when the student was reading an expository text. Mary finds some students are better readers when reading nonfiction, and some are more comfortable when reading fiction.

Change over Time: OTS Recordkeeping

Mary's recordkeeping for the students' miscue analysis consists of a file folder for each student that she keeps out on a table, accessible to all. She and the students both make additions to the folder: she saves all the OTS forms and anecdotal records from the teaching conversations; the students go through their OTS forms frequently, looking back over time to see how they have changed as readers. They write comments about their observations on sticky notes and put them on their forms. Parents, students, and the teacher can discuss these forms and the students' comments during conferences. Every nine weeks or so, she and the students fill out the Holistic Evaluation of the Reader form (see Appendix L) to summarize the information from the individual OTS forms; these completed forms are also shared during conferences.

To keep track of the students with whom she has conducted an OTS, Mary maintains a chart with students' names down one side and columns for the date across the top. Each time she reads with a student, she puts a check mark in the corresponding box. When all the students have worked with her in an OTS session, she draws a bold vertical line and begins going through the list again. This system ensures that she sees each student in an individual reading conference before she begins a new cycle. Usually it takes two to three weeks to conduct a reading conference and OTS with each student in the class.

How Can I Use Miscue Analysis Every Day?

The best reading assessments we can use are ongoing and embedded in our teaching (Bridges 1995; Routman 2000). Over the Shoulder miscue analysis is one such assessment. To use miscue analysis every day, we develop an overall reading program, establish organizational structures like reading workshop (Kaufman 2001), and conduct individual reading conferences (Routman 2000; Calkins 2001). Each of these is described in the following sections (see Figure 8–2).

The Global Context: An Informed Reading Program

Mary carefully considers her decisions about ways to use miscue analysis throughout the day and thoughtfully examines the choices she makes as she plans learning and teaching experiences for readers. She looks critically at questions such as What materials will I use? What are my guidelines for the quality and quantity of books I will make available? How do I choose the invitations I'll offer to readers? What do I accept as evidence for readers' successes? How do I thoughtfully select the assessments to use? What criteria do I use when selecting strategies to model?

When designing literacy engagements for learners, we develop lessons with clear goals in mind, consider the lives and background experiences of students, take personal interests into account, and accept certain mandates. I think teaching is a continual process of finding a balance between what we have to do and what we choose to do, based on what we believe is best for our learners.

The choice to use taped or untaped miscue analysis procedures as a means of assessing readers takes place within the context of other decisions. We can choose to frame our philosophy of teaching with knowledge about linguistics, language development, and the active nature of the reading process. We can choose to create an informed reading program that includes the following characteristics:

- Literacy learning engagements generated by students' needs, not prepackaged.
- Books that are relevant to students' lives, interests, and cultures.
- Literacy experiences with foundations in authentic social settings.
- Strategies modeled for students through think-alouds.
- Instruction focused on meaning-based reading strategies.
- Phonics taught in the context of authentic texts.
- Students have access to a variety of literature and informational texts
- Students read and respond to excellent literature.
- Ongoing assessment.
- A literacy learning partnership with families.
- Literacy learning engagements based on what we know about language development and how language works.

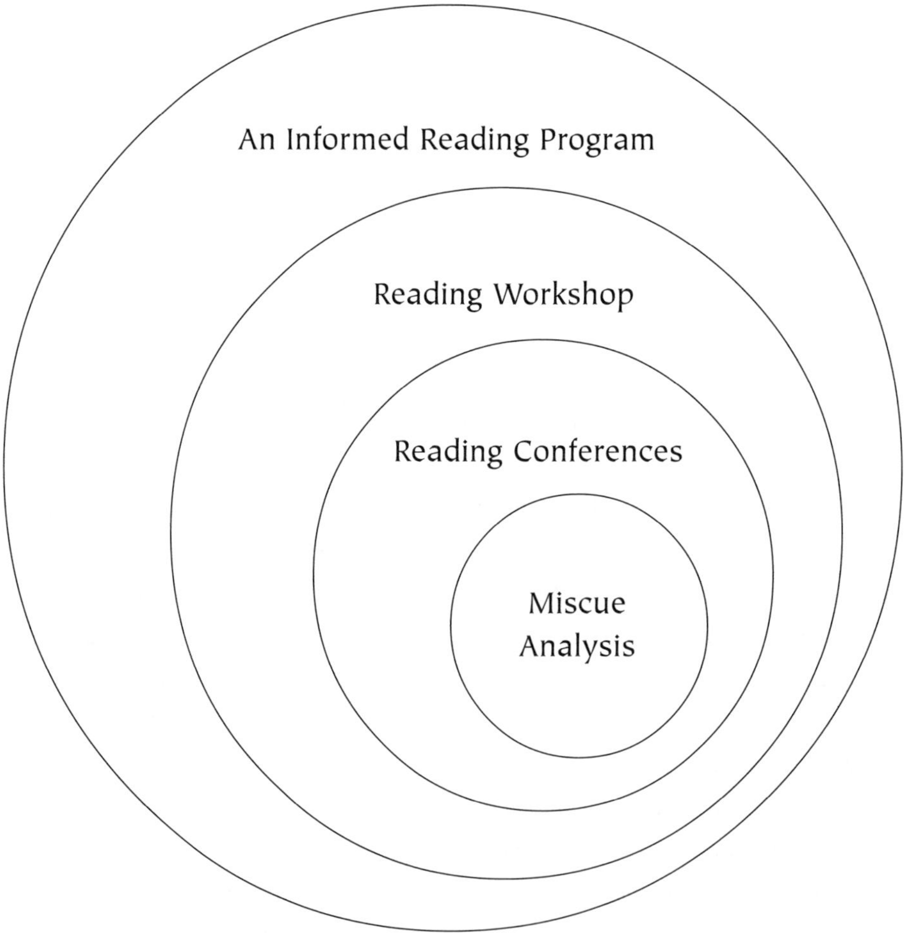

FIGURE 8–2 An Informed Reading Program

Literacy Learning Engagements Generated by Students' Needs, Not Prepackaged

Once we clarify goals for learners, we can design a reading program that will help students meet those objectives while reading authentic literature. We do not need to succumb to basal programs or computer-based reading programs that bribe kids with points, tell students what books to read, and tell teachers what students should think about them when they're done. If we find ourselves in a school district that requires us to use such programs, we must also offer learners a rich array of literature and literacy experiences. We should take ownership of our teaching and let the reading program emerge from our best judgment, trust in great books, knowledge of research, familiarity with best practice, and faith in learners as language users.

Books That Are Relevant to Students' Lives, Interests, and Cultures

Publishers in New York City or San Diego don't have a clue about the background experiences of Jacque Barthel-Hines' students in eastern Oregon, the interests of Mary Diener's students in central Illinois, the inquiry questions of Lynne Warren's kids in western Colorado, or the passions of Bob Shaw's third graders in southern Missouri. Each group of learners is unique. Each individual brings to the classroom community a different dialect or home language, hopes, dreams, interests, dislikes, talents, and hobbies. There is no one literacy curriculum that is going to meet all their needs. We provide a wide variety of relevant texts for students and generate our reading program based on the people they are and the learners they can be.

Literacy Experiences with Foundations in Authentic Social Settings

Every time we ask students to engage in reading, writing, speaking, or listening, we should ask ourselves, Is this something I would see someone do in the world outside the classroom? Would someone read a book and talk about it with others? Would someone create a play to teach youngsters about fire safety? Would someone underline nouns once and verbs twice? Would someone offer suggestions to a poet on her latest draft? Would someone write a thank-you note to a visitor who shared his expertise on insects? If we cannot honestly answer *Yes* to this type of question, we need to reflect critically on our actions as teachers of literacy.

Strategies Modeled for Students Through Think-Alouds

If we want students to do something, we need to show them how. When we want students to be strategic readers, we need to let them in on the workings of a mature learner's mind as he struggles with a difficult text (Davey 1983; Harvey and Goudvis 2000; Wilhelm 2001). We need to let them see that literacy does not spring forth, fully formed, in the mind of an adult. Nor does it leap from the pages of a basal reader or emerge from stacks of inane worksheets. Literacy blossoms slowly, over time, in fits and starts, through successes and approximations, with delight and triumph, resulting in a new power to interact with and make sense of the world.

Teachers come to literacy instruction with a vision of unlimited possibilities for learners' engagements as readers and writers, not a blind adherence to a packaged program in which someone else has selected the literature and made the teaching decisions for them. Teachers let kids in on their thinking as they try, plan, explore, stumble, question, and succeed as readers of the word and of the world. Teachers take the best of what they know about learners and the learning process and provide instruction in literacy strategies that propel learners forward to joy and independence.

Instruction Focused on Meaning-Based Reading Strategies

An informed reading program offers students strategies that keep them focused on making meaning. If students don't understand reading as the construction of meaning, we're not doing our job. How do we know how they define reading? We ask them. We discuss our actions as readers and post an ongoing list of strategies good readers use, which is generated from the students' ideas. How do we let them know how readers go about actively constructing meaning? We show them through our repeated modeling and think-alouds (Davey 1983). Wilhelm (2001) and Harvey and Goudvis (2000) offer clear examples of comprehension strategies that get students actively involved in thinking about, directing, and reflecting on their construction of meaning during reading.

Phonics Taught in the Context of Authentic Text

All readers need phonics (except perhaps students who are deaf). The graphophonic cueing system is made up of the complex relationships between what we see in written texts and what we hear in spoken language. As one of the language cueing systems, it is one of the reader's vital tools that is needed to make sense of what is being read. The critical issue is how we choose to teach phonics, and in an informed reading program, this is done within the context of authentic language such as stories, poems, songs, and rhymes (Dahl et al. 2001). We use the best of what we know from recent onset-rime research (Moustafa 1997) to convey ways to use their knowledge of graphophonics to assist students when reading.

To teach symbol–sound relationships within the context of authentic literature, we do not have to (and should not!) fragment language to the point that it becomes nonsense. We're not teaching helpful strategies for reading when that happens—we're teaching nonsense. Rather than show kids what reading is *not* ("sounding out all the words"), let's be committed to showing them that it *is*—constructing meaning through a personal transaction with text.

Student Access to a Variety of Literature and Informational Texts

For real estate, they say the three most important considerations are location, location, location. For literacy learning it is *access, access, access!* Studies have shown that literacy learners need access, at home and at school, to individuals who will read to them, read with them, and listen to them read. They need interested literacy mentors who will nurture their developing abilities as readers, writers, and thinkers, and they need to have many great books available in a variety of genres and levels of difficulty (McQuillan 1998; Harvey and Goudvis 2000; Allington 2000).

But which are the great books and where to we get them? Teachers can learn about new books for children and adolescents through publications such as Trelease's *Read Aloud Handbook* (2001) and the *Adventuring with Books* series from NCTE (e.g., Pierce 2000). Also, professional journals, such as *Reading Teacher,* regularly offer reviews of new children's books (e.g., Giorgis and Johnson 2001). Teachers can stock their classroom libraries by visiting auctions, garage sales, second-hand stores, and library sales; by using bonus points from their students' book club orders; and by inviting book donations from families in their children's names to honor birthdays. Our goal is to make available a multitude of great books, from a variety of genre and difficulty levels. Sometimes we have to be creative in achieving that goal.

Your classroom library can be a place for your students to find a new home as they become joyful readers, but only if they know their way around. In my multiage classroom, I let students organize the classroom library and determine how books should be grouped (e.g., author, genre, subject, level of difficulty). They quickly became familiar with the selections and knew where they could find the bin that held the text they were seeking. I also brought a few books at a time at the beginning of the school year so that students would not be overwhelmed at the number of choices. As I gradually added new books to our collection, I introduced them in the opening circle of reading workshop by selecting one and either reading the book to the class, reading parts of it, or leafing through it with the students. The students helped me decide where the book should be located in our library, and we labeled it accordingly.

Students Read and Respond to Excellent Literature

There is a critical link between classroom practices, the theories on which the practices are based, and the beliefs we hold about all we do with learners. If we have made the shift in our understanding of reading from "By saying all the words, the reader's job is to 'go get' the meaning, which is lying on the page" to "Through a transaction with text, meaning is personally constructed by the reader within a social context," then our practices will reflect this change. Rather than asking literal-level questions after reading a story in a basal anthology, we ask a student to respond as an individual, with her own opinions and interpretations of quality literature. We offer students interesting texts that have "something there to talk about" (Watson 2001). We ask students to respond to group members' insights as they reflect in a "grand conversation" about books they've read together (Peterson and Eeds 1990).

Teachers need to trust that great books have an infinite number of insights to enrich our lives. We read stories to reflect on the human experience, to relate to characters who solve real problems, to give our lives patterns and continuity, to allow us to impose order on random events, to learn in a meaningful context, and to share a common reference (Lauritzen and Jaeger 1997). Teachers need to believe that kids have important things to say about the books they read. They don't need to be assigned roles, or given jobs when meeting in literature study groups any more than we do. In an adult book club, who would dream of saying Today it's your job to share with the group some beautiful language that you read. Of course we're going to be doing that during our discussion, but we will do so in a natural, authentic manner, not because it was assigned to us (Serafini 2001).

Ongoing Assessment

For many years we have been aware of the value of being great "kidwatchers" (Y. Goodman 1985). To know our students well, we realize our best assessments are not separate from our teaching. They are ongoing and continuous. We place value on a teacher's knowledge and judgments; and we honor the awareness of students' abilities we gain by watching, not necessarily by testing (Rhodes and Shanklin 1993; Bridges 1995).

A Literacy Learning Partnership with Families

Many times the culture of the school differs from the students' home culture. If we can keep the door open and make students' family members feel welcome at school, a powerful partnership, which honors the students' literacy learning in each setting, can be formed (Freeman and Freeman 2000). We want to be sensitive to varied cultural literacies and how they impact students' views of what it means to be literate; we need to become aware of parents' perceptions of their role in helping with literacy learning; we can share with families our philosophy of teaching and learning; and we can help them understand what is being taught, the ways it is being taught, and how they can support literacy learning at home (Bialostok 1992; Taylor 1998).

Literacy Learning Engagements Based on What We Know About Language Development and How Language Works

If we see reading as a language process, we draw on the best of what is known about how young children acquire literacy and how we can provide the best environment for literacy learning (Cambourne 1988; Davenport and Eckberg 2001). When children come to school, they are already proficient language users. If we observe them carefully as they learn to read, we can support what they already know about how language works.

The Daily Context: Reading Workshop

The framework that seems to work best in providing the time to listen to and converse with each reader individually is a reading workshop (Butler and Turbill

1984; Hindley 1996; Serafini 2001). We give students extended periods of time for reading and provide strategies to help them be reflective about what they have read. As Harvey and Goudvis state: "Strategic reading takes hold in classrooms that value student thinking. . . . The reading workshop promotes thinking when reading" (2000, 29).

The following scheduling structure allows us to create an environment in which:

- We get readers to engage in reading a variety of texts for extended periods of time.
- We provide instruction in reading strategies for the whole group, for small groups, and for individuals.
- We invite students to read deeply and to read widely.
- We immerse readers in a wide range of genres, looking closely at authors, illustrators, and the literary craft.
- We gather assessment information as students read authentic texts.
- We invite students to talk about literature.
- We facilitate students' engagements in art, music, dance, and drama as ways of knowing and responding to their reading.

Depending on the age of students, workshops can last from thirty to ninety minutes. I have always thought of a workshop in my classroom as a cycle, whether it was writing workshop, inquiry workshop, or math workshop. Each one had a similar structure that consisted of an opening circle, a working time, and a reflection circle.

This pulling students together, nudging them out to working time, and pulling them together again for circle time created an ebb and flow—a rhythmic pulse to our day that students looked forward to and enjoyed. In reading workshop, they knew they could count on the working time to just be readers and they could rely on frequent conversations with the teacher. The sections that follow describe what a reading workshop might look like.

Opening Circle

Workshops begin when the teacher brings the students together in circle for about ten to fifteen minutes. We establish ways of conducting the opening and closing reading workshop circles by talking with students in class meetings (Developmental Studies Center 1996). I found there is a big difference between having children sit at your feet in a cluster and having them *really sit in a circle.*

A few years ago I worked with a group of Illinois second graders who had never before had the chance to sit in a circle. I was modeling how to conduct a reading workshop for their teacher, so I had the students stand in a circle holding hands, then drop their hands and sit down. There was an audible gasp of delight as, for the first time, they looked all their classmates in the eye. One boy exclaimed, Dr. D.! It's like we're all on the front row! These students were no longer vying for the teacher's attention—they had eye contact with everyone, they felt like valued members of a learning community, and they were not as likely to misbehave because of the increased visibility.

In the opening circle, the teacher uses a shared book or big book to give a brief lesson on some aspect of the reading process, a comprehension strategy, or a word-analysis technique. He may read a story and do a think-aloud procedure (Davey 1983), or "report out" as he is reading (Wilhelm 2001), to let kids in on his own thinking about the text and introduce the strategies good readers use. A teacher might also use a think-aloud to highlight the style of a particular author, or consider a favorite illustrator's technique. He provides support for readers in bringing the nature of the reading process to the conscious level. He gradually introduces a variety of reading strategies, starting with a few options, then increasing the repertoire as students become effective users of the strategies they know. There is a recursive quality to teaching reading strategies: Old favorites are revisited and discussed after new ones are introduced.

To end the opening circle, the teacher invites the students to think about what they will do during their working time. He asks them to make a plan for how they will spend their time today, and jots these ideas down on a class list. This process is similar to Atwell's idea of taking the "status of the class" in a writing workshop (1998). In order to make their plan, he asks students to consider one or more of the following:

- Their current work in the literature study group
- The current spot in a book they're reading individually
- Their current efforts on a book-related project
- A partner with whom they'd like to share a book during buddy reading
- Their current work on a selection of writing related to a book
- A reading strategy the teacher has demonstrated through a think-aloud procedure

Working Time

After the students have made a plan for how they'll use their working time, they are dismissed from circle. At the beginning of the school year, this part of reading workshop lasts from fifteen to twenty minutes and increases to longer periods of time, based on what students can comfortably handle. By the end of the year, my seven-, eight- and nine-year old students stayed engaged during their working time for sixty minutes and begged for more. I've found students are capable of sustained attention to focused work and reading for longer periods of time than we usually think they can.

During the working time, the teacher can be doing several things. I generally began by reading on my own for a few minutes, which showed students that I valued reading too. While I might occasionally need to walk around the room between conferences to help students refocus, I spent most of the working time dividing my time among the following activities:

- Meeting with Guided Reading groups—flexible instructional groups
- Participating in literature circles—flexible response groups
- Holding reading conferences and conducting OTS miscue analysis

During the working time the students may be:

- Reading silently by themselves in a self-selected text from any genre
- Reading quietly with a partner and talking about what they're reading
- Meeting in literature circles
- Preparing for the next literature circle, reading or rereading the next passage
- Writing in response to literature
- Engaging in an extension activity, such as art, drama, music, or writing that helps students revisit the text and consider new interpretations
- Meeting with the teacher for a reading conference

The working time allows students to be engaged in meaningful reading and writing while the teacher is reading with one student, or working with a small group of students (Cambourne 2001). Through teacher modeling and open discussions in circle (Developmental Studies Center 1996), students learn how to use their time appropriately; they become aware of the purposes of the lessons, the working time, and teacher conferences; they become empowered learners and readers as they come to see reading as a process of making meaning; and they come to understand the different strategies that help them improve as readers.

Reflection Circle

After working time, the teacher brings the students back together. This closing circle lasts about fifteen to twenty minutes and gives the teacher and students time to talk about what just took place during the working time. They may discuss their reading strategies, their miscues, the books they read, illustrations they enjoyed, and/or their behavior. Our question to ourselves and students at this time is How did it go? This may also be a time for another strategy lesson or a read-aloud.

Workshops and individual reading conferences will be most successful when you have negotiated with your students guidelines for the following:

- Conducting themselves respectfully during reading workshop
- Maintaining the negotiated logistics and time frames
- Using materials as demonstrated
- Respecting each other's space

- Finding an appropriate place to be
- Engaging in tasks, such as literature study, independent work, paired reading
- Practicing the strategies used by good readers

The reading workshop procedure is summarized in Figure 8–3.

The Conversational Context: The Reading Conference

Each day I designated two to four students with whom I'd like to meet individually during the working time. Similar to Mary Diener's recordkeeping method, I kept an ongoing class list so that I was sure to meet with each student for a reading conference. I usually could see each student in the class at least once during a two- to three-week period. I wrote the names of the students I would be calling for a conference on the board.

Once the big group of students was settled with their individual, buddy, or small-group work, I was able to go to my conferencing corner and begin reading with students one at a time. This is where the magic happens.

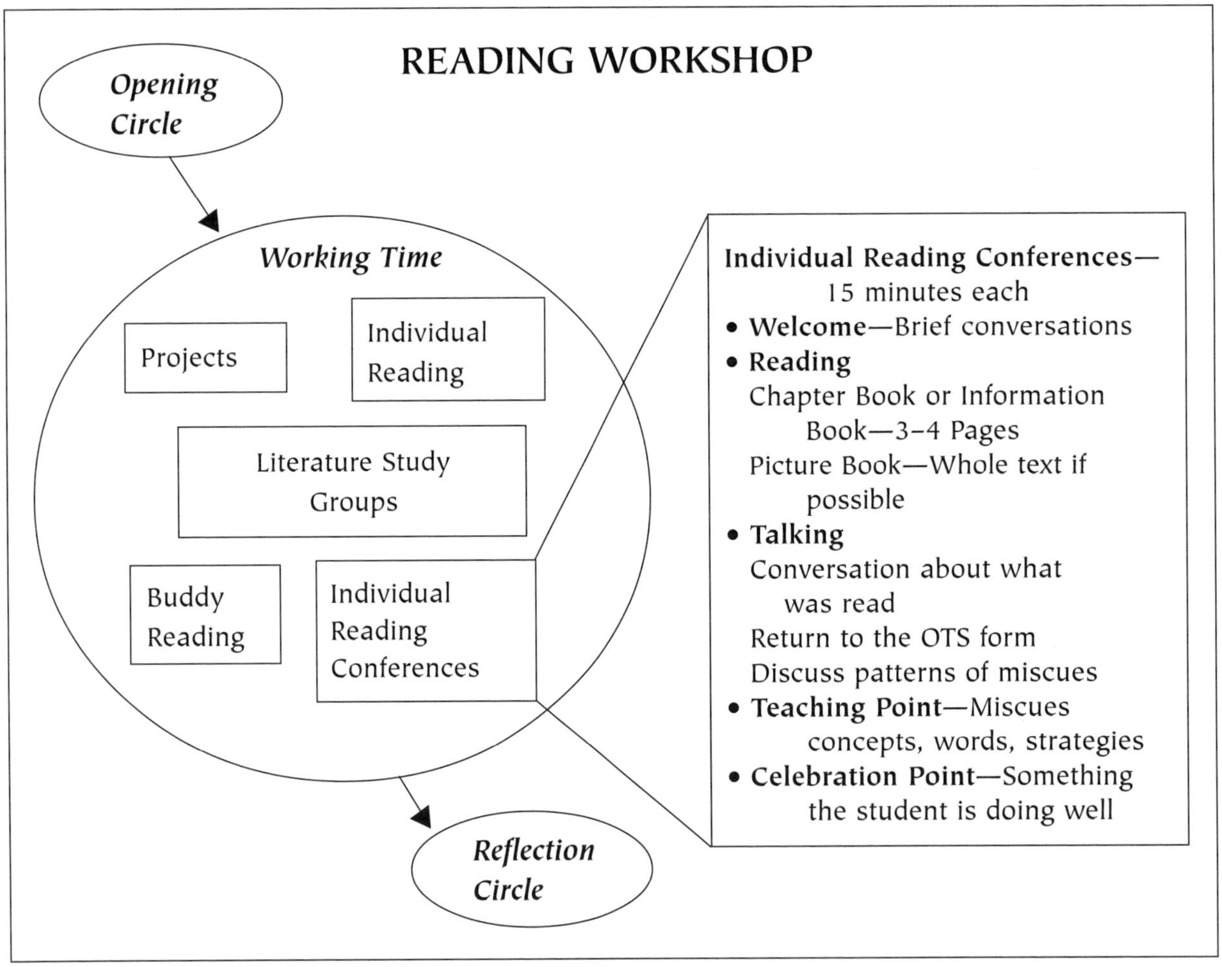

FIGURE 8–3 Reading Workshop

Even though these meetings with each student are brief, they are powerful exchanges between two learners. After observing me work with one of her students in a reading conference, fifth-grade teacher Jacque Barthel-Hines said: "I was surprised by how much you got done in such a short time" (2001). From these conversations I learn so much about how reading works and how kids think. Students also learn a great deal about what makes them tick as readers and what they're doing well. The reading conferences last approximately fifteen minutes each and consist of the elements described in the next sections.

Welcome

This is a moment of brief conversation to welcome the student to the conference, and in general, to see how things are going. The teacher asks what book she brought to read, and if it's a chapter book, she might bring the teacher up to date on what's been going on since their last meeting. During this conversation, the teacher makes notes about the reader's text on the OTS cover page.

Reading

The amount of text read during the conference depends on the age and ability level of the student. If he is an emergent reader or early reader, he may read an entire picture book. If reading a chapter book or information book, the student may read three or four pages. During this time, the teacher writes down information about the students, his miscues, and the book on the miscue page.

Talking

After the reading, the teaching conversation begins. This is an informal discussion about what was read that usually begins with the teacher's invitation: Let's talk about what you just read. The conversation may include a combination of sharing personal responses, asking questions, retelling detail, summarizing, or synthesizing (Harvey and Goudvis 2000). After the exchange about the story, the teacher takes the student back to the miscue page to discuss patterns of miscues and strategies observed.

As discussed earlier, I have been thinking a lot about the kinds of retellings we are looking for in the reading conference. Mary Diener and I discovered that we have had similar struggles with some of the same dilemmas regarding formal retellings that use a retelling guide like the one used in Procedure III. She has also moved to a more informal discussion format, inviting students to talk about your reading. Not only is she getting a better picture of what the student understood, remembered, and valued, she is modeling the kind of talk we'd like to hear in literature circles. She finds these discussions "a great way to model that type of conversation" and observes her students beginning to talk about their reading in a similar manner when working in pairs or small groups without her (Diener 2001).

Teaching Point

I usually choose one or two teaching points that allow the student to reexamine her reading (Routman 2000). We may go back to the text to explore and discuss particular miscues, concepts, words, or comprehension strategies. I remind her that the miscue page provides us evidence of her actions as a reader, and is not a list of her "mistakes."

Celebration Point

I keep the tone positive for these brief reading conferences and make a point to end by celebrating something the student is doing well. For more details on reading conferences, see Chapter 6.

"Doin' Workshop": A Culture of Reading

Many students may not have had the opportunity to participate in a reading workshop. They'll need a little help getting the feel of a functioning workshop, as the stance of the learner is very different. They may not have been invited to make personal choices about books, to talk with peers about what they're reading, to work independently, or to observe the teacher revealing her thinking while she engages in various reading strategies.

One of the foundational ideas that guides the way we set up and conduct a reading workshop comes from Bloome, who suggests reading "is a social process—a means to participate in and establish a community or social group" (1987, 123). Reading involves social relationships among teachers and students that include ways of interacting; gaining social status; and acquiring culturally accepted ways of thinking, solving problems, and feeling. "Reading and writing are viewed as manifestations and reflections of the culture in which the children's day-to-day activities are embedded" (Bloome 1987, 124); that is, a student comes to understand what he reads in ways that are appropriate within the culture of his own classroom. This social process of defining and practicing reading will influence the ways he interacts with and interprets various texts.

As teachers, we need to consider the messages we send to students about reading within the cultural context of our classrooms. Particularly, Bloome (1985, 1987) believes we need to be aware of "what counts as reading" within our classrooms. For example, do students just see "reading" as an activity we do in school, during a basal reading lesson, or to prepare for a literature discussion? Or do students see all engagements with text as reading, regardless of what genre they are reading or where the reading takes place? As we establish guidelines and expectations for "doin' workshop," we are facilitating the social and cultural processes of reading. Together, students and teachers define what are acceptable behaviors whether reading alone, with a partner, or in a small group. We are establishing the culture of reading in our classrooms when we help students understand the reading engagements in which they can participate, the acceptable ways to conduct each activity, and the expectations for how we will respect each other during the workshop.

Teaching conversations can lead students to a new definition of reading as the construction of meaning, and they may also lead to changes in their self-concept as readers. Suzi Dixon found that one of her first graders, who thought he was a "perfect" reader, at first didn't want to talk about the OTS form or examine his miscues. He interpreted the miscue page as a list of everything he had done "wrong," so Suzi continued talking with him about the meaning of the columns on the miscue page. She discussed his strengths as a reader and showed him the patterns of miscues she observed.

A few weeks later, this same student asked her in the middle of a conference, Do you have enough written down [on the miscue page] so we can see my patterns now? Over time, he came to trust that Suzi was interested in what he was doing "right," and he realized that she was going to share with him everything she knew about him as a reader. He also saw that while he was doing many things well as a reader, there were still areas in which he could improve (Dixon 2001).

First-/second-grade teacher Angie Arriola heard similar comments when beginning to use the OTS with her students, and she saw the need for the same kind of sensitivity to students' perspectives. She observed "it's a trust thing"; that is, students need to come to trust that we are not writing down what they're doing "wrong," but we are observing their overall reading process through the lens of individual miscues (Arriola 2001).

Maybe this is one of the values of using the OTS: We put students into a little bit of cognitive dissonance so that they can reconsider some personal views and tacit understandings about the reading process. If the student sees herself differently as a reader (I'm making miscues that don't change meaning, I'm self-correcting miscues, I'm using these strategies . . . , which are things that good readers do), then she starts to see reading differently (Reading doesn't mean reading fast or saying all the words on the page—it means making sense and those things I'm doing show that I'm making sense when I read). The end result is the OTS procedure allows students to rethink the reading process and themselves as readers, and it refocuses the teachers' listening on what kids are doing well as readers.

What Is My Evidence from OTS Miscue Analysis and How Does It Inform My Teaching?

Once we develop "miscue ears" and have a new appreciation for the complexity of the reading process, we hear self-corrections we never noticed before, nonwords we weren't aware of, and uncorrected miscues that maintain meaning; and we have a new "lens" through which to know readers. We even know things at a tacit level about our readers that we never write down. As shown in Figure 8–4, there is a variety of documentation from the three miscue analysis procedures we've examined.

	PROCEDURE III	OVER THE SHOULDER	PROCEDURE IV
Documentation	• Typescript markings • Sentence codings • Graphic similarity • Retelling guide • Reader profile	• Cover page—scribing retelling • Miscue pages • Insights page	• Procedure IV form
Qualitative Information	• Concern for making meaning • Ability to use strategies independently • Ability to draw on appropriate background • Fluency • Affect	• Concern for making meaning • Ability to use strategies independently • Ability to draw on appropriate background • Fluency • Affect • Book choice • General sense of comprehension	• Concern for making meaning • Ability to use strategies independently • Ability to draw on appropriate background • Fluency • Affect • Book choice • General sense of comprehension
Quantitative Information	• Comprehending score (in process) • Comprehension score • Percentage of syntactic and semantic acceptability • Percentage of meaning change • Percentage of graphic similarity • Percentage of miscues that were self-corrected • Percentage of miscues uncorrected with no meaning change • Percentage of miscues uncorrected with a meaning change	• Percentage of self-corrections • Percentage of High, Some or No graphic similarity • Percentage of uncorrected miscues with no meaning change (high-quality miscues) • Percentage of uncorrected miscues with a meaning change	• Number of sentences that are semantically acceptable • Number of sentences that are not semantically acceptable • Percentage of comprehending score
Linguistic Information	• Use of all cueing systems	• Use of all cueing systems	• Direct: Use of semantic cueing system • Informal: Use of syntactic and graphophonic cueing systems

FIGURE 8–4 Information Gained from Three Different Miscue Analysis Procedures

higher anxiety

Let's closely examine the evidence we gain from the OTS and how we move from this documentation of readers' actions to our instruction. There are several sources within the reading conference and the OTS procedure from which we draw information to guide our teaching. By examining the evidence we gather from OTS sessions and teaching conversations, we can select strategies for individual or whole-group lessons that our students need right now (Y. Goodman, Watson, and Burke 1996; Harvey and Goudvis 2000; Hoyt 2000). These lessons can offer metalinguistic support by helping students take on the vocabulary they need to talk about language and themselves as readers, or the lessons can highlight a particular strategy and make visible what good readers do. From the reading conference, the OTS form, and the teaching conversation, the sources of assessment evidence include: the reading, the patterns of miscues, the talking, and the insights.

The Reading

One of the first observations I can make about a student when he comes to a reading conference is his *book choice*. I ask myself questions such as: Has he selected a text that is understandable? Is this interesting to him and conceptually within his grasp? Does he return to a favorite author? Does he take a risk and try new genres? Often students choose a book solely because someone they admire has read it, but it exceeds their current range as a reader. Here is an opportunity to talk with students about book selection (Fountas and Pinnell 1999; Peterson 2001). Another thing I am watching for is the student's *affect*—Is reading a chore? Is it something he seems to enjoy? The answers to these questions are dependent on the match between the reader, his abilities, and the book he chooses.

The flow of the reading, or *fluency*, is also dependent on these factors. We want to help students find books that allow them to read "easily and smoothly, and with expression when reading aloud. When students read fluently, aloud or silently, the reading appears automatic and effortless" (Routman 2000, 128). But as Routman reminds us, some miscues are made when reading aloud because students feel self-conscious and act like they are *performing*. Within the reading conference and within the learning community as a whole, the goal is to keep this anxiety to a minimum.

Students who lack fluency may have selected a book that is too difficult, they may be overfocusing on accuracy, or they may perceive the reading process as one of saying all the words rather than constructing meaning. We can help students develop fluency by allowing them to repeatedly reread books with which they are very comfortable. They can take these familiar books and make up puppet shows, conduct a Readers' Theatre, or read books to younger students to build their confidence and develop a flow to their reading.

One of the most important observations I can make about a student during the reading is her ability to *use strategies independently*. My evidence for lacking this

Reader Said	Text Said	Self - Corrected	Uncorrected - No Meaning Change	Uncorrected - With Meaning Change	Graphic Similarity High	Graphic Similarity Some	Graphic Similarity None	Self-Corrected During Conversation
Be-	Beside	✓				—		
s-	sadly	✓				—		
un-	unicorn	✓				—		
trav-	traversed	✓				—		

FIGURE 8–5 Corrected Partials

ability is when a student gets "roadblocked." Does the student come to an unfamiliar word and just shut down, or is she able to use a strategy that will help her through a difficult passage? Is she able to use a naming strategy on a difficult name, or does she sit there and stare at the name until I intercede? Does she have at her fingertips the ability to skip a difficult word, read to the end of the sentence, then speculate on what word might make sense there? Does she use chunking strategies, looking inside the unfamiliar word for smaller words, prefixes, or suffixes she knows? Is she able to flexibly use a variety of strategies, or does she rely solely on "sounding out"? The goal is to help students develop the ability to be volitional and strategic readers.

The Patterns of Miscues

When looking at the miscue page, I tell folks: Hold the sheet out away from you and squint! What *patterns* emerge? The evidence we are looking for here comes from the column totals and the percentage of the total number of miscues they represent in this instance of reading. If I see a high number of *self-corrections*, I first pay attention to what kinds of miscues were corrected. If a reader is making a lot of corrected partials, I would work on fluency to help him develop a flow to his language and to trust his hunches as a reader. A lot of these corrections indicate a less-confident reader, yet one who is paying attention to meaning (see Figure 8–5).

If I see a lot of corrected substitutions, then this is strong evidence that the reader is self-monitoring her reading and concerned with making sense of the text. If I see a low number of self-corrections, I want to look at the next two columns to see whether the miscues that were left uncorrected changed the meaning. If not, the reader is making sense as she is reading. If those miscues should have been corrected, then we should help her develop some metacognitive skills and attend more closely to the meaning. At this point, I would also look at her definition of reading, because if she defines reading as saying all the words, she won't be concerned with making meaning and therefore won't attend to the miscues that do need to be fixed (see Figure 8–6).

I also pay attention to the pattern of miscues that were left uncorrected but did not change the author's intended meaning. These indicate to me that a reader is making the leap to meaning by picking up just enough visual cues to make an appropriate prediction. These miscues don't need to be corrected because the reader is constructing meaning. For these miscues, I am interested to see how much graphic similarity there is between the miscue and the text item; often, there is little (see Figure 8–7).

Another pattern I want to watch for is a high number of miscues that were uncorrected with a meaning change. I am particularly concerned when these miscues are a different part of speech, for example, squirrels/scarlet. This type of miscue indicates the reader is having difficulty picking up cues from both the meaning (semantics) and from the sentence structure (syntax). In other words, he is not able to recognize that his word choice wouldn't make sense right there or

Reader Said	Text Said	Self - Corrected	Uncorrected - No Meaning Change	Uncorrected - With Meaning Change	Graphic Similarity			Self-Corrected During Conversation
					High	Some	None	
but	between	✓				✓		
seen	laid eyes on	✓			—	—	—	
hopped	hoped	✓			✓			
$ gapping	gaping	✓			✓			

FIGURE 8–6 Corrected Substitutions

Reader Said	Text Said	Self - Corrected	Uncorrected - No Meaning Change	Uncorrected - With Meaning Change	Graphic Similarity			Self-Corrected During Conversation
					High	Some	None	
rather content	— content		✓		—	—	—	
a	the		✓				✓	
Mom	Ma		✓			✓		
through the year	throughout the year		✓		✓			

FIGURE 8–7 Uncorrected Miscues—No Meaning Change

Reader Said	Text Said	Self - Corrected	Uncorrected - No Meaning Change	Uncorrected - With Meaning Change	Graphic Similarity			Self-Corrected During Conversation
					High	Some	None	
Never	Near			✓	✓			
or	our			✓	✓			
squirrels	scarlet			✓		✓		
well	walls			✓	✓			

FIGURE 8–8 Uncorrected Miscues—With Meaning Change

that the word he chose is in the wrong position in the sentence. My questions to students when discussing this type of miscue are: Did that sound like the way we talk? Did that make sense?

For this student, I might invite him to listen to a tape of himself reading and listen for this kind of miscue. We are also seeing here a student who is overrelying on the graphophonic cueing system; that is, he is paying more attention to the letters on the page than to the meaning of the passage. A helpful strategy for this type of reader is the cloze procedure, in which selected nouns in a text are covered up and the student doesn't have any graphic information available. He must make a prediction based solely on the meaning and the syntactic structure (see Figure 8–8).

The pattern I am looking for in the next section on the miscue page is the graphic similarity between the miscue and the text item. Remember, we *don't try* to complete this section *during the reading*; we return to the form later to make the determination about graphic similarity. If the uncorrected miscues show little or no graphic similarity but they don't change meaning, then the reader has picked up a minimal amount of graphic cues and prioritized constructing meaning. If the uncorrected miscues have High graphic similarity and they do change meaning, we are seeing a reader who is overrelying on the graphic information (see Figure 8–9). Again, a cloze procedure is helpful for this type of reader.

Checks in the last column on the miscue page, Self-Corrected During Conversation, indicate that when revisiting the text during the teaching conversation, the reader realized what the word should have been. Sometimes this type of miscue is one that was made in haste or is a mispronunciation of a word for which the reader knew the meaning.

Here is a summary of the miscue patterns to keep in mind:

- *High percentage of self-corrections*: This pattern generally indicates the student is self-monitoring her reading for meaning. She self-corrects miscues that change meaning and doesn't accept nonwords. It is interesting to

Reader Said	Text Said	Self - Corrected	Uncorrected - No Meaning Change	Uncorrected - With Meaning Change	Graphic Similarity: High	Some	None	Self-Corrected During Conversation
three	there			✓	✓			
grand	garden			✓	✓			
$apparted	appeared			✓	✓			
impossibility	impossibly			✓	✓			

FIGURE 8–9 Uncorrected Miscues—High Graphic Similarity

note whether she is correcting miscues she doesn't necessarily need to (high-quality miscues) (like seen/laid eyes on). If so, she may be an effective reader (constructing the meaning), but not particularly efficient (doing so with the least effort) (Y. Goodman, Watson, and Burke 1987).

- *Low percentage of self-corrections:* If miscues were not self-corrected, I ask, Did they change meaning? If the reader is making sense of the text, he may leave miscues uncorrected that were not significant enough to alter the meaning (for example cannot/can't). If the miscues do change meaning and the reader leaves them uncorrected, I want to invite the reader to go back to some of these and if possible, discuss his thinking at the time he made the miscue. Sometimes I find the reader has corrected these miscues in his head.
- *High percentage of miscues uncorrected with no meaning change:* When miscues that don't change meaning are left uncorrected, the reader is efficiently leaping to meaning with less attention to graphic information. There may be little or no graphic similarity between these miscues and their related text items. The reader doesn't need to correct these miscues because they didn't interrupt the construction of meaning.
- *Low percentage of miscues uncorrected with no meaning change:* Generally this pattern indicates a reader is overly bound to print. Either she reads what is on the page correctly, self-corrects most miscues, or doesn't correct miscues that do change meaning. There are few high-quality miscues.
- *High percentage of miscues uncorrected with meaning change:* This pattern is a concern because it indicates that the student is not focused on making sense of the text. The reader is not able to monitor the reading, stop when meaning is lost, and use appropriate strategies to construct meaning. Often, this reader accepts nonwords as well.
- *Low percentage of miscues uncorrected with meaning change:* This is a very desirable pattern. The reader is self-correcting or making high-quality miscues.

- *Graphic similarity:*
  - If miscues are mostly in the High and Some columns, or if they are evenly distributed across the three columns (High, Some, None), then there are probably few concerns here. The reader is well aware of symbol–sound relationships.
  - If there are a lot of miscues with High graphic similarity that do change meaning, this is a concern. The reader is overusing graphic cues to the detriment of making meaning.
  - If there are a lot of miscues with no graphic similarity and they don't change meaning, the reader is selecting a word that makes sense, but it doesn't necessarily look like the word in the text. For example, a/the is a miscue that often doesn't change the meaning, and there are no letters in common.
  - If there are a lot of miscues with no graphic similarity that do change meaning, the reader is having trouble attending to both graphic cues and meaning cues.

The Talking

Another source of evidence from the OTS sessions is the talk that takes place during the teaching conversations. We attend to students' talk in two main areas: Do they have *metalinguistic* skills?—that is, Do they have the language to talk about language? Are they comfortable discussing strategies? Do they know what good readers do? Are they able to use the language of miscue analysis?

We are also interested in students' *metacognitive* skills, that is: Can they access and articulate their thinking when reflecting on their miscues? Do they understand the nature of their own reading process? Y. Goodman and Flurkey found that both proficient and less proficient middle school students "were able to articulate not only beliefs about the reading process and about their strengths and weaknesses as readers but were able to make statements that reveal their concepts or knowledge about the reading process" (1996, 92–93).

Wilhelm (2001) offers various ways of conducting think-alouds during reading to help students develop these important skills. Most important, the teacher must become aware of his own reading process first and be able to talk through his own use of reading strategies. Then, he will be able to model these active engagements with text in front of his students.

When students take on this reflective stance as readers, their think-alouds offer the teacher valuable assessment information. We want students to come to realize the value of activating background knowledge before they start reading, setting purposes for reading, making predictions, visualizing as they read, asking questions of the text, summarizing as they go, monitoring and self-checking to see if they're comprehending, and using fix-up strategies when they're not making sense of the text.

During reading conferences, students are either engaged in conversation with the teacher or they are reading aloud. In the talking that takes place *before reading*, we might model for the reader how we set a purpose for reading, choose a particular text, make predictions based on the title or cover pictures, and recognize and draw on appropriate background knowledge.

Recently Jacque Barthel-Hines and I were modeling the OTS procedure for her fifth graders with her as the reader. As we talked before she read, she did all of those things. She had selected a collection of Greek myths for her next literature group and decided to read the first story in a fishbowl setting. Her purpose was to become familiar with the myth before she talked about it with her group, she chose the text because she doesn't know a lot about Greek myths, and she predicted the story would be about weavers because of the picture of a woman at a loom. She mentioned she knew a lot of Native American legends and, drawing on this background, she predicted she would see similarities between those stories and Greek myths.

As students are talking *during reading*, we listen to their side comments about the strategies they use, their thinking about the story, their attempts on unfamiliar words, and their questions. Examples of this kind of talk include:

- Second-grader Claire's Oops, I mean before each of her self-corrections
- Second-grader Josh's That's funny, because she's thinking about Clifford thinking about her when he noticed the picture of Emily Elizabeth who had a thought bubble above her head, and in the thought bubble was Clifford with his own thought bubble showing he was thinking of her
- First-grader Matt's I can't figure out this [*sic*] when he was trying to sound out tomato sauce and after repeated tries still didn't know what it was
- Second-grader LaMar's shouldn't there be a "with" right there, "with him"? He was trying to say catch up with him when the text said catch him.

Students are invited to talk *after reading* as they engage with the teacher in the teaching conversation. The evidence we are gathering in this part of the OTS procedure is captured through our notes on the cover page as we scribe the discussion. We are interested in hearing how the student responds to Let's talk about what you just read. Some students begin to talk about the text in the middle, noting an exciting part or the climax of the story, then they may tell an experience one of the characters had, and then tell how the story started. Some cut to the chase and give a brief gist statement, much as an adult would. Some may tell you everything that happened, in great detail, in order, from the beginning to the end.

Some may mention important information, then move to a sophisticated synthesis by which they gain a new perspective or combine several ideas, perhaps drawing on events both from their lives and from the story. Some students will say, This reminds me of . . . and make reference to events from earlier in the text or make connections between the book and the world, or between the book and other texts. Some will point out interesting or unusual language the author used or make other comments about the author's craft. Each of these types of discussion informs us regarding the reader's comprehension of what was read (see Figure 8–10).

There are two other main settings in which students have the opportunity to talk about their reading. During both of these, the teacher can collect assessment information. In *literature circles,* the interactions between peers is centered on the talk they share. We listen for students' talk to reveal their understanding of the text, their questions about the actions of the characters, their personal connections to the events, their ability to take the perspective of another, their willingness to agree to disagree, and their ability to regard the ideas of others with respect.

In *fishbowl* discussions, we listen for a student's observations of another reader and consider how these insights reveal her own view of the reading process. We make note of her awareness of the reader and determine the appropriateness of the strategies she suggests. We also pay attention to her comparisons between what she observed the fishbowler do and what she does herself as a reader, and how she values certain actions and strategies.

The Insights

After the reader has left the conferencing setting and the miscue and insights pages have been completed, the teacher can now take a minute to *reflect* on each reading. I try to jot down a few notes that summarize my global observations of a reader and an area or two I'd like to keep an eye on when working with this student. For example, when fourth-grader Tyler and I were talking after his reading, I noticed there was an unusual syntactic structure to his speech. He was also very text-bound; that is, he was reluctant to move away from a reliance on the text during our discussion and to talk comfortably about what he had just read.

If Tyler were a student in my class, I would watch his speech and writing for his understanding of the syntactic structure of standard English. If he's having difficulty in his generative language, he won't be able to ask himself when he's reading, Does that sound like the way we talk? Also, I was concerned that he wasn't comfortable making decisions about what was important to talk about in the story. This was either an issue of his short-term memory or it was related to his difficulty understanding story structure and knowing what to hang on to after reading something.

Generally, my global observations focus on the reader's (1) concern for making meaning, and (2) use of the language cueing systems. My observations in the first area usually fall into two big categories. I see students who are self-

SOURCE	EVIDENCE	SUGGESTED STRATEGIES
Book brought to conference	Book choice	Choosing a book
The reading	Affect	Identifying interests Choosing a book
	Fluency/expression	Choosing a book Rereading Reading to younger students Performing a Readers' Theatre
	Independent use of strategies	Choosing an appropriate strategy when you come to an unfamiliar word Using a naming strategy Using a placeholder strategy Chunking Decoding by analogy Using context cues Defining reading Noticing when you lose focus Rereading to clarify Reading ahead to clarify Articulating what's confusing
The patterns of miscues	Uncorrected miscues that change meaning	Monitoring meaning Defining reading Picking up cues from semantic and syntactic cueing systems Listening to own tape Using a cloze procedure
	Accepts nonwords	Monitoring meaning Defining reading Listening to own tape
The talking before reading	Metalinguistic skills Metacognitive skills	Setting purposes for reading Choosing a book Making predictions from title and pictures Activating prior knowledge Discussing genre and types of strategies needed

Figure 8–10 Evidence from OTS and Related Strategies

SOURCE	EVIDENCE	SUGGESTED STRATEGIES
The talking during reading	Metalinguistic skills Metacognitive skills	Using appropriate language to talk about language and miscues Accessing and articulating thinking during reading Asking questions during reading Making inferences and predictions Making connections between the text and self, other texts, and the world
The talking after reading	Metalinguistic skills Metacognitive skills	Identifying story structure Sequencing Identifying important information Summarizing Synthesizing Extending understanding Making connections Creating visual images Identifying author's craft Asking questions Making inferences
The insights	Reader's concern for making meaning Reader's use of language cueing systems	Defining reading Observing think-alouds by proficient readers

FIGURE 8–10 (continued)

monitoring their reading and constructing meaning as they go, as shown by a high number of self-corrections or uncorrected miscues that don't change meaning. I also see students who need to be more concerned with the construction of meaning, as shown by a high number of uncorrected miscues that do change meaning, or the acceptance of nonwords.

When attending to the student's balanced use of the language cueing systems, I look at the relationships between the miscues, the corrections, and the graphic similarity. The most telling of these is High graphic similarity on miscues that do change meaning. This is evidence that the student is overattending to the graphic information and is paying less attention to the meaning. I am also concerned when a student overrelies on the "sounding-it-out" strategy and has few other options available when encountering unfamiliar words.

I also look at several OTS forms with the same reader and consider my reflections *over time*. I ask the student to do so as well, and to put sticky notes on their forms to capture their observations. In looking at their patterns of miscues across several instances of reading, do we see similar patterns? Are they consistently concerned with making meaning? Do they use similar strategies in different genres? These insights over time are very helpful in informing conferences with parents and colleagues.

The Holistic Evaluation of the Reader form (see Appendix L) allows us to summarize our ongoing observations of a reader and to pull together insights from several reading conferences. The Burke Reading Interview (see Appendix H) can also provide information over time about students' understanding of reading strategies, what good readers do, and their own reading process. These documents are helpful during conferences because they provide evidence to share with parents.

Once we summarize our observations from the OTS sessions and determine the reader's strengths and areas of concern, we turn our attention to the selection of strategies that will be helpful in moving this reader along. Although there is not room here to go into depth, I would like to recommend the texts summarized next and the strategies that they offer.

Stephanie Harvey and Anne Goudvis, in their book *Strategies That Work: Teaching Comprehension to Enhance Understanding* (2000), suggest working with short texts and helping students make connections between the text and themselves, the text and other texts, and the text and the world. They offer many excellent strategies for helping students develop the following: the ability to make connections and bridge from the new to the known, to ask questions during reading, to create visual images and to make inferences, to determine what is important in the text, and to synthesize information. The authors advocate thinking aloud to demonstrate the actions of a proficient reader, helping students learn to monitor their comprehension, using all aspects of the story to infer meaning, asking questions of the author, applying specific strategies for content-area texts, and learning to summarize and synthesize text information.

In *Snapshots*, Linda Hoyt presents a compendium of literacy minilessons that help the teacher see the progression from showing what you want students to do through think-alouds and modeling, to supporting them during guided practice, to helping students move to independence in the use of reading strategies. She suggests that "deliberate, purposeful, intentional teaching in a short period of time" can offer "high-impact teaching/learning opportunities" (2000, 7). She offers procedural minilessons in areas such as taking care of books and the rules of reading workshop. She has specific lessons on strategies and skills —connecting reading to your life, using context with unfamiliar words, self-correcting, using letters and word parts, making inferences, and determining key ideas. She presents strategies to help students when reading content-area texts, such as note-taking, skimming and scanning, and understanding the structure of expository texts. She also has minilessons to help call students' attention to literary features (e.g., structure of stories, figurative language, foreshadowing and character development).

While there are other great books on reading strategies, one of the most detailed is *Reading Strategies: Focus on Comprehension* by Yetta Goodman, Dorothy Watson, and Carolyn Burke (1996). Not only do they offer an excellent discussion of the reading process itself, but they also provide teachers with numerous strategies to share with students. They organize these strategies according to the different language cueing systems. For example, if a student needed to focus more on the semantic cueing system, we might help them understand their purposes for reading, or to *give them permission* to reread and rethink. We could help students see how different genres have different text structures and help them become aware of text organization. If students need to focus more on the syntactic cueing system, we might offer a cloze procedure, and highlight dialogue carriers or punctuation. We could also help students see how some structures are hard to predict. For those students needing more focus on the graphophonic cueing system, we might have them work with synonym substitutions, make meaning with selected deletions (as in the cloze procedure), or work on print and format variations.

All these texts, and others, offer strategies to support readers once we have determined through various miscue analysis procedures where they most need our help.

Final Questions

When developing a new procedure, there are endless questions. The most important one for me is "Am I being *true to* the principles that guide miscue analysis?" I have made every effort to do so. Colleagues learning OTS ask me questions such as the following:

- *"Is it OK to do an OTS with a book the student has already read?"*—Sure! We'll still get a few miscues and still get insights into the reader's strategies.
- *"Do I only write down the first attempt the reader makes?"*—That's fine. It's also OK to write down as much as you can catch. A few extra words can make all the difference in recalling the context when viewing the forms later.

- *"What if the student is too nervous because I'm writing things down as they read?"* Reflect on the groundwork that you have laid for this engagement. Have you modeled the OTS conference in front of the students? Be patient. Keep explaining, have them listen in as you work with confident readers. They'll get the idea that you're interested in what they're doing well as a reader, they know you'll talk over the form with them, and they will begin to trust that you have their best interest in mind.

I'm sure there will be many, many more questions as I continue to learn more about the procedure and continue to share it with colleagues, teachers, and college students. In the following sections I discuss some of the questions that have been asked most frequently.

Can I Use OTS with Speakers of Other Languages?

Yes. My student Sonja Fuglestad helped me understand how the OTS form can be adapted when listening to Spanish-speaking students. She teaches a literacy block class in a bilingual school and helps students maintain their ability to read in Spanish while learning to read in English. Reflecting on her use of the OTS to get to know her students as readers, she finds she can identify her students' strengths and areas of concern. When working with second-grader Joselin, Sonja realized that comprehension was a strong area for her, both in her ability to retell with detail and in her skill in *getting the gist* of the passage. When she was reading the Spanish translation of *The Paper Bag Princess* (Munsch 1988—1991 *La Princesa Vestida con una Bolsa*, trans. Langer), she said: Todo lo que le importaba fue mirar a las princesas bonitas (All that was important [to the prince] was to look at beautiful princesses), although this idea was never directly stated in the text.

Sonja also observed that Joselin had a fairly balanced use of the language cueing systems, even noting a second miscue in a sentence that was *necessary* in order to keep the correct syntactic structure in light of the first miscue. She commented on Joselin's habit of subvocalizing difficult words before she made an attempt at them, and the occasions when she left nonwords uncorrected. Sonja pondered the High graphic similarity of most of Joselin's miscues to their related text items, and thought this indicated an over-reliance on graphophonic cues on some miscues, particularly those that changed meaning and were left uncorrected.

We made an interesting discovery as Sonja was learning miscue analysis—we needed to add a column to the OTS form for gender change. For example, Joselin said una dragon/un dragon, which she corrected, and una castillo/un castillo, which she did not. Technically, these changed the meaning from masculine to feminine, but Joselin seemed to realize a determiner was needed, used one, and was satisfied with the mismatch. So did the second miscue change meaning? Not significantly. An extra column on the OTS form would have allowed Sonja to quickly make note of this type of miscue without repeatedly revisiting this question of gender change.

This is an example of taking ownership of the OTS form and adapting it to your personal needs. If you are using this procedure with speakers of other languages, there may be certain characteristics of that language about which it would be helpful to make notes. Sonja also realized that the evidence she gathered about Joselin through the OTS form gave her "some interesting fodder for reflection" about herself as a teacher. She questions whether, in her instruction, she had overemphasized the use of phonics and the strategy of sounding out unfamiliar words. She believes the goals of her instruction include helping students to improve their reading in Spanish, to begin reading in English, to enjoy reading, and to develop comprehension skills that move them beyond "the strategy of sounding it out." Sonja found, as many other teachers have:

> The only concern I have with the Procedure III is the amount of time it takes to go through the process of typing the retelling guide, finding a time to read with the students, typing the hard copy {typescript}, listening again and marking and sentence coding the hard copy, transferring the information to the miscue tally form, and then crunching the numbers. I believe with the mental progress I've made by going through this, I will use the information through the form of the Over the Shoulder process, which is more practical. (Fuglestad 2001)

Peregoy and Boyle believe that, when examining the miscues made by Spanish speaking students, "it is most helpful to look for *persistent miscue patterns*. If a student makes the same kind of miscue repeatedly, the pattern often provides a direction for instruction" (2001, 295). They also believe that "English learner pronunciation differences *per se* should not be considered a reading problem with either beginning or intermediate learners. Only miscues that impede meaning should be cause for concern" (296, emphases in original).

How Can I Talk with Parents About Miscue Analysis?

The parents of our students can become great kidwatchers and develop their own miscue ears if we take a little time to share with them the fundamentals of miscue analysis. Mary Diener holds an orientation night for parents early in the year during which she discusses basic questions such as: What is reading? What are miscues? What is miscue analysis? She invites parents to the meeting with a letter similar to the one in Figure 8-11.

What Is Reading?

As adults, we forget how actively we engage as readers and may not be aware that we make miscues. Being sensitive to the group of parents with whom we're working, their cultural backgrounds, and perhaps their own experiences in schools as young students, we can invite them to explore reading with us. By asking parents to observe their own reading strategies as they read a challenging text (as I asked you to do in Chapter 2), we can help them become aware of the com-

Dear Families,

I am delighted your child will be in my classroom this year. I'm looking forward to lots of exciting learning together. You and I will be communicating weekly through the homework folders and newsletters. In this letter, I'd like to invite you to our first Open House Night, and to tell you a little bit about how I get to know your child as a reader.

When your child is reading aloud to me, I listen for miscues, which are changes in the text that every reader makes. I use a procedure called Over the Shoulder Miscue Analysis that allows me to write down the miscues and what the text said at the point of miscue. There are a lot of different kinds of miscues. For example, I might hear one word substituted for another word, a word put in that's not there, or I might notice there's a word left out. I don't view miscues as mistakes, because they give me valuable information about what your child is doing with language. Miscues help me see how your child is understanding of the structure of sentences, the meaning of words, and the sounds of letters.

After your child has read aloud with me in a reading conference, we go back over my notes and talk about what we heard. I help your child understand that there are lots of different kinds of miscues and we all make them. We don't call these changes "mistakes" or "errors" because they tell us a lot about how your child is using language to make sense of what is read. The important questions we ask when we hear miscues are: "Did that sound like the way we talk (like the English language)?" and "Did that make sense?" Ultimately, these are the questions we want your child to ask when reading alone.

Open House Night is going to be Monday, October 22, 2003, at 6:30 PM in our classroom. I'm looking forward to meeting you and sharing more with you about miscue analysis. I'll show you the form I use and we'll try it out together as I read aloud. See you then!

FIGURE 8–11 Letter to Families

plex nature of the reading process. We can demonstrate how we use cues from the sentence structure, word meanings, and letters on the page to make sense of what we're reading. We can do a think-aloud in front of parents and show them our own thought processes and use of strategies as we read a difficult text. Our goal is to help parents come to understand that reading is an active process of constructing meaning, not just sounding out words.

What Are Miscues?

It's difficult for me to remember how I viewed reading before I learned about miscue analysis. Other than realizing it was a struggle for me and I wasn't much good at it, I don't think I thought about it much in terms of a *process.* It was just what I did when I plowed laboriously through a difficult text, and what I asked kids to do when they opened their basal readers. After all, that's what I had done when I was in school and what I had been taught to do in my teacher preparation program. It wasn't until graduate school that anyone asked me to consider how I viewed reading. It was then that I began to realize how I could help my students come to understand reading as well. If we recognize our own perceptions of the reading process, it will be easier to find ways to facilitate for parents a similar shift in their thinking.

For most parents, their view of reading is likely based on what they were asked to do as young students. Our task is to help them understand that all readers make miscues and to show them how informative those miscues can be. We can use examples from the students in our class, as well as from their own reading, to help them see that miscues are a natural part of the reading process for all readers. Miscues are not mistakes, but valuable sources of linguistic information.

What Is Miscue Analysis?

Mary shows her parents the OTS form on an overhead transparency and lets them know `You're going to be seeing this`. She explains the columns on the miscue page to help the parents understand what she's listening for when she asks a student to read with her in a reading conference. She discusses graphic similarity and "basic theory points" with parents. She finds parents receptive to this kind of informational meeting for the same reasons her students appreciate the discussion of their miscues: There are no secrets. What Mary knows about her students as readers, she shares with both the kids and the parents.

In the first student–parent–teacher conference held in November, Mary finds that while the students are beginning to take on the language of miscue analysis and are starting to get comfortable discussing their miscues in reading conferences with her, they generally prefer that she take the lead in explaining the OTS forms to parents. Mary shares with parents, `This is where I see your child as a reader. Here's what he's strong in and here are some examples`. She finds the miscue pages provide powerful evidence of students' actions as readers and can "guide the whole conference." By the time parents come in for the second conference in April, students "are really comfortable with the OTS and can explain it themselves" (Diener 2001).

One way Mary helps her students grow as readers is by guiding them as they revisit their portfolio of OTS forms and reflect on their growth over time. They put sticky notes on their forms when they notice changes such as more self-corrections or fewer miscues that change meaning. They make comments on individual miscues. Every few weeks, she has them complete a form with the headings `I used to. . . . But now I . . .` This is another document she uses in her parent conferences. By the second conference, students are comfortable talking about the sticky notes on their OTS forms (their own reflections) and they can explain how they've changed, what strategies they use, and what they're continuing to work on. Parents "are able to see what their child has done to improve as a reader."

We can also talk with parents about listening for miscues when they are reading with their children at home. Again, we need to remember that we react to any reading situation based on our experiences as readers. The most common response when one hears a miscue is to interpret it as a mistake that needs to be fixed. A natural reaction is to correct the child, right at the point the miscue is made. We can help parents learn to pause a second and ask themselves, Yes, I heard a miscue, but does the reading still sound like language? Did that miscue change the meaning of the sentence? We can have activities on parent night to help them come to understand the importance of these questions and the different stance it offers us as listeners when children are reading. We also help them understand we're trying to get kids to ask those same questions when reading alone.

It is important for parents to understand it is a great thing to talk with their children about miscues, but only after they have finished the sentence or maybe even two or three sentences. The discussion isn't a pejorative one, but one of curiosity and discovery. I wonder why you said that? Do you remember what you were thinking? Do you think that still makes sense? When children hear these same discussions at school and at home, it reinforces for them a meaning-making stance as a reader and conveys a consistent message about the reading process.

How Can Miscue Analysis Help Readers Become Self-Reflective?

I believe one of the strengths of miscue analysis is that it allows students, in conversation with the teacher, then independently, to become reflective about their own reading process. Retrospective Miscue Analysis allows us to revisit the reading with the reader, by listening again to a tape recording and thinking about individual miscues (Y. Goodman and Marek 1996). Procedure III in the fishbowl setting allows students to look back at their marked typescript and to see a clear graphic representation of their actions as a reader. They notice patterns in their miscues and in the sentence codings.

In the conferencing setting, returning to the OTS form or the tallies used in Procedure IV allows the teacher and student to talk about miscues they select and to discuss new strategies that "help readers interact more completely with their reading, bringing themselves to the text to engage in a richer, deeper, more thoughtful reading experience" (Harvey and Goudvis 2000, 1).

Miscue analysis not only gives students the chance for self-evaluation, but when we teach students to conduct these procedures themselves, they also become more proficient at interpreting the reading of their peers.

In their introduction, Harvey and Goudvis write (2000, xi, xiii):

> We love to hear what kids think about their reading—their questions, reactions, interpretations, opinions, inferences, arguments, and celebrations. . . . Schools need to be havens for thinking, classrooms incubators for deep thought. Thinking thrives when readers connect to books and to each other.

The teaching conversation that takes place after the reading allows students the chance to talk through their understandings. Jennings and Di remind us of the vital importance of giving students this time to talk (1996, 83):

> In order to learn, children need the opportunity to think and talk about what they are doing. As they talk, they hear themselves, and others learn to recognize that which they understand or do not understand. Talking out loud helps children clarify their own thinking about thinking.

Bringing It All Together: Making Miscue Analysis Your Own

Now it is time for you to make some personal choices about the use of miscue analysis and the reading assessments that make sense for you. I invite you to return to thinking about the relationships between the beliefs we hold, the theories and paradigms that guide us, and the practices in which we engage (refer to Figure 3–5).

Serafini (2000/2001) describes the following three paradigms of assessment:

1. Assessment as measurement
    - Associated with a positivist or modernist view of reality
    - Knowledge exists separately from the learner
    - An example is a norm-referenced standardized test
2. Assessment as procedure
    - Has characteristics of both the assessment as measurement paradigm and the assessment as inquiry paradigm
    - Knowledge is separate from the learner and can be directly transmitted and objectively measured
    - An example is a mandated portfolio in which the students and teachers have no choices
3. Assessment as inquiry
    - Associated with a constructivist theory of knowledge, student-centered learning, and the inquiry process
    - Knowledge is constructed by the individual in social contexts; multiple interpretations are encouraged and accepted
    - An example is a portfolio that promotes reflections, student ownership, and self-evaluation, and that allows the teacher and student to work together to set goals

I believe miscue analysis and OTS can be classified as "assessment as inquiry," because, as Serafini notes (2000/2001, 387):

> [T]he teacher uses various qualitative and quantitative assessment techniques to inquire about particular learners and their learning processes.

> [Assessment] is a process of inquiry, and a process of interpretation, used to promote reflection concerning students' understandings, attitudes, and literate abilities.

From this perspective, assessment is a social, interpretive activity, the purpose of which "is a deeper understanding of individual learners in their specific learning contexts" (387). The audience for these assessments includes teachers, parents, and students, not just external authorities. Teachers and students are "active creators of knowledge" and teachers use classroom-based assessments "to facilitate learning, direct curricular decisions and communicate more effectively with students and parents" (Serafini 2000/2001, 387). I believe miscue analysis is one such assessment.

I'd like to close by reminding you of, or perhaps introducing you to, a delightful story about a lizard who makes up a song about his home (Shannon 1994). In the story, Bear wants to learn the song and asks Lizard to teach it to him. Bear keeps forgetting the song, and after teaching his song to Bear several times, Lizard wisely realizes that one reason Bear is having such difficulty is that the song is not about his own home. Once Bear makes up his own song, he never forgets it.

What I have shared here about miscue analysis is my song, composed by borrowing notes from many others' tunes, melodies, and symphonies. It is my hope that you will take the song and make it your own.

Appendices

A: LaMar's Procedure III Typescript and Blank Typescript

B: LaMar's Procedure III Miscue Tally Form

C: Blank Procedure III Miscue Tally Form

D: LaMar's Retelling

E: LaMar's Retelling Guide

F: LaMar's Reader Profile

G: Blank Reader Profile

H: Burke Reading Interview

I: Josh's OTS Form

J: Blank OTS Form

K: Blank Miscue Analysis Procedure IV Form

L: Blank Holistic Evaluation of the Reader Form

M: Story Text—"The Old Man, His Son, and the Donkey"

Appendix A: LaMar's Procedure III Typescript

The Old Man, His Son, and the Donkey

Name LaMar Date October 12

An old farmer and his son were taking their donkey to town to sell. They had not gone far when they saw some girls at a well.

"Look at them!" said one of the girls. "Summer's here and the day is hot. And those two walk when they might ride. What fools they are!"

All the girls laughed at this. The old man heard them laugh. "Get up and ride," he said to his son.

So the son got on the donkey's back. The old man walked. Soon they came to some men in a field. "Look at that!" one of the men shouted. "That big boy rides while his poor old father must walk."

The old man heard their words. "Get right down," he said to his son. "I will ride." The son got down, and the old man got on the donkey's back.

1 to sell
"That doesn't make sense"
to sell
(I adjust his microphone "I know")
donkey to
"oh yeah"

4 $serm-eh
$serm
s-s-summer.
summer.
Her and
"wait"
Her
Her and the day is hot.
Summer
her
"That doesn't make sense"
Look at them
s- said one of the girls,
Summer.
Her and the day's

1 NN-
2 YYN
3 YYN
4 NN-
5 YYN
6 YYN
7 YYN
8 YYN
9 YYN
10 YYN
11 YYN
12 YYN
13 YYN
14 YYP
15 YYN
16 YYN
17 YYN
18 YYN

C

f/eels

19 *$feeled*

"It feels good to ride," the old farmer   *man* *C*

       isn't   *son,*   CHANGED

20   21 *son.*   INTONATION

said, "It wasn't right for me to walk." Soon   **19 YYN**

        ^

                          child   **20 YYN**

they came to a woman and her children walking on

                d

the road. *well*   **21 YYP**

UC 22 *well*   *C* *old*

"Will you look at him!" the woman said.   **22 YYN**

23   *RM*

              well

"That man rides while, his poor little son must

           ^

      24   *the woman* 25

walk." The old man heard her words. "Get up   **23 YYP**

                                             24 YYN

                        26   **25 YYN**

here with me," he said to his son. The son got

          R   *R*

up on the donkey in back of his father.   *donkey in*   **26 YYN**

SEE   27   *donkey in*

MARGIN Soon they saw a man and his wife standing *in back of*

                        C *It's*

                     28 *It*

by their house. "Is that your donkey?" the man   **27 YYN**

asked the old man.   **28 YYN**

        29

"Yes, it is," said the old man.   **29 YYN**

       30   *C*

                   s-

"How can you be so mean?" asked the wife.   **30 YYN**

R 31   *"wait"*   *C*

"The two of you up there on one poor little   *The two of*

SEE MARGIN 32   *The two of*

donkey!" Then she went on to say, "Two big   *The two of* **31 YYN**

          couldn't   *"wait"*

people like you could carry him."   *The two* **32 YYY**

      R 33   *C* *w-*

CHANGES "Very well," said the old man, "we'll try that." *The two of...* **33 YYN**

INTONATION 34

     The old man and his son got off the donkey

C

                        35

and tried to pick him up. The old man picked up   **34 YYN**

leg the / said, "Son, pick

two legs, and his son picked up the other two legs." — 35 YYN

36 poor

But just then, some more people came by. — 36 YYP

37 RM man ©the

And when they saw the old farmer and his son,

they all started laughing. — 37 YYN

UC 38 Ha Ha Ha Ha Ha 39 40

"Oh, oh, oh!" they laughed. "Look! The — 38 YYN, 39 YYN

fools are carrying the donkey!" — 40 YYN

41

The donkey didn't like the noise and didn't

42

like to be carried. So he pulled loose and ran — 41 YYN

43

out into the fields. The old man and the son — 42 YYN

© to tie

tried and tried, but they couldn't catch him. — 43 YYN

SEE MARGIN

44

So now they had no donkey to sell. — 44 YYN

45

At last, the old man turned to his son. — 45 YYN

© 46 so ® ©ple- ©very very 47

"Son," he said, "You cannot please everyone. If — 46 YYN

SEE BELOW

you try, you only make a donkey of yourself." — 47 YYN

tried to tie and
tired and tired
but they
couldn't catch
tried and tried to
tried and tried but
they couldn't
catch up
they couldn't catch up him
"Shouldn't there be a
'with' right there,
'with him'?"
they couldn't catch up him
they couldn't catch him
"oh"
catch him

you cannot ple-, please
you cannot please
very
very
everyone

The Old Man, His Son, and the Donkey

Name ____________________________ Date_____________

An old farmer and his son were taking their donkey to town to sell. They had not gone far when they saw some girls at a well.

"Look at them!" said one of the girls.

"Summer's here and the day is hot. And those two walk when they might ride. What fools they are!"

All the girls laughed at this. The old man heard them laugh. "Get up and ride," he said to his son.

So the son got on the donkey's back. The old man walked. Soon they came to some men in a field. "Look at that!" one of the men shouted. "That big boy rides while his poor old father must walk."

The old man heard their words. "Get right down," he said to his son. "I will ride." The son got down, and the old man got on the donkey's back.

19 "It feels good to ride," the old farmer
said. 20 "It wasn't right for me to walk." 21 Soon 19 ______
20 ______
they came to a woman and her children walking on
the road. 21 ______

22 "Will you look at him!" the woman said. 22 ______
23 "That man rides while his poor little son must
walk." 24 The old man heard her words. 25 "Get up 23 ______
24 ______
here with me," he said to his son. 26 The son got 25 ______
up on the donkey in back of his father. 26 ______

27 Soon they saw a man and his wife standing
by their house. 28 "Is that your donkey?" the man 27 ______
asked the old man. 28 ______

29 "Yes, it is," said the old man. 29 ______

30 "How can you be so mean?" asked the wife. 30 ______
31 "The two of you up there on one poor little
donkey!" 32 Then she went on to say, "Two big 31 ______
people like you could carry him." 32 ______

33 "Very well," said the old man, "we'll try that." 33 ______

34 The old man and his son got off the donkey
and tried to pick him up. 35 The old man picked up 34 ______

two legs, and his son picked up the other two legs. 35

36 But just then, some more people came by. 36

37 And when they saw the old farmer and his son,

they all started laughing. 37

38 "Oh, oh, oh!" they laughed. 39 "Look! 40 The 38

39

fools are carrying the donkey!" 40

41 The donkey didn't like the noise and didn't

like to be carried. 42 So he pulled loose and ran 41

out into the fields. 43 The old man and the son 42

tried and tried, but they couldn't catch him. 43

44 So now they had no donkey to sell. 44

45 At last, the old man turned to his son. 45

46 "Son," he said, "You cannot please everyone. 47 If 46

you try, you only make a donkey of yourself." 47

Appendix B. LaMar's Procedure III Miscue Tally Form

PROCEDURE III MISCUE TALLY FORM

Name LaMar Page 1 **Date** October 12

Selection Read The Old Man, His Son, and the Donkey

Sentence #	Reader Said (Record first Attempt) I began with Sentence 7	Text Said	Self - Corrected	Uncorrected: No Meaning Change	Uncorrected: Partial Meaning Change	Uncorrected: With Meaning Change	Graphic Similarity: High	Graphic Similarity: Some	Graphic Similarity: None
7	the	this.	✓				✓		
8	the	them	✓				✓		
9	a	and	✓				✓		
	h-	he	✓					—	
13	shuh-aw	shouted.	✓					—	
14	well‸	while			✓			✓	
15	the	their	✓				✓		
	word	words.	✓				✓		
19	$feeled	feel	✓				✓		
	man	farmer	✓					✓	
20	isn't	wasn't		✓			✓		
21	son‸	soon	✓				✓		
	child	children			✓		✓		
22	well	will		✓			✓		
	old	—	✓					—	
24	the woman	her words.		✓				—	
28	It	Is	✓				✓		
Page Column Totals:			12	3	2	0	11	2	0

Total Miscues this page: 17 Total Miscues this page coded for Graphic Similarity: 13

Cannot code for graphic similarity: Complex miscues, omissions, insertions, partials

PROCEDURE III MISCUE TALLY FORM

Name LaMar   Page 2 **Date** October 12

Selection Read The Old Man, His Son, and the Donkey

Sentence #	Reader Said (Record first Attempt)	Text Said	Self - Corrected	Uncorrected: No Meaning Change	Uncorrected: Partial Meaning Change	Uncorrected: With Meaning Change	Graphic Similarity: High	Graphic Similarity: Some	Graphic Similarity: None
30	s-	so	✓					—	
31	one on	on one	✓					—	
32	couldn't	could				✓	✓		
33	w-	we'll	✓					—	
35	leg	legs	✓				✓		
	the	and	✓						✓
	said, "Son, pick	his son picked		✓				—	
36	poor	more			✓			✓	
37	the	his	✓					✓	
38	Ha, ha!	Oh, oh, oh!		✓				—	
43	tried to tie	tried and tried	✓					—	
46	so	son	✓				✓		
	ple-	please	✓					—	
	very	everyone.	✓				✓		
Page Column Totals:		Page 2	10	2	1	1	4	2	1

Total Miscues this page: 14   Total Miscues this page coded for Graphic Similarity: 7   + 13 = 20

Page 1 TOTALS	17	12	3	2	0	11	2	0

Cannot code for graphic similarity: Complex miscues, omissions, insertions, partials

OVERALL TOTALS	31	22	5	3	1	15	4	1

Appendix C: Blank Form

PROCEDURE III MISCUE TALLY FORM

Name________________________ **Date** ________________

Selection Read ________________________________

Sentence #	Reader Said (Record first Attempt)	Text Said	Self-Corrected	Uncorrected: No Meaning Change	Uncorrected: Partial Meaning Change	Uncorrected: With Meaning Change	Graphic Similarity: High	Graphic Similarity: Some	Graphic Similarity: None
Page Column Totals:									

Total Miscues this page: Total Miscues this page coded for Graphic Similarity:

Cannot code for graphic similarity: Complex miscues, omissions, insertions, partials

Appendix D: LaMar's Retelling

R: Super reading, LaMar, very good job. OK, I want you to tell me everything you can remember about that story.

L: Well, there was an old man and his son and they had a donkey, is it, do we, do we have to say every word?

R: No, just tell me the events in the story, what happened in the story, who was in the story.

L: Well, there was an old man and his son and they were going to sell a donkey and they were going to town and first they met some girls, and they, and they were both, and both the man and the son were walking the donkey and the girls laughed at them because they weren't both on, because they both weren't on the donkey, and so first he said, "Son, get up on the donkey."

And then they met some other people and they were walking because, um, wait, and they said, "Your s-" and then they met some men and they shouted, "Um, your s-, your son is re-, is a very good rider and, but um, but poor, but his poor fath – father isn't very, isn't very good." They said that all he did was walk.

And then he, um, and then they met some other people and they said, and then he, then the old man said, "Get down from there, I want to do it." And then they met some other people and they said, um, the, the other way around, they said that the, the man, the old man was a pretty good rider and the son was a not very, that the poor son just walked, and then he said, "Get up, son, get up here with me."

And then they met some people, a man and his wife, and they said, how, that the wife said that that's mean because, um, they were both on there and they said how, "I bet you both," and then the wife said, "I bet you can't carry the donkey" and donkey, and then they said, "OK, we will" and then they tried to pick him up and they couldn't and then they met some poor people and they laughed and laughed and then the donkey didn't like that sound, so, and he didn't like being carried very well and then he ran off and then the old man and his son they couldn't, um, they couldn't catch the donkey and then they had to go to town without the donkey and they didn't have anything to sell.

R: Such a good job. If there was sort of a moral to this story, what would you say that'd be?

L: What a moral mean?

R: Well, what's the last thing the father said, it's kind of the lesson you learn from the story.

L: That they, that the people, that if you try to carry the donkey, you're just making a fool out of yourself. And if you try to please all the people, you're making a fool out of yourself.

Appendix E: LaMar's Retelling Guide

Retelling Guide
The Old Man, His Son, and the Donkey

Name LaMar Date October 12

Characters 28 / 32 (4 points each)

- ✓ old farmer *old man*
- ✓ his son
- ✓ donkey
- ✓ girls at the well *some girls*
- ✓ men in the field *met some men*
- 1/2 woman and her children *other people*
- ✓ man and his wife
- 1/2 more people *poor people*

Setting 10 / 10

- ✓ on the road to town *they were going to town*

Events 38 / 48 (4 points each)

- ✓ farmer and son walking to town with donkey to sell
- ✓ girls at well laugh because they're walking *they weren't both on*
- ✓ farmer tells son to ride
- ___ men in field say not right for son to ride and father to walk *said son was a good rider and all the father does is walk*
- ✓ son gets down and farmer rides
- ___ woman tells children not right for father to ride while son walks *old man was a good rider, the son just walks*
- ✓ both ride donkey
- ✓ man and wife say two people are too heavy for the donkey
- 1/2 wife says they could carry the donkey *"I bet you can't carry the donkey"*
- ✓ people laugh at them
- ✓ noise bothers donkey – he runs away
- ✓ farmer and son can't catch him so they have no donkey to sell

Moral / Main idea / Lesson from story 10 / 10
You can't please everyone. If you try, you make a donkey of yourself.
If you try to please all the people, you're making a fool of yourself

Characters	28 / 32
Setting	10 / 10
Events	38 / 48
Main idea	10 / 10
Total	86 / 100

86 % Comprehension Score

Appendix F. LaMar's Reader Profile

Reader LaMar Date October 12
Selection Read The Old Man, His Son, and the Donkey
Number of Sentences Coded 47

INFORMATION FROM TYPESCRIPT

Comprehending in Process (Sentence Codings)

40	85	% YYN
4	9	% YYP
1	2	% YYY
0	0	% YN-
2	4	% NN-

Syntactic Acceptability

45	96	% Acceptable
2	4	% Unacceptable

Semantic Acceptability

45	96	% Acceptable
2	4	% Unacceptable

Meaning Change

40	85	% No Meaning Change (N)
4	9	% Partial Meaning Change (P)
3	6	% With Meaning Change (Y and Dash)

INFORMATION FROM RETELLING GUIDE

Comprehension 86 %

INFORMATION FROM MISCUE TALLY FORM

Total Number of Miscues Tallied 31

Corrections

22	71	% Self-Corrected
5	16	% Uncorrected, No Meaning Change
3	10	% Uncorrected, Partial Meaning Change
1	3	% Uncorrected, With Meaning Change

Total Number of Miscues Coded for Graphic Similarity 20

Graphic Similarity

15	75	% High
4	20	% Some
1	5	% None

COMMENTS

Proficient reader - Maintains meaning during reading - Good recall of details - Could attend more to word endings

Appendix G: Blank Reader Profile

READING MISCUE INVENTORY
Procedure III—Reader Profile

Reader ______________________________ **Date**______________

Selection read ______________________________________

Number of sentences coded ________

INFORMATION FROM TYPESCRIPT

Comprehending in Process (Sentence Codings)

_____ _____ % YYN
_____ _____ % YYP
_____ _____ % YYY
_____ _____ % YN–
_____ _____ % NN–

Syntactic Acceptability

_____ _____ % Acceptable
_____ _____ % Unacceptable

Semantic Acceptability

_____ _____ % Acceptable
_____ _____ % Unacceptable

Meaning Change

_____ _____ % No Change (N)
_____ _____ % Partial Change (P)
_____ _____ % Change (Y and Dash)

INFORMATION FROM RETELLING GUIDE

Comprehension _____ %

INFORMATION FROM MISCUE TALLY FORM

Total Number of miscues tallied _____

Corrections

_____ _____ % Self-Corrected
_____ _____ % Uncorrected, No Meaning Change
_____ _____ % Uncorrected, Partial Meaning Change
_____ _____ % Uncorrected, With Meaning Change

Total Number of miscues coded for graphic similarity _____

Graphic Similarity

_____ _____ % High
_____ _____ % Some
_____ _____ % None

COMMENTS

Appendix H: Burke Reading Interview

1. When you are reading and come to something you don't know, what do you do?

   Do you ever do anything else?

2. Who is a good reader you know?

3. What makes ____________________ a good reader?

4. Do you think ____________________ ever comes to something she/he doesn't know?

5. "Yes"—When ____________________ does come to something she/he doesn't know, what do you think he/she does?

   "No"—Suppose ____________________ comes to something she/he doesn't know. What do you think she/he would do?

6. If you knew someone was having trouble reading how would you help that person?

7. What would a/your teacher do to help that person?

8. How did you learn to read?

9. What would you like to do better as a reader?

10. Do you think you are a good reader? Why?

Appendix I: Josh's OTS Form

Over the Shoulder Miscue Analysis
Cover Page

Student Josh **Grade** 2nd **Date** October 23

Selection Read Clifford's Thanksgiving **Type of Text** Easy Picture Book

Amount Read Whole story in two sections **Comments on Text** 2-3 lines per page, large pictures

Notes from Teaching Conversation – Scribe as much as possible – Continue on back if needed
These are **suggestions** for the conversation, which **may** include **any or all** of the following (**or other discussion**):

- *Tell me about what you just read – Anything you'd like to add? – Do you remember what happened here?* (if something significant was omitted) – *Does this remind you of anything? – Do you have any questions about this?*
- Take back to OTS form – Discuss patterns of miscues – Go back to individual miscues (teacher-selected or student-selected) - *What were you thinking when you said...? How did you get that?*
- Go back and clarify concepts or words where meaning may have been lost
- Select a brief Teaching Point – Model or remind student of a strategy – Suggest something to work on
- End with a Celebration Point – Point out what the student is doing well

First Part:
he wanted to spend TG w/ his mom
set out to find her - bumped into a lot of cars
he fell into ocean
he went into tunnel & got bumped by train
? who was he staying with
the next door neighbors

Second Part:
got onto street
in a town he didn't recognize
climbed a bunch of buildings
saw his mom's house
he walked there
he got involved in a football game on the way
he found his mom's house - he ate dinner
he went home - he saw Mary Elizabeth because they got home at the same time

Over the Shoulder Miscue Analysis
Miscue Page

Student Josh **Date** Oct. 23 **Selection Read** Clifford's Thanksgiving

Page 1

	Reader Said	Text Said	Self - Corrected	Uncorrected - No Meaning Change	Uncorrected - With Meaning Change	Graphic Similarity: High	Graphic Similarity: Some	Graphic Similarity: None	Self-Corrected During Conversation	Notes
	First Part									
1.	lots of	a lot of		✓			—	—		
2.	on our next	our	✓				—	—		
3.	he	his	✓				✓			
4.	is	his	✓			✓				
5.	sister	sisters			✓	✓				
6.	Bone	Bonnie			✓	✓				– discussed naming strategy
7.	Nor	Nero			✓		✓			
8.	dis-	decided			✓		—	—		
9.	set	started		✓			✓			
10.	— ↔	to			✓		—	—		– insertion
11.	Er-	Everybody	✓				—	—		
12.	smiled	seemed	✓				✓			
13.	—	see		✓			—	—		
14.	beeped	bumped	✓			✓				– made "Beep" noises
15.	was	were	d				✓			– verb form
16.	wanted way	wondered why			✓		—	—		
17.	—	drawbridge			✓		—	—	✓	– "Uh oh – this can't be good" later – SC and "It opens. when a boat comes"
18.	road	roar								
	Total Miscues this page	18	7	3	7	4	5	0	1	

Over the Shoulder Miscue Analysis
Miscue Page

Student Josh **Date** Oct. 23 **Selection Read** Clifford's Thanksgiving

Page 2

	Reader Said (Second Part)	Text Said	Self - Corrected	Uncorrected -No Meaning Change	Uncorrected - With Meaning Change	Graphic Similarity: High	Graphic Similarity: Some	Graphic Similarity: None	Self-Corrected During Conversation
19.	there	the			✓	✓			
20.	so	to	✓			✓			
21.	the	a	✓					✓	
22.	where he was:	where was his Mom	✓				—		
23.	always (likes parades)	usually (likes parades)		✓			✓		
24.	—	to			✓		—		
25.	He	She			✓	✓			
26.	to see	too	✓				—		
27.	worried	wondered	✓			✓			
28.	called	could			AC		✓		
29.	thinking of	thankful for		P			—		
Total Miscues this page		11	5	2	4	4	2	1	0

"he's gonna get stuck"

"Oh, there's a balloon of him."

"Ah! Get it! Get it! Look at all of them! Touchdown! Look! Clifford-down!" (Football game)

"Man, his mom's tiny"

"Man, his mom's <u>really</u> tiny!"

Over the Shoulder Miscue Analysis
Insights Page

Josh		SC	Unc No Chg	Unc With Chg	H	S	N	SC During Conv.
Overall Totals	29 Miscues	12	5	11	8	7	1	1
Percentages		41	18	41	53	41	6	

Cannot code for graphic similarity: Complex miscues, omissions, insertions, partials — Number of miscues coded for graphic similarity 17

Observations about Comprehension During this Reading (Not all will be observed during each reading)

Mentions important information when I asked "and then what" prompts he had details

Able to summarize, gets the gist didn't summarize – I didn't ask for one

Able to synthesize text information – Gains a new perspective – Combines ideas – indicated by "thinking of / thankful for"

Able to extend understanding through connections to self football to the world drawbridge to other texts (or movies) Knew character

Refers to making visual images of the text during reading no, but interprets levels of meaning in picture

Able to analyze the author's craft (interesting words, metaphors, similes, colorful images) makes his own play on words

Asks questions ____ Makes inferences and predictions "he's gonna get stuck" "this can't be good"

Global Observations

X **Reader is self-monitoring his/her reading and constructing meaning**
High number of self-corrections, uncorrected miscues don't change meaning (*it's* for *it is*, *Mother* for *Mom*)

X **Reader needs to be more concerned with the construction of meaning**
High number of uncorrected miscues that change meaning, accepts nonwords

___ **Reader is over-relying on print – Sounding out is strategy most commonly used**
Graphic similarity is high on miscues that change meaning (*house* for *horse*)

Additional Insights about this Reader and Suggestions for Instruction

He made a lot of noises and side comments - indicating he is understanding, making connections, creating sensory images and making inferences - Used sophisticated language

Josh is a developing reader and shows characteristics of both
59% sc or unc - no mng chg
41% chg in meaning
I think he is compensating through his use of picture cues
Changed character's name

Appendix J: Blank OTS Form

Over the Shoulder Miscue Analysis
Cover Page

Student____________________ **Grade**____________ **Date**________

Selection Read__________________ **Type of Text**______________

Amount Read__________ **Comments on Text**____________________

Notes from Teaching Conversation – Scribe as much as possible – Continue on back if needed
These are **suggestions** for the conversation, which **may** include **any or all** of the following (**or other discussion**):

- *Tell me about what you just read – Anything you'd like to add? – Do you remember what happened here?* (if something significant was omitted) – *Does this remind you of anything? – Do you have any questions about this?*
- Take back to OTS form – Discuss patterns of miscues – Go back to individual miscues (teacher-selected or student-selected) - *What were you thinking when you said...? How did you get that?*
- Go back and clarify concepts or words where meaning may have been lost
- Select a brief Teaching Point – Model or remind student of a strategy – Suggest something to work on
- End with a Celebration Point – Point out what the student is doing well

Over the Shoulder Miscue Analysis
Miscue Page

Student____________________________ **Date**___________ **Selection Read**_________________________

Reader Said	Text Said	Self - Corrected	Uncorrected -No Meaning Change	Uncorrected - With Meaning Change	Graphic Similarity			Self-Corrected During Conversation
					High	Some	None	
Total Miscues this page								

Over the Shoulder Miscue Analysis
Insights Page

		SC	Unc No Chg	Unc With Chg	H	S	N	SC During Conv.
Overall Totals								
Percentages								

Cannot code for graphic similarity: Complex miscues, omissions, insertions, partials   Number of miscues coded for graphic similarity________

Observations about Comprehension During this Reading (Not all will be observed during each reading)

Mentions important information____

Able to summarize, gets the gist____

Able to synthesize text information – Gains a new perspective – Combines ideas - ________________________

Able to extend understanding through connections to self__________ to the world__________ to other texts (or movies)__________

Refers to making visual images of the text during reading________________________________

Able to analyze the author's craft (interesting words, metaphors, similes, colorful images)________________________

Asks questions____________________Makes inferences and predictions____________________

Global Observations

_____ **Reader is self-monitoring his/her reading and constructing meaning**
High number of self-corrections, uncorrected miscues don't change meaning (*it's* for *it is*, *Mother* for *Mom*)

_____ **Reader needs to be more concerned with the construction of meaning**
High number of uncorrected miscues that change meaning, accepts nonwords

_____ **Reader is over-relying on print – Sounding out is strategy most commonly used**
Graphic similarity is high on miscues that change meaning (*house* for *horse*)

Additional Insights about this Reader and Suggestions for Instruction

Appendix K: Blank Miscue Analysis

MISCUE ANALYSIS PROCEDURE IV
Individual Conference Form

Reader ______________________________ **Date** ______________

Teacher ______________________________ **Age/Grade** ______________

Selection ____

Does the sentence, as the reader left it, make sense within the context of the story?

Yes ______________________________________ **Total** __________

No ______________________________________ **Total** __________

Number of Sentences ______________ **Comprehending Score** ______________

Divide the Total Yes by the Total Number of Sentences for Comprehending Score

Retelling Information

Comments

Appendix L: Blank Holistic Evaluation of the Reader Form

Name ______________________________ Date ____________________

	Seldom	Some-times	Often	Usually	Always
I. In what ways is the reader constructing meaning?					
• Recognizes when miscues have changed meaning	1	2	3	4	5
• Makes high-level substitutions that don't change meaning	1	2	3	4	5
• Self-corrects miscues that change meaning	1	2	3	4	5
• Uses pictures and/or other visual cues	1	2	3	4	5
• Uses strategies flexibly; Employs all the language cueing systems	1	2	3	4	5
• Influences from first language or dialect do not change meaning	1	2	3	4	5
• Other					
II. In what ways is the reader disrupting meaning?					
• Substitutes words that don't make sense	1	2	3	4	5
• Makes omissions or insertions that change meaning	1	2	3	4	5
• Relies too heavily on graphic cues—Miscues look like text item but don't make sense	1	2	3	4	5
• Other					

Appendix L (continued)

HOLISTIC EVALUATION OF THE READER (continued)	**Seldom**	**Some-times**	**Often**	**Usually**	**Always**
III. Observations of retelling—If narrative text is used	**No**		**Partially**		**Yes**
• Recalls main characters	1	2	3	4	5
• Develops characters	1	2	3	4	5
• Describes setting	1	2	3	4	5
• Recalls main events	1	2	3	4	5
• Sequences main events	1	2	3	4	5
• Identifies theme	1	2	3	4	5
Comments					
IV. Observations of retelling— If expository text is used					
• Explains major concepts	1	2	3	4	5
• Makes generalizations	1	2	3	4	5
• Gives specific information	1	2	3	4	5
• Retells in a logical sequence	1	2	3	4	5
Comments					
V. In what ways is the reader using background knowledge?					
• Brings background knowledge to the reading	1	2	3	4	5
• Uses linguistic knowledge / Makes appropriate predictions	1	2	3	4	5
• Uses memory to help make predictions (On familiar text)	1	2	3	4	5
Comments					

Appendix M: Story Text—
"The Old Man, His Son, and the Donkey"

An old farmer and his son were taking their donkey to town to sell. They had not gone far when they saw some girls at a well.

"Look at them!" said one of the girls.

"Summer's here and the day is hot. And those two walk when they might ride. What fools they are!"

All the girls laughed at this. The old man heard them laugh. "Get up and ride," he said to his son.

So the son got on the donkey's back. The old man walked. Soon they came to some men in a field. "Look at that!" one of the men shouted. "That big boy rides while his poor old father must walk."

The old man heard their words. "Get right down," he said to his son. "I will ride." The son got down, and the old man got on the donkey's back.

"It feels good to ride," the old farmer said. "It wasn't right for me to walk." Soon they came to a woman and her children walking on the road.

"Will you look at him!" the woman said. "That man rides while his poor little son must walk." The old man heard her words. "Get up here with me," he said to his son. The son got up on the donkey in back of his father.

Soon they saw a man and his wife standing by their house. "Is that your donkey?" the man asked the old man.

"Yes, it is," said the old man.

"How can you be so mean?" asked the wife. "The two of you up there on one poor little donkey!" Then she went on to say, "Two big people like you could carry him."

"Very well," said the old man, "we'll try that."

The old man and his son got off the donkey and tried to pick him up. The old man picked up two legs, and his son picked up the other two legs. But just then, some more people came by. And when they saw the old farmer and his son, they all started laughing.

"Oh, oh, oh!" they laughed. "Look! The fools are carrying the donkey!"

The donkey didn't like the noise and didn't like to be carried. So he pulled loose and ran out into the fields. The old man and the son tried and tried, but they couldn't catch him. So now they had no donkey to sell.

At last, the old man turned to his son. "Son," he said, "You cannot please everyone. If you try, you only make a donkey of yourself."

Bibliography

Adams, M. J. 1994. "Modeling the Connections Between Word Recognition and Reading." In *Theoretical Models and Processes of Reading,* 4th ed., eds. R. B. Ruddell, M. R. Ruddell, and H. Singer, 838–863. Newark, DE: International Reading Association.

Allen, J., and K. Gonzalez. 1998. *There's Room for Me Here: Literacy Workshop in the Middle School.* York, ME: Stenhouse.

Allington, R. L. 2000. *What Really Matters for Struggling Readers: Designing Research-Based Programs.* New York: Longman.

Arriola, A. Conversation with author, 10 April 2001.

Atwell, N. 1998. *In the Middle: New Understandings About Writing, Reading, and Learning*. 2nd ed. Portsmouth, NH: Boynton/Cook.

Barnes, D., J. Britton, and H. Rosen. 1969. *Language, the Learner and the School.* London: Penguin.

Barthel-Hines, J. Conversation with author, 25 September 2001.

Bialostok, S. 1992. *Raising Readers: Helping Your Child to Literacy.* Winnipeg: Peguis.

Birchak, B., C. Connor, K. M. Crawford, L. Kahn, S. Kaser, S. Turner, and K. G. Short. 1999. *Teacher Study Groups: Building Community Through Dialogue and Reflection.* Urbana, IL: National Council of Teachers of English.

Bloome, D. 1985. "Reading as a Social Process." *Language Arts* 62 (2):134–142.

————. 1987. "Reading as a Social Process in a Middle School Classroom." In *Literacy and Schooling,* ed. D. Bloome, 123–149. Norwood, NJ: Ablex.

Bloome, D., and A. R. K. Dail. 1997. "Toward (Re)Defining Miscue Analysis: Reading as a Social and Cultural Process." *Language Arts* 74 (8): 610–617.

Bridges, L. 1995. *Assessment: Continuous Learning.* York, ME: Stenhouse; Los Angeles: The Galef Institute.

Brown, J., K. S. Goodman, and A. M. Marek. 1996. *Studies in Miscue Analysis: An Annotated Bibliography.* Newark, DE: International Reading Association.

Brummett, B., and L. B. Maras. 1995. "Liberated by Miscues: Students and Teachers Rediscovering the Reading Process." *Primary Voices K–6* 3 (4): 23–31.

Butler, A., and J. Turbill. 1984. *Towards a Reading–Writing Classroom.* Portsmouth, NH: Heinemann.

Calkins, L. M. 2001. *The Art of Teaching Reading.* New York: Longman.

Cambourne, B. 1988. *The Whole Story: Natural Learning and the Acquisition of Literacy in the Classroom.* Auckland: Ashton Scholastic.

————. 2001. "What Do I Do with the Rest of the Class?: The Nature of Teaching-Learning Activities." *Language Arts* 79 (2): 124–135.

Clay, M. M. 1991. *Becoming Literate: The Construction of Inner Control.* Portsmouth, NH: Heinemann.

————. 1993. *An Observation Survey of Early Literacy Achievement.* Portsmouth, NH: Heinemann.

————. 2000. *Running Records for Classroom Teachers.* Portsmouth, NH: Heinemann.

Crowell, C. G. 1995. "Documenting the Strengths of Bilingual Readers." *Primary Voices K–6* 3 (4): 32–37.

Cummins, S. Conversation with author, 20 September 2000.

Dahl, K. L., P. L. Scharer, L. L. Lawson, and P. R. Grogan. 2001. *Rethinking Phonics: Making the Best Teaching Decisions.* Portsmouth, NH: Heinemann.

Davenport, M. R. 1993. "Talking Through the Text: Selected Sixth-Grade Students' Metacognitive Awareness of Their Learning and Reading Processes." Ph.D. diss., University of Missouri, Columbia.

————. 1998. "Miscues, Not Mistakes: Analyzing Oral Reading." *College of Education News, Illinois State University* 5 (3): 3, 9.

Davenport, M. R., and J. Eckberg. 2001. "'Put an Idea Together': Collaboration and Composition in the Writing Workshop." *Reading Teacher* 54 (6): 562–566.

Davenport, M. R. and C. Lauritzen (2002). "Inviting Reflection on Reading through Over the Shoulder Miscue Analysis." *Language Arts.* In Press. (November)

Davenport, M. R. and D. J. Watson (1993). "Whole Language: Philosophy and Work—In Process." In *Whole Language: History, Philosophy, Practice,* eds. S. K. Brady and T. M. Sills, 1–17. Dubuque, IA: Kendall/Hunt.

Davey, B. 1983. "Think Aloud—Modeling the Cognitive Processes of Reading Comprehension." *Journal of Reading* 27 (1): 44–47.

Developmental Studies Center. 1996. *Ways We Want Our Class to Be: Class Meetings That Build Commitment to Kindness and Learning.* Oakland, CA: Developmental Studies Center.

Diener, M. Conversation with author, 19 July 2001.

Dixon, S. Conversation with author, 10 April 2001.

Farris, P. J. 2001. *Language Arts: Process, Product, and Assessment.* Boston: McGraw-Hill.

Flurkey, A. D. 1995. "Taking Another Look at (Listen to) Shari." *Primary Voices K–6* 3 (4): 10–15.

Fountas, I. C., and G. S. Pinnell. 1996. *Guided Reading: Good First Teaching for All Children.* Portsmouth, NH: Heinemann.

———. 1999. *Matching Books to Readers: Using Leveled Books in Guided Reading, K–3.* Portsmouth, NH: Heinemann.

Frazier, C. 1997. *Cold Mountain.* New York: Atlantic Monthly Press.

Freeman, D. E., and Y. S. Freeman. 2000. *Teaching Reading in Multilingual Classrooms.* Portsmouth, NH: Heinemann.

Freire, P. 1985. *The Politics of Education.* South Hadley, MA: Bergin and Garvey.

Fuglestad, S. 2001. Conversation with author. 19 July.

Giorgis, C., and N. J. Johnson. 2001. "Creativity." *Reading Teacher* 54 (6): 632–640.

Goodman, K. S. 1968. "Study of Children's Behavior While Reading Orally" (Contract No. OE-6-10-136). Washington, D.C.: Department of Health, Education, and Welfare.

———. 1969. "Analysis of Reading Miscues: Applied Psycholinguistics." *Reading Research Quarterly* 5 (1): 652–658.

———. 1973. "Miscues: Windows on the Reading Process." In *Miscue Analysis: Applications to Reading Instruction*, ed. K. S. Goodman, 3–14. Urbana, IL: ERIC Clearinghouse on Reading and Communication Skills and the National Council of Teachers of English.

———. 1993. *Phonics Phacts.* Portsmouth, NH: Heinemann.

———. 1994. "Reading, Writing, and Written Texts: A Transactional Sociopsycholinguistic View." In *Theoretical Models and Processes of Reading*, 4th ed., eds. R. B. Ruddell, M. R. Ruddell, and H. Singer, 1093–1130. Newark, DE: International Reading Association.

———. 1996. *On Reading: A Common-Sense Look at the Nature of Language and the Science of Reading*. Portsmouth, NH: Heinemann.

Goodman, Y. M. 1985. "Kidwatching: Observing Children in the Classroom." In *Observing the Language Learner*, eds. A. Jagger and M. R. Smith-Burke, 9–18. Urbana, IL: National Council of Teachers of English; Newark, DE: International Reading Association.

———. 1995. "Miscue Analysis for Classroom Teachers: Some History and Some Procedures." *Primary Voices K–6* 3 (4): 2–9.

———. Conversation with author, 14 December 2000.

Goodman, Y. M., and A. Flurkey. 1996. "Retrospective Miscue Analysis in the Middle School." In *Retrospective Miscue Analysis: Revaluing Readers and Reading*, eds. Y. M. Goodman and A. M. Marek, 87–105. Katonah, NH: Richard C. Owen.

Goodman, Y. M., and A. M. Marek. 1996. *Retrospective Miscue Analysis: Revaluing Readers and Reading.* Katonah, NY: Richard C. Owen.

Goodman, Y. M., and D. J. Watson. 1998. "A Sociopsycholinguistic Model of the Reading Process and Reading Strategy Instruction." In *Practicing What We Know: Informed Reading Instruction*, ed. C. Weaver, 113–139. Urbana, IL: National Council of Teachers of English.

Goodman, Y. M., D. J. Watson, and C. L. Burke. 1987. *Reading Miscue Inventory: Alternative Procedures.* New York: Richard C. Owen.

———. 1996. *Reading Strategies: Focus on Comprehension.* Katonah, NY: Richard C. Owen.

Hagerty, P. 1992. *Reader's Workshop: Real Reading.* Richmond Hill, Ontario: Scholastic Canada.

Halliday, M. A. K. 1985. *An Introduction to Functional Grammar.* London: Edward Arnold.

Hamilton, S. Conversation with author, 2 August 2000.

Harvey, S., and A. Goudvis. 2000. *Strategies That Work: Teaching Comprehension to Enhance Understanding.* York, ME: Stenhouse.

Hindley, J. 1996. *In the Company of Children.* York, ME: Stenhouse.

Hoyt, L. 2000. *Snapshots: Literacy Minilessons Up Close.* Portsmouth, NH: Heinemann.

Jennings, C. M., and X. Di. 1996. "Collaborative Learning and Thinking: The Vygotskian Approach." In *Vygotsky in the Classroom: Mediated Literacy Instruction and Assessment*, ed. L. Dixon-Krauss, 77–91. White Plains, NY: Longman.

Jung, C. G. 1957. *The Undiscovered Self.* New York: The New American Library.

Kaufman, D. 2001. "Organizing and Managing the Language Arts Workshop: A Matter of Motion." *Language Arts* 79 (2): 114–123.

Keolker, S. Conversation with author, 2 August 2000.

Lauritzen, C., and M. Jaeger. 1997. *Integrating Learning Through Story: The Narrative Curriculum.* Albany, NY: Delmar.

Macmillan Company, The. 1970. "The Old Man, His Son—and the Donkey." In *Country and City Book.* New York: Bank Street College of Education.

Martens, P. 1995. "Empowering Teachers and Empowering Students." *Primary Voices K–3* 3 (4): 39–42.

McQuillan, J. 1998. *The Literacy Crisis: False Claims, Real Solutions.* Portsmouth, NH: Heinemann.

Merriam-Webster. 1990. *Merriam-Webster's New Collegiate Dictionary, Ninth Edition.* Springfield, MA: Merriam-Webster.

Menosky, D. M. 1971. "A Psycholinguistic Description of Oral Reading Miscues Generated During the Reading of Varying Portions of Text by Selected Readers from Grades Two, Four, Six, and Eight." Ph.D. diss., Wayne State University, Detroit.

Moustafa, M. 1997. *Beyond Traditional Phonics: Research Discoveries and Reading Instruction.* Portsmouth, NH: Heinemann.

Nice, K. Conversation with author, 2 August 2000.

Peregoy, S. F., and O. F. Boyle. 2001. *Reading, Writing, and Learning in ESL.* New York: Longman.

Peters, S. Conversation with author, 15 August 2000.

Peterson, B. 2001. *Literary Pathways: Selecting Books to Support New Readers.* Portsmouth, NH: Heinemann.

Peterson, R., and M. Eeds. 1990. *Grand Conversations: Literature Groups in Action.* New York: Scholastic.

Pierce, K. M., ed. 2000. *Adventuring with Books: A Booklist for Pre-K–Grade 6.* 12th ed. Urbana, IL: National Council of Teachers of English.

Pierce, V. E. Conversation with author, 2 August 2000.

Rahn, K. K. Conversation with author, 20 June 2000.

Rhodes, L. K., and N. L. Shanklin. 1990. "Miscue Analysis in the Classroom." *Reading Teacher* 44 (3): 252–254.

———. 1993. *Windows into Literacy: Assessing Learners, K–8.* Portsmouth, NH: Heinemann.

Rosenblatt, L. M. 1978. *The Reader, the Text, the Poem: The Transactional Theory of the Literary Work.* Carbondale, IL: Southern Illinois University Press.

Routman, R. 2000. *Conversations: Strategies for Teaching, Learning and Evaluating.* Portsmouth, NH: Heinemann.

Scherer, P. 1997. "Book Club Through a Fishbowl: Extensions to Early Elementary Classrooms." In *The Book Club Connection: Literacy Learning and Classroom Talk,* eds. S. I. McMahon and T. E. Rafael, with V. J. Goatley and L. S. Pardo, 250–263. Newark, DE: International Reading Association; New York: Teachers College Press.

Serafini, F. 2000/2001. "Three Paradigms of Assessment: Measurement, Procedure and Inquiry." *Reading Teacher* 54 (4): 384–393.

———. 2001. *The Reading Workshop: Creating Space for Readers.* Portsmouth, NH: Heinemann.

Shadle-Talbert, D. Conversation with author, 3 October 2000.

Short, K. G., J. Schroeder, J. Laird, G. Kauffman, M. J. Ferguson, and K. M. Crawford. 1996. *Learning Together Through Inquiry: From Columbus to Integrated Curriculum.* York, ME: Stenhouse.

Short, K.G., and J. C. Harste, with C. Burke. 1996. *Creating Classrooms for Authors and Inquirers.* 2nd ed. Portsmouth, NH: Heinemann.

Smith, F. 1973. *Psycholinguistics and Reading.* New York: Holt, Rinehart and Winston.

Stack, K. Conversation with author, 6 June 2000.

Street, B. 1984. *Literacy in Theory and Practice.* New York: Cambridge University Press.

Taberski, S. 2000. *On Solid Ground: Strategies for Teaching Reading K–3.* Portsmouth, NH: Heinemann.

Taylor, D. 1998. *Family Literacy.* Portsmouth, NH: Heinemann.

Trelease, J. 2001. *Read Aloud Handbook,* 5th ed. New York: Penguin Books.

Watson, D. J. 1988. "Knowing Where We're Coming From." In *Whole Language Strategies for Secondary Students*, eds. C. Gilles, M. Bixby, P. Crowley, S. R. Crenshaw, M. Henrichs, F. E. Reynolds, and D. Pyle, 3–10. New York: Richard C. Owen.

———. Conversation with author, 15 September 1989.

———. 1994. "Whole Language: Why Bother?" *Reading Teacher* 47 (8): 600–607.

———. 1997. "Beyond Decodable Texts—Supportive and Workable Literature." *Language Arts* 74 (4): 635–643.

———. 1999. "A Whole Language Journey: Are We There Yet?" In *Reflections and Connections: Essays in Honor of Kenneth S. Goodman's Influence on Language Education,* eds. A. M. Marek and C. Edelsky, 51–66. Cresskill, NJ: Hampton Press.

———. Conversation with author, 5 October 2001.

Weaver, C. 1980. *Psycholinguistics and Reading: From Process to Practice.* Cambridge, MA: Winthrop.

Wilde, S. 1997. *What's a Schwa Sound Anyway?* Portsmouth, NH: Heinemann.

———. 2000. *Miscue Analysis Made Easy: Building on Student Strengths.* Portsmouth, NH: Heinemann.

Wilhelm, J. D. 2001. *Improving Comprehension with Think-Aloud Strategies: Modeling What Good Readers Do.* New York: Scholastic.

Wilson, J. Conversation with author, 20 September 2000.

Children's Books Cited

Bridwell, N. 1993. *Clifford's Thanksgiving.* New York: Scholastic.

Hoffman, M. 1991. *Amazing Grace.* New York. Dial Books for Young Readers.

Munsch, R. N. 1991. *La Princesa Vestida con una Bolsa*, trans. S. Langer. Toronto: Annick Press.

Naylor, P. R. 1991. *Shiloh.* New York: Bantam Doubleday Dell Books for Young Readers.

Raskin, E. 1991. *The Westing Game.* New York: Dutton.

Shannon, G. 1994. *Lizard's Song.* New York: Mulberry.

Index